Literacy and Written Culture
in Early Modern Central Europe

Literacy and Written Culture in Early Modern Central Europe

István György Tóth

CEU PRESS

Central European University Press

First published in Hungarian as *Mivelhogy magad írást nem tudsz...* in 1996 by
MTA Történettudományi Intézete

English edition published in 2000 by
Central European University Press

Nádor utca 15
H-1051 Budapest
Hungary

400 West 59th Street
New York, NY 10019
USA

Translated by Tünde Vajda and Miklós Bodóczky

Distributed in the United Kingdom and Western Europe by
Plymbridge Distributors Ltd., Estover Road, Plymouth PL6 7PZ, United Kingdom

ISBN 963 9116 85 8 Cloth

Library of Congress Cataloging in Publication Data
A CIP catalog record for this book is available upon request

Printed in Hungary by Akadémiai Nyomda

CONTENTS

List of Figure and Tables   vii

List of Maps   ix

List of Illustrations   xi

INTRODUCTION   1

Chapter 1
A WINDOW TO THE WORLD OF LITERACY: A SOCIAL
HISTORY OF ELEMENTARY SCHOOLS   5

Chapter 2
THE SLOW ADVANCE OF LITERACY IN PEASANT
CULTURE   47

Chapter 3
LITERACY AMONG THE NOBILITY   95

Chapter 4
THE LOWER NOBILITY AND THE ORAL TRADITION   147

Chapter 5
AN OUTLOOK IN TIME: NATIONALITIES AND THE
SPREAD OF LITERACY AFTER THE AUSTRO–HUNGARIAN
COMPROMISE   193

Conclusion   209

Appendix   213

Notes   221

References   245

Index   263

LIST OF FIGURE AND TABLES

Fig 1. Percentage of Elementary School-Goers within the Total
Population in the Provinces of the Habsburg Empire (1781)   39

Table 1.1. Age at which Teachers in Vas County Started to Teach
(1778)   14
Table 1.2. Years Spent in Teaching Profession by Registered
Teachers in Vas County (1778)   14
Table 1.3. Number of Years Spent at One School by Teachers in Vas
County (1778)   15
Table 1.4. Tuition Fees as a Proportion of Schoolmasters' Income in
Vas County (1770)   16
Table 1.5. Schoolmasters' Income in Vas County (1770)   17
Table 1.6. Income of Schoolmasters in the Outer Parishes as a
Percentage of Those Teaching in Parish Villages (1770)   17
Table 1.7. Number of Schoolchildren in Vas County (1770)   19
Table 1.8. Number of Schoolchildren in the Villages of the Győr
Archdeaconry (1698)   33
Table 1.9. Percentage of School-Goers in the Győr Archdeaconry (1698)   34
Table 1.10. School-Goers in Eastern Styria (1617 and 1805)   36
Table 1.11. Percentage of Elementary School-Goers within the Total
Population in Provinces of the Habsburg Empire (1781)   38

Table 2.1. Peasant Literacy in Vas County in the Seventeenth Century   48

Table 2.2. Peasant Literacy in Vas County in the Eighteenth   49
Century

Table 2.3. Peasant Literacy in Eighteenth-Century Vas County by
Nationality   50

Table 2.4. Peasant Literacy in Vas County in the First Half of the
Nineteenth Century   52

Table 2.5. Peasant Literacy in Vas County in the First Half of the
Nineteenth Century by Nationality   53

Table 2.6. Villages in Vas County with More than Five Literate
Peasants (1800–48)   53

Table 2.7. Peasant Literacy in Villages of the Körmend Estates
(1600–1848)   55

Table 2.8. Literacy among the Protestant Peasants in Vas County in
1732   56

Table 2.9. Dates Specified by Witnesses in Eighteenth-Century
Witchcraft Trials (Sopron and Zala Counties)   75

Table 2.10. Dates Specified by Witnesses in Eighteenth-Century
Criminal Trials (Western Transdanubia and Nagykőrös)   75

Table 3.1. Literacy of the Lower Nobility in Vas County in the
Eighteenth Century (Males Only)   108

Table 3.2. Literacy of the Lower Nobility in Vas County According
to Size of Estate Mentioned in Testaments (1721–1800)   109

Table 3.3. Literacy among Lower Noblewomen in Vas County as
Mirrored in Their Testaments (1721–1880)   127

Table 5.1. Proportion of Literates in Hungary by Nationality in 1890   196

Table 5.2. Percentage of Illiterates in Vas County in 1870 (of the
Entire Population)   197

Table 5.3. Percentage of Illiterates in Transdanubia in 1870 (of the
Entire Population, Excluding Royal Towns)   198

Table 5.4. Percentage of Readers-Only in Hungary in 1870   201

Table A1. Literacy in the Counties of Hungary (1870)   213

Table A2. Proportion of Those Able to Write in the Counties and
Towns of Hungary   215

LIST OF MAPS

Map 5.1. Proportion of Illiterates among Males over 6 in the
Hungarian Kingdom   194
Map 5.2. Proportion of Illiterates among Females over 6 in the
Hungarian Kingdom   195

LIST OF ILLUSTRATIONS

(Selected by Anna Jávor)

1. Hungarian noble boy with his primer (17th century)

2. A Roman Catholick student in Siculia (17th century)

3. School-children learning to write

4. Difficult signatures from documents of the Eger and Miskolc County Archives (18th century)

5. A Hungarian Calvinist student (17th century)

6. a. Letters patent of Stephen Bocskay, prince of Hungary and Transylvania (1606), **b.** Hungarian peasant of noble origin reading the letters patent of his ancestor (1943)

7. a–c. Hungarian noble and aristocrat girls learning to read and wirte, **d.** Young boy learning his first letters

8. Hungarian documents deposited in the Central State Archives in Vienna (1686)

INTRODUCTION

The European Early Modern Age, from the early sixteenth century to the end of the eighteenth century, saw a veritable revolution in cultural history. In the Middle Ages, it was deemed natural that only a select few knew how to read and write and that many of these individuals made their living from these skills as scribes and clerks. Not only peasants but often the nobility viewed written text as incomprehensible. By the late eighteenth century, however, about fifty percent of the male population in the most developed regions of Europe was able to gather information by reading newspapers, and the number of those capable of conducting correspondence in writing increased steadily. Reading and writing skills and the use of literacy in general gained ground rapidly to the detriment of oral communication. The body of written documents available drastically expanded, and literacy increasingly made its presence felt. The number of printed books grew while their price became cheaper, and more events and ideas were thought to be worth committing to paper. In addition, literacy extended its influence to new sectors of the developing state administration and bureaucracy: surveys and certificates were drafted, and the use of written documents gradually replaced oral testimony. Although difficult to demonstrate—let alone measure—styles of thinking and general mentalities simultaneously changed. Orally transmitted information and the memory of the elderly lost a great deal of their former prestige while respect for details put down in writing, which were comprehensible to increasing numbers of people (even among the peasantry), strengthened. With the spread of calendars and printed maps, the concepts of space and time altered; numerically articulated, measurable time came to replace an image of the past drawn with vague, uncertain outlines.

The changes that took place were indeed revolutionary, and their significance in the social development of the Early Modern Age cannot be overestimated. Yet these changes were not rapid—it took centuries for mass literacy and the everyday use of writing to triumph in Europe, and the old ways and new fashions coexisted for hundreds of years. Travelers were quick to note that, while in certain regions, almost everyone could read and write, literate persons were few and far between in other parts of Europe. Central Europe Hungary attempted to follow in the footsteps of the developed sections of Europe in overcoming illiteracy. Although perceivably lagging behind the Netherlands and Britain, Central Europe's relative state of development was evident in contrast to other regions of Europe to the east, including the Balkan peninsula and Russia.

The goal of this book is to examine the gradual spread of literacy and written culture among the peasants, market town burghers, the landed gentry and the landless and impoverished nobles in the territory of the Hungarian Kingdom from the sixteenth to the eighteenth century. In addition, the book explores the role written documents played in the lives of the members of these social strata, who represented the great majority of the population in early modern Central Europe. The Hungarian Kingdom, part of the Habsburg Empire, comprised territories inhabited by Hungarians, Roumanians, Slovaks, Germans, Serbs, Croats, Slovenes and Ukrainians, making possible the comparison in the development of literacy. In the course of this examination, both statistically analyzable and descriptive sources are utilized. Efforts were made to avoid the gathering of colorful stories that freely roam in space and time—a method often found in the abundant literature on the development of literacy—but rather to identify material that commands the power of evidence. By way of a starting point and a case study, the author mapped and statistically processed the sources on literacy in a definable and especially well-documented area: the large and populous Vas County in western Hungary. Four nationalities—Hungarians, Slovenes, Croatians and Germans—lived in this county, representing three religious denominations: Catholicism, Lutheranism and Calvinism. When completed, the results of the analysis of this county and its exceptionally rich source material hopefully will provide a firm basis on which to make generalizations. Thus the results of the analysis of Vas

County will be compared first to other territories of the Hungarian Kingdom, then to other provinces of the Habsburg Empire and finally to other European countries.

This analysis must be preceded by an examination of elementary schools in the region and the chances children from various social strata had to acquire reading and writing skills in order to leave the world of oral culture behind and join the literate minority.

CHAPTER 1

A WINDOW TO THE WORLD OF LITERACY:
A SOCIAL HISTORY OF ELEMENTARY SCHOOLS

Schoolmasters Who Did Not Teach

A detailed register of teachers can be found in the records of the Catholic and Lutheran Church visitations, this publication's primary sources on village schools. At the end of the seventeenth century, in 1696, there were eighty-nine schoolmasters and eighty-five schools in Vas County. By 1754 their numbers had increased to 181 and 169 respectively.[1] The contemporary designation of these teachers, *magister scholae* (schoolmaster), was, however, grossly deceptive. The main task schoolmasters performed was not teaching, as one might assume, but serving as cantors. This is quite obvious when their sources of income are examined, clearer still from what passed as their job descriptions, and most evident from the distinction the Catholic Church visitations made between a schoolmaster and an instructor.

The church visitation of Bishop Szily in 1778 documented eleven villages in which teaching was conducted, although he found there no schoolmasters. In nine villages the bell ringer taught: "his main task was teaching children", the church visitor wrote in the village of Neustift. There were bell ringers in two other villages, but they did not teach, as they were obviously unfit for the job. In these locations school-age children were taught how to read and write by a separate *instructor puerorum* (instructor of children). One might think that these "substitute" teachers performed their duties poorly, acting as occasional assistants, but three of them were recorded as having taught arithmetic in an age when, according to the same church visitations, only twenty percent of the teachers in the region's parish villages were capable of doing so.[2] The question arises as to why these bell ringers and instructors were *not* called schoolmasters.

The explanation is that the main function a schoolmaster performed at this time was that of a cantor rather than of a teacher of this village. "The schoolmaster may be called none other than a *præceptor* (assistant teacher), as he has no income other than what he receives from his pupils"; thus, he received nothing as a cantor according to the records of the village of Frakunó, Sopron County, at the time of the 1651 visitation.[3] The concept of a schoolmaster was defined fairly clearly for this survey: a person who only engaged in teaching but was not a cantor could not be labeled a schoolmaster. In Tótság, the southern, Slovene-populated part of Vas County, eleven teachers were registered in 1770, while the number of pupils was a mere *eight* in the entire region, all of whom attended the same school. The other schoolmasters may have sung ever so beautifully in church or at funerals yet hardly contributed to improving literacy. The schoolmasters were primarily cantors who looked upon teaching as a complementary task, and this was not unique to western Hungary. Abbot Johann Ignaz Felbiger, the father of Austrian school reform, noted in despair that "whoever applies to the schoolmaster's post is deemed fit for the job, provided he is well enough versed in music to sing, conduct a choir, play the organ a little and perhaps know a little something about writing".[4]

Who may be viewed as a teacher from the sixteenth century to the eighteenth century? There were several schoolmasters who did not teach because they lacked pupils. The *licentiatus* (a married layman who attended to some of a Catholic priest's tasks with permission from the bishop when the parish lacked an ordained priest), however, taught. Church visitors clearly described some of them as such, whereas in other cases one may surmise that if there was no schoolmaster in the village and the village community paid a fee to a *licentiatus* (who often had a secondary education), then he was expected to teach children, provided he was capable of doing so, in addition to attending to baptisms, funerals and Sunday sermons. When, in the first third of the eighteenth century, the organization of the Catholic Church gradually was restored and the *licentiatus* were replaced by ordained parish priests, many of the latter opted to earn their livings as schoolmasters—and thus as cantors—a task they had performed earlier to complement their primary work.[5]

Lutheran Pastors Who Did Not Know How to Write

The situation was no less complex among the Protestants. If there was a Lutheran pastor who studied theology and a Lutheran schoolmaster who had a secondary education in a village, the division of labor was clear. The Lutheran Church, however, was as lacking in educated men as the Catholic Church, in which *licentiatus* substituted for parish priests. In most villages, at most one Lutheran master could be found, and he usually had completed grammar school. The Catholic visitors were apparently at a loss as to how to place them, once registering them in the category of pastor, and at another time in that of schoolmaster. The latter did attend to some of a pastor's duties, as is clear from a Catholic visitor's indignant notes describing how on Sundays a Lutheran schoolmaster read and sermonized to the congregation in 1697. A pastor, in turn, would instruct the children on reading and writing if there was no teacher in the area. In 1778, well after the victory of Catholicism in the region, Bishop Szily noted that the Lutherans refused to pay school fees for the Catholic schoolmaster, saying the Catholic parish priest should ensure his upkeep and relinquish part of his own income for the schoolmaster's benefit, just as Lutheran pastors had done "when [they] did not want to fulfill the post of schoolmaster at the same time".[6]

In later periods, specific criteria were set up and the duties of the priest and the schoolmaster were separated and defined clearly. However, projecting the orderly circumstances of the late eighteenth century back onto this period in which men of education were so scarce would be anachronistic. In the late seventeenth century, for example, János Hercegszőllősi, age fifty-eight, functioned as a Catholic *licentiatus* in Rábagyarmat for eleven years. Originally a Lutheran pastor, he came to the village from the Turkish-occupied county of Baranya, converted to Catholicism and remained in the same position for another denomination. Despite the ecclesiastical functions Hercegszőllősi attended to for two different churches, he was not educated and could read but not write.[7] Hercegszőllősi was not the only one in this situation: Mihály Smodics, the Lutheran pastor of the village of Nádasd, was visited by a Lutheran church visitor in 1659. In 1698, four decades later, the Catholic archdeacon visited him, as, at this time, he had been serving in the same village for fifteen years as a Catholic *licenciatus*. He did not leave the village or job during the turbulent Counter Reformation period of the 1670s but changed denominations instead. Despite four decades in the service of two churches, Mihály Smodics was not an educated man—he could read but was not able to write.[8]

To summarize, therefore, the full number of elementary school-teachers in villages in which there were schools must also include the *licentiati* and Lutherans who did not deal directly with theology and had, at best, a secondary education.

A Sociological Description of Schoolmasters

Based on the records of Catholic Church visitations, a portrait of teachers as a social group in the Early Modern Age can be pieced together. At the end of the seventeenth century, a Catholic Church visitor recorded the place of birth of thirty-three Catholic schoolmasters. Unfortunately, though, he only made a point of doing so near the end of his tour. More than half the masters were born in the county, but only two of them stayed and taught in their own villages. The others found posts farther from their birthplaces, in settlements lying at distances of twenty to thirty kilometers or more. This is a clear indication that not just individuals from the same village were entrusted with instructing local children; these people, some of whom were grammar school graduates, were professional teachers.

After examining data on the forty Lutheran schoolmasters recorded by the same Catholic visitor in the late seventeenth century, the picture is entirely different. In many respects, the situation of Lutheran schoolmasters in Vas County was similar to that of the Protestant inhabitants of overpopulated French Alpine villages. Each year they set out in search of employment, heading towards the south of France and usually settling in Provençal villages as teachers.[9] Of the forty schoolmasters in Vas County, no fewer than twenty-two came from Upper Hungary (now Slovakia), and, with the exception of one Hungarian, were all actually Slovaks. Eight were from Turóc, six from Trencsén and three from Árva County—from the poor northern Slovak-speaking part of Upper Hungary. They all taught in Hungarian villages, most likely after receiving their secondary education in a Lutheran grammar school (probably the famous school of Pozsony [now Bratislava]) where they learned Hungarian. From there they traveled south to Vas County, which lacked a Lutheran grammar school at the time.[10]

The 1778 church visitation provides a portrait of schoolmasters in the entire territory of Vas County. Of the 238 Catholic teachers, 116 (about one-half) were born in the county, but only 23 schoolmasters (one-fifth) found posts in either their own birthplaces or nearby villages affiliated with the same parish. It is striking that only two teachers were from the developed town of Kőszeg, the only free royal town in the county. These schoolmasters found employment in two tiny villages on the other side of the county. The low social prestige of teaching and the meager income explain why so few urban graduates sought employment in village schools.

Seventeen teachers in Vas County were from Austria and Styria, one each from Mainz and Salzburg, and an additional eight from the provinces of the Bohemian crown—one from Bohemia, two from Silesia and five from Moravia. Those teachers from German-speaking territories and the hereditary provinces of the Habsburg Empire practiced their profession in German-speaking villages in the western part of Vas County, which now forms part of the Burgenland in Austria. When crossing the border between Styria and Hungary, some did nothing more than go to the adjacent village, as did the teacher in Hidegkút, who was from Burgau, ten kilometers beyond the creek that marked the border between Styria and Hungary. Anton Gros, the schoolmaster in Keresztes, came from a Styrian village lying only forty kilometers away.

Language was the decisive element in the choice of places for teachers rather than geographical proximity, which explains why Anton Gros later went on to teach in German-speaking villages in another county. The schoolmasters from Linz, Salzburg, Mainz and Moravia worked where they could find jobs, but as they could not speak Hungarian, they only taught German speakers.[11]

Those teachers who came from a distance did not do so at random; usually one teacher invited another. Schoolmaster Johann Gerhardt came from Kirchschlag, Austria, near the Hungarian border, as did Joseph Gerhardt, six years his junior, who taught in another village twenty-five kilometers away. Most likely Johann, who started teaching earlier, invited Joseph (who may have been his brother) to follow his example. Before coming to Hungary, both acted as the schoolmaster of Hochneukirchen, where, once again, Johann may have recommended Joseph for the job.

Kinship between the two Gerhardts seems likely enough but is certain in the case of the Holtzapfel brothers. Márton Holtzapfel was the son of a serf from Kagran (today an outlying district of Vienna) and immigrated to Hungary at the age of nineteen. He began his career as an innkeeper in Vasvár, opting for a schoolmaster's job only two years later. He taught in a German-speaking village for two years. Having learned to speak Hungarian "better than middling", he then went on to Körmend, a Hungarian market town with a sizable German-speaking minority. He was an assistant teacher to begin with and then became a schoolmaster for forty years. Owing to the poverty of his family, his younger brother József followed him to Körmend. József learned to write from his brother so that, according to the records of the elder sibling, "he too was suited to become a schoolmaster in both the German and the Hungarian tongues". The underlying idea could not have been stated more clearly: whoever commanded writing skills also was fit to teach. The younger brother, then, followed in the footsteps of the elder—he came to Hungary where he received his training from his brother and went on to start his own career as schoolmaster. In 1782, however, Joseph impregnated a girl from Körmend and was forced to move to a village in Zala County and begin his own career as a schoolmaster.[12]

Bernhart Jacob Herbst, the schoolmaster of Rohonc, a German-speaking market town in Vas County, was from Sankt Leonard, Austria. Before assuming his post in Rohonc he acted as a schoolmaster in various Austrian towns and taught at an orphanage in Vienna for four years. Both of the assistant teachers he employed in Rohonc were Moravian Germans; the elder one taught in the village for three years when his seventeen-year-old brother joined him. There was a market for German-speaking schoolmasters in western Hungary, a demand that these teachers promptly realized.[13]

Teachers: Illiterates and Grammar School Graduates

When comparing the qualifications of the Catholic and Lutheran teachers in Vas County at the end of the seventeenth century, their portraits are surprisingly similar. Of the Lutheran as well as of the Catholic schoolmasters, no less than sixteen percent were illiterate in 1697. These teachers could read but not write and thus were only capable of teaching children to read at best. The number of teachers of both denominations who had finished some form of grammar school was similar and included, according to the Latin names of the different forms, seven and eight *syntaxists* respectively, two *poets* each, and five and six *rhetors* respectively. One Catholic and three Lutheran teachers also studied logic—that is, they began academic training. Unfortunately, later church visitations did not focus on the qualifications of teachers. In 1754 a church visitor noted that three schoolmasters were ignoramuses, unfit to instruct children and qualified only to sing or ring the church bells. In consideration of the low standards of the time, one may assume that these teachers could not even write. Of the other teachers, the visitor merely recorded that they carried out their jobs well. In the national school survey of 1770, which was in many respects much stricter than the ecclesiastical ones, a village teacher summarily was dismissed as an idiot, yet he went on teaching children to write, "insofar as a man of such feeble capabilities could indeed do so". At the same time, five of the schoolmasters taught children only to read, since they could only write with difficulty, if at all.[14]

The schoolteacher in Tana may have been unqualified as well; it was noted that "he does not have a single pupil to teach, as the schoolteacher himself knows but little". In the case of other villages, the survey was more unambiguous and described schoolteachers who only taught reading, as they themselves could not write. The schoolteacher in Nick, for example, was described as being "unfit to teach anything beyond reading and syllabification". In Bögöte "the master, being of meager knowledge, teaches his pupils to read from prayer-books"; the master in nearby Szergény was "capable only of teaching reading". The schoolteacher in Árokszállás was also a sexton and cobbler, and in wintertime he usually taught thirty pupils reading but not writing, as he was unable to do the latter. The figure of the *illiterate schoolmaster*, therefore, was still a reality in the second half of the eighteenth century.[15]

Bishop Szily also recorded whether or not particular schoolteachers knew Latin. Such data indicate a great deal about their qualifications, since some knowledge of Latin presupposed at least one or two forms of grammar school. Judging Latin language skills is certainly somewhat subjective. The four-year visitation did not and could not depict perfectly the Catholic Church in the county; in many cases the schoolmasters migrated during the period of the church visitation and therefore figure twice in the records. A schoolmaster was first registered in Gencs and again in Sitke a year later; while he was described as a Latin scholar in the first case, at his new post the same visitor described him as speaking only his mother tongue. Similarly, schoolmaster József István, who moved to a new village while the visitation was in progress, seemed to have forgotten Latin by the time he arrived at his new home: he had been registered as speaking Latin in the first village and as not in the second village.[16] Therefore, Bishop Szily's estimate, which indicated that one-fifth of the schoolmasters (forty-six) knew Latin around 1778, must be an approximation. At the same time, however, the number was confirmed by a state school survey taken eight years earlier, according to which seventeen percent of the teachers (thirty-six) did teach Latin, although mostly only Latin declensions. At the same time, the Latin teaching in the schools of Jánosháza, Sárvár and Károlypátty was of such high standard that graduates easily could pursue their studies in the second or third

form of the Jesuit grammar school. It was in vain that the 1777 school reform act of the enlightened state of Queen Maria Theresia, *Ratio Educationis*, stipulated that the children of village nobles and brighter peasant offspring had to be taught some Latin; about eighty percent of the schoolmasters in Vas County were unfit for the job due to their lack of knowledge of
the language. The reformist endeavors of Enlightened Absolutism thus
conflicted with reality.[17]

Both illiterate and grammar school-educated teachers could be found in
the county in the second half of the eighteenth century. Although there
always have been good and bad teachers, the magnitude of differences
among the group during this period was conceivable only before the advent
of regular teacher training.

Of the schoolmasters registered by Bishop Szily in 1778, not all had been
teachers for their entire careers. As noted earlier, one was an innkeeper, and
two were itinerant craftsmen—one joiner traveled from Mainz to Vas
County, where he settled and became the schoolmaster of an elementary
school. Another schoolmaster made his living as a locksmith in Trencsén
County before becoming a teacher in a village school. Scribes or notaries
"turned schoolmasters" continued to live on their knowledge of reading and
writing. There were two former servicemen among the teachers as well: one
discharged soldier retired near his native village, while Johann Fleischer
from Silesia played the trumpet in the imperial army for seventeen years
before settling in a German-speaking village in Vas County at the time of
the Austrian War of Succession. Most likely he did not want to return to his
birthplace, which was occupied by the Prussians after the war.[18]

The schoolmaster's duties were primarily those of a cantor rather than of
a teacher. Unsurprisingly, musicians and sacristans also turned to teaching.
There was a coal burner who previously was a sacristan at the Augustinians
of Buda; another teacher used to play the organ at the Dominicans of
Szombathely; two others had been musicians for the chapter in Szombathely. The son of the trumpeter of the town of Kőszeg became a village
teacher. The soldier mentioned earlier, Johann Fleischer, also may be
counted among the musicians, as he played the horn in the army. There
were no proper teachers in Dömölk or the neighboring villages, so the job
was performed by two musicians from the Benedictine abbey. One of them
instructed pupils, and the other only sang at funerals—a further indication
that this was the most important criterion of being a schoolmaster.[19]

For the schoolmaster, teaching was complementary to performing the
duties of a cantor. There were some, however, who pursued even school-

masterships in addition to their original occupations for additional income. In the village of Kám, the schoolmaster's primary occupation was tailoring, and in winter he also taught six pupils to read. Nor did the schoolmaster of Szecsőd, familiarly nicknamed Jankó Mester (Master Johnny), abandon tailoring—depositions indicate that peasants came to him to have clothes made. The schoolmaster at Óvár was mainly a cobbler, although he also "did a little bit of teaching".[20]

These examples are certainly more colorful than the career of the average teacher, but they are the few exceptions. The majority of teachers in Vas County prepared to become teachers and remained in the profession. In the course of his 1778 visitation, Bishop János Szily recorded the careers of 131 teachers (fifty-five percent) of the 238 he encountered in Vas County.[21]

According to the data presented in table 1.1, two-thirds of the Vas County teachers started teaching by the time they were twenty-five years old. They did not view the time they spent teaching as transitional periods in their lives: in 1778, one-third were over forty, and 41.2 percent had taught for more than fifteen years (see table 1.2).

Based on the 1778 canonical visitation, it is possible to reconstruct the movements and earlier posts of the schoolmasters. There were some, such as the master of Szentpéterfa, who taught in the same village for decades. In a 1754 court case he stated that although he was not from the village, he still was eligible to offer evidence as "he had come to Szentpéterfa to become a schoolmaster forty-five years before, from which time he dwelled there continuously". At that time he was sixty-six years old and had taught in the village from the age of twenty-one.[22] It was more common, however, for schoolmasters to change posts, if not annually, at least every third to fifth year on average. Sixty-two percent spent less than five years at any given school (see table 1.3).

Schoolteachers often moved in search of new posts in hope of higher salaries. In general they found new jobs within one day's walking distance, twenty to thirty kilometers from their previous posts.

In the Vas County villages, not only the locals or random visitors were entrusted to teach children. There was an established group of people who were educated, although not at a very high level, from which teachers were chosen. There may have been former soldiers, trumpeters or joiners among the Vas teachers, but this was not typical. For the overwhelming majority, teaching was a lifelong occupation. Many may have changed their teaching posts, but only a few abandoned the profession altogether. This is confirmed by the fact that many took over the profession from their fathers.

Table 1.1

Age at which Teachers in Vas County Started to Teach (1778)[a]

Age	Number	Percent
16–20	46	35.1
21–25	44	33.6
26–30	21	16.0
31–35	11	8.4
36–40	6	4.6
41 and over	3	2.3
Total	131	100.0

[a] No data available for additional 107 teachers.

Table 1.2

Years Spent in Teaching Profession by Registered Teachers
in Vas County (1778)[a]

Number of Years	Number of Teachers
1–5	28
6–10	33
11–15	16
16–20	17
21–25	20
26–30	5
31–35	6
36–40	3
41 and over	3
Total	131

[a] No data available for additional 107 teachers.

Table 1.3

Number of Years Spent at One School by Teachers in Vas County (1778)

Number of Years	Number of Teachers	Percent
1–5	136	62.4
6–10	43	19.8
11–20	21	9.6
21–30	9	4.1
31 and over	9	4.1
Total	218	100.0

In 1778, Bishop Szily found seven Vas County schoolmasters who were continuing their fathers' professions. The schoolmasters of Léka and Kőszeg left their fairly well paid posts to their sons. Three other masters had served previously as assistants to their fathers and later became independent schoolmasters elsewhere.[23]

Schoolmasters: The Poor and the Well-off

In the course of the church visitations, schoolmasters' incomes were recorded carefully. Nevertheless, this information does not lend itself to comparison. In order to be able to analyze the financial positions of schoolmasters, one must consider the average number of funerals held in a particular village each year, the value of food and goods provided in kind or how much they could make on a plot of land—neither of them is known to us. A clear picture can be formed only on the basis of national school surveys, and even within these, only for those villages where the locals made a cash estimate of the schoolmaster's varied dues. These records plainly reveal that there was no connection between the number of pupils and the income of a schoolmaster; even though parents were expected to pay for their children's education, teaching was only a supplementary activity for the schoolmaster. In fact, only ten to twenty percent of a teacher's income came from school fees.[24]

The income of the schoolmasters in two districts, including amounts earned from tuition, was recorded in 1770. In two other districts, the total income of schoolmasters was recorded, although tuition fees were not specified. However, if their income is compared to the number of pupils, it is clear that there was no connection whatsoever between the number of students (that is, the tuition fees received) and the teacher's income. This is not surprising in view of table 1.4, as tuition fees comprised only a fraction of a schoolmaster's income.

Table 1.4

Tuition Fees as a Proportion of Schoolmasters' Income in
Vas County (1770)

Percentage of Total Income from Tuition Fees	Instances
0–10.0	11
10.1–20.0	7
20.1–30.0	7
30.1–40.0	3
40.1 and over	0
Total	28

Those schoolmasters living in larger market towns or receiving salaries from the local landlord (for which they were obliged to play music for him) had higher incomes—over one hundred forints (see table 1.5). The one in Szentgotthárd received payments from the local Cistercians; the masters at Rohonc, Körmend and Borostyánkő drew salaries from the ducal Batthyány family. The Szombathely schoolteacher's income was supplemented from the foundation of the Counts Széchényi, and in Sároslak, from the foundation of a wealthy Körmend merchant. Some of the schoolmasters in the outer parishes (*filiæ*, villages without parish churches), however, only earned an annual salary of ten to twelve forints. It is no surprise, therefore, that one record indicates that the schoolmaster of an outer parish in Vas County, Porpác, "earns his bread in a miserable way, reaping and threshing, begging other people's mercy".[25]

On average the schoolmasters in the outer parishes did not earn more than forty to sixty percent of the income of schoolteachers in parish villages (see table 1.6). This was due to the fact that the duties of a schoolmaster primarily consisted of cantorship, the main source of income, and performing beside the parish priest during funerals.

Table 1.5

Schoolmasters' Income in Vas County (1770)

Districts	Number of Teachers	Annual Average Income (Forints)
1. Teachers in Parish Villages		
Rohonc	12	69.1
Szombathely	19	62.5
Őrség	21	42.1
Németújvár	20	36.2
2. Teachers in Outer Parishes		
Rohonc	14	28.4
Szombathely	13	26.2
Őrség	4	25.9
Németújvár	13	22.6

Table 1.6

Income of Schoolmasters in the Outer Parishes as a Percentage of Those Teaching in Parish Villages (1770)

District	Percent
Rohonc	41.1
Szombathely	41.9
Őrség	61.5
Németújvár	62.4

On the estate of György Bernáth, a Vas County middle nobleman, at the end of the eighteenth century, a gamekeeper or a farm hand received twenty-three forints per year, and an ox herder, twenty-four; this was complemented by a payment in kind of equal value. With approximately twenty-five forints, the teachers' annual income in the outer parishes remained well below that of the gamekeepers and ox herders. In the parish villages, the income of schoolmasters teaching and, more importantly, serving as cantors was comparable to that of tenant farmers, who received forty-six forints in addition to payments due in kind. In the entire county, only the incomes of a few privileged schoolmasters approached the Bernáth estate purser's pay-ment of two hundred forints.[26]

It is understandable then that the prestige of the teaching profession was low during this period. In 1770 it was noted in Sitke that, while it would be desirable for their teacher to have the aptitude to instruct children not only in reading and writing but also in arithmetic, "they are compelled to employ people in the schoolmaster's post with lower capabilities, owing to the mea-ger income". The archdeacon executing the register in Keresztúr blamed the local nobles for tolerating the schoolmaster, whom he simply called an idiot. "Not even the hope of any progress glimmers in hiring a better schoolmaster, for the village, inhabited purely by nobles, is backwards in other respects too; therefore a more educated schoolmaster cannot be brought here for so meager an income as they are willing to pay him." In addition, it should be mentioned that in this village the nobles were all Catholic, so the poor state of affairs cannot be blamed on the resistance shown by the Protestants against Catholic schoolmasters. In the next village the implication was that "they will never be able to employ an educated schoolmaster for this money". In Nick the inhabitants bitterly said that, owing to the schoolmaster's poor pay, no decent man would endeavor to come to the village.[27] One peasant in Pozsony County, recalling his teacher from 1740, said that after an earlier schoolmaster's departure he attended the class of "a schoolmaster called Farkasdi, whom they also called 'the rag-ged' because of being so poor".[28]

As noted earlier, tuition fees did not comprise a sizable part of a school-master's income. How great was the burden of the children's tuition on a peasant family? School fees, fixed on the basis of customary law, were twenty-five *denarii* quarterly in the seventeenth and eighteenth centuries. In addition, the children's parents were expected to contribute to the heating of the school building, as most teaching was done in the winter. The twenty-five *denarii* fee remained fixed for centuries and did not follow changes in the value of the currency. Accordingly, school fees increasingly became less of a burden for peasant households but at the same time repre-sented decreasing income for teachers.

In the 1780s in the villages around the market town of Szentgotthárd, a cobbler mended shoes for fifty *denarii*. For this sum, his child could attend school for half of a year. The smith charged six to ten *denarii* for shoeing a horse; for the price of three horseshoes, then, a child could learn to read and write for a quarter of a year. The price of a hatchet, twenty-five *denarii*, equaled a quarter-year of studying reading, and the price of two pitchforks (thirty *denarii*) paid for a quarter-year of writing instruction. For one forint, the price of a sow, a serf could have his child taught for a full year at the end of the eighteenth century. However, only a few children attended school for a full year; they pursued schooling mostly in the winter. For the price of two day's labor, thirty-two *denarii*, a peasant could finance his son's tuition for an entire winter.[29] The fees in village elementary schools, therefore, did not really present an obstacle for rural peasant households, except perhaps for the most destitute families with many children, cottars or widows. The work missed by children while attending school was a much greater burden, though difficult to measure in monetary terms. This explains why in nineteenth-century Russia peasants demanded payment from the teachers for keeping schoolchildren away from work, and quite rightly according to their logic.[30]

The Proportion of Children Actually Attending Schools

Before the introduction of general and *de facto* compulsory education, the efficiency of the educational system largely depended on the percentage of school-goers among school-age children. Unfortunately, neither national surveys nor canonical visitations recorded this type of information. Therefore, the index can be approximated only by collating several sources. In 1770 the survey conducted by the governor-general's council noted the number of children attending school (see table 1.7).

Table 1.7

Number of Schoolchildren in Vas County (1770)

District	Number of		Pupils per School	Teachers without Pupils
	Schools	Pupils		
Kemenesalja	43	588	13.67	4
Sárvár	25	355	14.20	4
Szombathely	45	828	18.40	5
Németújvár	34	835	24.50	1
Őrség	23	316	13.70	3
Rohonc	27	688	25.40	0
Tótság	11	8	–	10
Total	208	3.618	17.3	27

In Vas County in 1770, a total of 3,618 children attended elementary schools. However, the number of children learning to read and write was greater, as reading and writing were taught also in the lower forms of the two grammar schools in this county, in the towns of Kőszeg and Szombathely.

The number of those learning to write in the first form (*parva-principia*) of the two grammar schools certainly should be included. Data is available on the Jesuit school of Kőszeg from 1741 when it had five hundred pupils, at least half of whom may be counted as learning at an elementary level. At the time of its foundation in 1771, the Franciscan grammar school of Szombathely had fifty-six pupils in the first form, one hundred the next year and one hundred thirty in subsequent years; therefore, a figure of one hundred elementary school-age pupils may be used.[31]

In the 1770 national school survey, all elementary schools in Vas County in principle were supposed to be registered. However, as it was conducted by Catholic deacons, the Protestant schools were omitted, and data on the Lutheran and Calvinist schools are, therefore, missing. Thus, the number of pupils in these schools is unknown but obviously was higher than in Catholic elementary schools, as there were only one Calvinist and two Lutheran schools in the entire county. The number of pupils can be estimated safely as approximately one hundred fifty.

Including the two hundred fifty pupils of the Kőszeg and the one hundred of the Szombathely grammar schools, plus the number of registered pupils attending elementary schools (3,618) and the one hundred fifty pupils of the three Protestant schools, the total is 4,118. Rounded, the number of elementary school pupils in Vas County in the 1770s may be estimated as 4,100.

There are two methods of estimating the percentage of all school-age children in the county that these 4,100 pupils comprised. Children in eighteenth-century Hungary were considered to be of school age up to nine years old. In 1779 Gáspár Pál, the inspector of elementary schools and a driving force behind the Enlightened Absolutist reform of elementary education, submitted a lengthy petition in which he stated that "the entire youth, from the age of six to eight and nine, should be made to attend school".[32] If the enthusiastic reformer merely wanted to achieve this much, one may assume that the children in Vas County did not attend school past the age of nine. It is clear from the national school surveys and from the teachers' complaints that children attended school for three years on average—in fact, this meant three (occasionally four, but often not more than two) *winters*. The registered number of pupils, therefore, should be compared to the total number of children six to nine years of age, which will yield the percentage of children actually attending schools.

One method of calculation is comparing the number of pupils to the total population.[33] In the demographic structure of this period, one age group comprised approximately 2.5 percent of the total population. Consequently, the percentage of those between six and ten years of age constituted about ten percent of the population. In other words, had all members of the age group attended school, every tenth inhabitant of Hungary would have been a pupil in any given year. The census taken under Emperor Joseph II from 1784 to 1787, fifteen years after the survey mentioned above, registered approximately 220 thousand inhabitants in Vas County. The 4,100 elementary school pupils comprised 1.86 percent of this number, indicating that only some 18.6 percent of school-age children attended school.

Another method of checking the calculation above is to consider the number of inhabitants specified in the canonical visitation that took place closest to the national school survey. The visitors recorded the number of souls too "immature to be shriven"—too young to go to confession, which meant children under the age of seven. In view of the high rate of infant mortality of the time, the number of children under seven may have been roughly twice as many as those from six to nine years old. Collating the number of pupils registered in 1770 with *half* the number of children from one to six years old as recorded by Bishop Szily during his 1778 visitation, one may arrive at an estimate of the percentage of those attending school within the age group under discussion.

According to Bishop Szily's records, the number of children below the age of seven in Vas County was 55,021 in 1778. As noted earlier, the number of those attending school in 1770 was 3,618, to which the students of the three Protestant schools and the first forms of the two grammar schools are added, rounding the number to 4,100. Comparing these numbers, the result is that 14.9 percent of school-age children in Vas in fact did attend elementary school. Taking into account the factor of uncertainty in both calculations, the data obtained by the two methods confirm one another. In the 1770s—the decade of the Enlightened Absolutism's school reform, *Ratio Educationis* (1777), which stipulated compulsory education—according to a calculation based on the total population, only every fifth or sixth child, or according to another, based on the number of children under seven, every sixth or seventh child attended elementary school.

There are huge discrepancies underlying the average number of students in Vas County. There were many villages in which not a single child attended school; in others, as many as half the children of the appropriate age went to school. However, no clear territorial divisions or trends may be ascertained by comparing the data on the various parishes. The children may have been absent from school for two reasons. First, owing to the backwardness of the region, peasant parents may not have felt a need to educate their children. A second reason might be that Protestant parents refused to let their children attend a Catholic school, as they were afraid the schoolmaster would convert them to Catholicism.

A small percentage of children, on average one-sixth of the county, did attend school in the second half of the eighteenth century. In view of descriptions of the tiny school buildings, it is clear that if all school-age children wanted to acquire reading and writing skills as stipulated by Queen Maria Theresa's education reform plans, they simply would not have had enough room.

Illiterate School-Leavers

Not all of those who made it to school acquired writing skills. In 1770 twenty-four elementary schools in Vas County did not teach writing as a regular part of instruction; children were taught only to read. In the other schools, teachers taught writing only for an extra fee.[34]

When examining the effect schools had on literacy, it is important to ascertain the number of those who learned to write in comparison with the total number of school attendees. Unfortunately, this was recorded only very rarely. From the church visitations and school surveys, however, it is clear that a greater portion of pupils learned only to read. The schoolteacher in Szerdahely taught the basics of Latin and arithmetic, and the church visitation recorded that "he mainly teaches reading". It was noted that five other teachers also taught "reading and, in some few cases, also writing". The master in Lövő taught children how to read, "but hardly anybody to write"; the teacher in Keresztes "only teaches reading and, for a few children whose parents ask him especially to do so, also writing". In 1770 in Récse in Pozsony County, which was somewhat more advanced than Vas, ten of the forty-six pupils were taught to write; the remaining thirty-six learned only "syllabification and the knowledge of letters". How many students did sit in the other corner of the classroom the following year (as the expression "passing to the next form" would be a gross anachronism) and learn to write is not known, but it is quite clear that those learning to write were in the minority. At the same time in Csáva, Sopron County, three out of twenty-five children were studying writing.

As noted, schoolteachers in several Vas County villages did not teach writing because they themselves lacked the skill of forming characters. In other places, writing was a complementary activity teachers had to undertake to support themselves due to the meager income provided for teaching, which prevented the schoolmaster from offering a more thorough curriculum. In 1771 it was noted of the schoolmaster in Prácsa, Pozsony County, that he was teaching his forty-one pupils "only to read, nothing more", as his duties as village notary distracted him from school, and he could not pay an assistant from the little money he made. This was the same reason given by another schoolmaster in Gurab, Pozsony County, who did not teach writing.[35]

Learning to write demanded a great deal more time from both teachers and pupils than the passive learning of reading. Most children attended school for only two or three months in the winter and even then intermittently. Pupils were often absent from school, which was especially detrimental to learning to write, as the skill called for greater and more systematic efforts than reading. It was easier for children to learn prayers, songs and reading in the course of the disrupted scholastic year (which might better be called a "scholastic winter"), but it took more to acquire the active skill of tracing letters. The schoolmasters themselves deemed that the greatest obstacle was that in summer parents sent their children to "look after the beasts of the meadow" or to carry out other minor jobs in the fields instead of to school. Consequently, the children soon forgot what they had learned in the winter. In 1770 the teacher in Óhíd, Zala County, related that although he had fourteen pupils, "it is not possible to teach them more than just reading since they are not attending school continuously".[36]

No data can be offered to answer the decisive question from the perspective of the history of literacy: what percentage of the registered number of pupils acquired writing skills, and what percentage were content with learning the passive ability to read. However, it is clear from the remarks above that the majority of pupils left school without ever learning to write. Only a fraction of school-age children did attend school, and even of these, the majority stopped studying at the level of semi-literacy, acquiring the skill of reading without beginning to learn to write. Only a small portion of children attending elementary school in the eighteenth century learned to write, and even fewer attained proficiency in arithmetic.

Another manifestation of the lack of education in rural society was "mathematical illiteracy" or "innumeracy". Only forty-five schoolmasters—barely twenty-one percent—taught arithmetic in Vas County in 1770; in their schools only a few pupils who could afford to pay higher fees became acquainted with the first four rules of arithmetic. Most teachers did not teach multiplication tables because they themselves had difficulties with basic arithmetic. In contrast to Latin, the arithmetic skills of teachers were not examined during the church visitations in Vas County. In one district of neighboring Sopron County, however, the church visitors did review the teaching of arithmetic; thus, the master in Vitnyéd, who instructed children to read and write, himself knew only addition and subtraction—multiplication and division were beyond his skills. Even those teachers who knew some Latin failed to understand arithmetic. In the market town of Mihályi, the teacher knew some Latin, "though not arithmetic, nor can he therefore instruct the children in numeracy". Similarly, the schoolmaster in Németi was unqualified to teach arithmetic, even if he knew "some" Latin. The teacher in Páli also spoke Latin but was entirely ignorant of arithmetic. The teacher in Jobaháza knew very little Latin and knew only the first two operations of arithmetic. The master in Keresztúr knew how to add, sub- tract and multiply but failed when it came to division. The teacher at Kisfalud was *absolutus rhetor*—that is, he finished all six forms of grammar school—but could at best grapple with three of the four arithmetical operations.[37]

In 1777, seven years after the survey quoted above, *Ratio Educationis* pre- scribed the compulsory teaching of the four rules of arithmetic in village elementary schools.[38] The small number of schoolmasters who knew arith- metic and could teach it, however, indicates that it must have taken a long time, perhaps decades, before teachers well versed in arithmetic were found to teach in the village schools.

It is also true that all peasants were capable of counting the quantity of wine sold by scoring notches or selling their produce at the market by counting with fingers. However, when it came to counting larger sums or more intricate calculations due to the complicated changing of contempo- rary coins and measures, those who never learned arithmetic were as much at a disadvantage, compared to those who knew the four basic op- erations, as the illiterate majority was compared to those who could read and write.

Peasant Children Attending School in Neighboring Villages

One of the most important questions in the history of schools is whether village elementary schools were attended only by local children or also by those from neighboring villages. An answer to this question is not readily available; teachers did not keep diaries or registers, as was the practice in urban grammar schools. It is generally accepted that children did not travel to another village simply to learn, not even from a neighboring village. "To cover a distance of several kilometers daily, amid the vicissitudes of the weather, would have been a totally unfulfillable wish", states the definitive history of Hungarian schools.[39]

Had this been the practice, the history of schools would be much simpler. In Vas County, a region of small settlements, the majority of children who lived in villages with no school would not have been able to learn writing and reading skills. On rare occasions the schoolmasters of the parish villages visited other villages attached to their parishes primarily for the purpose of teaching the basics of religion to the local children on Sunday afternoons. In 1770 there were 622 settlements (towns, market towns and villages) in Vas County, while there were only 213 schoolmasters. Therefore, the inhabitants of four hundred settlements, the majority of the county's population, would not have had the opportunity to learn to read and write. Sources, however, including records of church visitations, law suits and correspondence concerning schools, reveal that, in contrast to what is indicated in the school history studies, children in western Hungary *did* attend schools in villages other than their own in the seventeenth and eighteenth centuries.

In the course of the Lutheran visitations carried out in northern Vas County in 1633, 1642 and 1650, the income of schoolmasters was recorded. Accordingly, frequent notes appear to the effect that the schoolmaster received a quarterly fee of twenty-five *denarii* from local children, while "he took as much as could be bargained from those coming from elsewhere"—thus, there *were* children coming "from elsewhere".[40]

In addition, it was not rare for a schoolboy from neighboring Sopron County to go to school in another village. In the mid-seventeenth century, the villagers of Márc sent their sons to the Lutheran school in a neighboring village, partly because they did not wish to put them under the hands of the local "Papist" schoolmaster and partly because there, "a man of appropriate knowledge, who is well versed in the writing of German and Latin, singing and even counting will take care of their instruction". The Lutherans of Nagymarton also were inclined to send their children to this school even though it meant a daily walk of two kilometers, because the schoolmaster at Nagymarton was, in addition to being a Catholic, "a drunkard who was not very knowledgeable about the teaching of children".[41] There were some children who went to school in another country, although all this involved was crossing the Leitha River. In 1651, for example, the children in Wimpassing, Hungary, had to go to the first village in Lower Austria across the Lajta River to study, as there was no school in their own village. In 1770 the residents of Lajtafalu in Moson County similarly sent their sons to the other bank of the Leitha River if they were not content with the local teaching of writing and reading. As it was noted in the school survey, "those who are better-off will send their children to the neighboring Austrian village of Haslau in order to learn German and arithmetic".[42] In 1770 the pupils from Engerau, a village facing the town of Pozsony (Bratislava) across the Danube River, would cross the frozen river until the winter became too severe or the ice started drifting to attend the school in Pozsony.[43] A nobleman attended school in the village of Simaháza, Sopron County, in the 1710s. However, the expression "attended school" is rather anachronistic since in Simaháza, "not having a schoolhouse", the master held classes at a different house each week. The pupil, age ten at the time, did not live in Simaháza but in the neighboring village of Szopor from which he would walk, if not to school, at least to learn.[44]

Most likely those children who went to school in another village in winter began their studies at a somewhat later age than their local peers; it took larger boys to set out on the muddy, snow-blown roads. The children might have been gathered and transported to the next village by cart, but this is merely a hypothesis, as neither the national school survey nor the canonical visitations noted the age of the pupils or the means by which they reached their schools.

In 1774 the county authorities reviewed the school of Hódos in Pozsony County because the Calvinist schoolmasters also instructed Catholic children, even though this was strictly forbidden. Evidence indicates that the Hódos children attended the village school from the age of eight "for some two years, only in winter though", while the children from a neighboring village two kilometers away began commuting to Hódos at the age of ten or eleven, pursuing their studies for two or three winters (this account goes on to confirm that schooling generally did not last longer than this). Parents most likely did not allow their children to walk to school in other villages in

snow and rain before they were ten, which is why they began their education at a later age than the locals did.[45]

This is confirmed by the notes of the Catholic archdeacon on the school
in Réte, Pozsony County. This Calvinist school was a solid one and even
taught the basics of the Latin language. The local Catholics, however, refused to let their children attend the "heretic" school, and they did not send
them to another village either. Owing to the lack of a schoolmaster, one
barely could find someone among the Catholics who knew how to read,
much less who knew how to write, since the children in the Catholic households were "too small to be sent elsewhere to learn the basics".[46]

Learning Outside School

It is very probable that the majority of children in Vas County and in Hungary in general did not attend any school. The rate of learning may have
been improved somewhat by the fact that learning to read and write was
possible outside of school as well. Those who knew these skills may have
passed their talents on to others.[47] Some artisans, for example, must have
instructed apprentices in the use of pens and tools. The occasional tutor and
his disciple did not, however, enter into a written agreement, nor did they
fall under the authority of the state or a denomination; they did not make
reports or statements or issue certificates. Therefore, it is extremely difficult
to gather data on private education of this nature. Education of this kind
remains obscure in most time periods, and it is no wonder that this question
has never been examined in Hungary. It may be assumed that some Protestants who refused to let their children attend Catholic schools in Vas
County, as the Catholic archdeacons reproachfully recorded, did not resign
themselves to having their children remain uneducated. More detailed records on other counties provide evidence that Protestant children also were
tutored at home: "*Domi instruitur*" (he is taught at home) was the entry for
many children from Lutheran families in Csetnek, Gömör County, in
1753.[48]

In his autobiography, the writer and revolutionary Mihály Táncsics
(1799–1884), a prominent figure in the 1848–49 War of Independence,
wrote "I used to teach the little daughter of the bread maker next door to
read outside school, for which I was granted no salary other than the pair of
buns that I took and devoured on the spot while hot". In 1838, a button
maker in Vienna requested that Táncsics teach him to write, as he could not

write out his accounts, and offered Táncsics free lunch at his house every day as payment.[49]

Apart from memoirs, depositions also provide evidence that the skill of writing and reading could be obtained outside school. In 1746 in the market town Vásárhely, a peasant woman being interrogated denied that a certain Mathias had fornicated with the wife of András Polya. The judges suspiciously noted that Mátyás often visited the Polyas' house, and they went on to interrogate the witness: "'Is it true that the husband, András Polya, taught Mátyás the alphabet?' 'Tis very true,' she replied, 'I saw them handle the book of the alphabet together.'" Unfortunately, the rest of the records were lost, so no more information about the occasional tutor or his pupil is available. It is clear from the court account that the protagonists were not part of the social elite. It is also clear that András Polya taught an adult man the alphabet outside of school. Similarly, in 1726 an "old maid" in the market town of Kissáros in Upper Hungary recounted that a student named Péter instructed the young maid at the pub, Marinka, to read throughout the night. Marinka, charged with fornication, probably was not spending her nights studying, but it is obvious from a sarcastic hint that she could not read to begin with, and more importantly, it was not seen as inconceivable that an adult could begin learning to read in Sáros County.[50]

Another case of a private pupil appears in the records of a crime. In December 1734 Ferenc Nagy, a nobleman, impregnated his stepdaughter and abandoned the mother and the baby in a public house in Komárom. As the stepdaughter was bathing her child in the pub, an eyewitness stated that the farmer who ran the pub "was tutoring his own child to read from a book". At this point Ferenc Nagy addressed the farmer, saying: "Tis truly a clever child. Were he mine I would not give him for the town of Komárom." Upon which the farmer-publican replied: "You ought to give instruction to that little infant too, my lord." Ferenc Nagy then responded: "That I shall do, indeed, if I live to see him grow up." This exchange assumed great importance in the court case, as Ferenc Nagy later, "beating his breast", denied that the baby was his. The publican, then, was teaching his little son to read from a book, although it is not known whether this was in lieu of or in addition to attending school. It is clear, however, that schoolmasters were not the only possible sources of learning to read and write. The alphabet book that was stolen from a maid of the public house in Deméte, Sáros County, also may have been used for education outside the school. While on her way from Eperjes to her village, two men attacked and raped her, robbing her not only of her virginity but also of a necklace and an alphabet book. Similarly, in 1753 in the market town, Tiszaladány, a peasant woman told the judge that another peasant woman, who was accused of witchcraft, "came to her to teach her to read; she bought a primer for herself and then even a psalm book". Despite these examples, illiteracy was widespread in the seventeenth and eighteenth centuries, and few learned to write either in or outside of school. There were some, however, who did not attend school because they had private tutors to teach them in their homes.[51]

Schooling of Nobles

The children of lower nobles who did not own land or possessed only a villein's plot (taxalists) attended the same local elementary school as the peasants, if at all. During ancestry investigations, a process in which the nobility's genealogy was examined by county authorities when the lowest stratum of the nobles of uncertain legal status sought their due, elderly peasants often would testify that they recalled the nobles in question, as they attended the same school.

This was the case in 1778 when a delegation from the county authorities investigated the genealogy of the Osváld family of Andrásfa, Vas County, who tried to prove its status. This was not an easy task—the noble who could provide evidence about his kin's lineage, István Osváld, "was deranged in his mind" and could not answer questions. Rather, he was "walking up and down, rambling, as was in line with his demented state". Eventually a sixty-nine-year-old shepherd spoke up and recounted the genealogy of the Osválds. The records indicate that "he knew all this to be true, as he dwelt for several years in the same village and attended the same school as did the above-named Osválds". Therefore, peasant and noble offspring attended the same school, although they later parted ways.[52]

In Transylvania it was customary for the children of the nobility to attend the same village school as peasant boys. In letters from exile in Turkey, the Transylvanian noble Kelemen Mikes (1690–1761) wrote about the education of nobles, saying reproachfully that only Latin was taught at the college rather than some more useful field. "Having studied the Latin language for so many years and nothing else, the young nobleman had not much use of it at his house", he wrote. But Mikes, while condemning the nobles who "amid the merry-making, hounding and drinking till the small hours of the night" forgot everything they learned in college, held less modern views about elementary schooling for noble youths. He believed that the noble children became assimilated by young peasants in the rural elementary schools: "in Transylvania, the noble youths in general did not leave their villages until they were ten or eleven, attending till then the village school. In the course of this time they would learn how to read, but together with reading skills, they also acquired peasant customs … owing to their education amid the many peasants, they often forgot that they were of noble lineage."[53]

The wealthy landed gentry, however, did not allow their children to intermingle with those of the peasants. Instead, they employed private tutors before sending their children to grammar schools in town. As he himself wrote in his testament in 1753, József Tallián, a wealthy landed noble from Vas County, employed "clever, God-fearing, pious teaching tutors" to instruct his sons at home, but all this was in vain according to the reproaches he included in his last will.[54]

Other landed nobles attempted to have their offspring tutored by a teacher in residence in an aristocratic court. Consequently, contacts between the young lords and would-be courtiers were established in childhood, and the nobles could be assured that the children were put in the care of competent tutors.

In the early seventeenth century, the county elite sent their offspring to study in the grammar schools of nearby Vienna or Graz. This is confirmed by an incident in 1616 in which Palatine György Thurzó, a follower of Luther's tenets, requested that the local gentry give grants for the Lutheran grammar school under construction in Galgóc. The nobles hesitated, stating that other financial burdens weighed down heavily on the inhabitants but also claiming that they had no need for the school because both Catholic and Lutheran students pursued their studies in Vienna or Graz, which were much closer than Galgóc.[55]

In the mid-seventeenth century, Jesuit grammar schools were opened in Győr and Sopron (in 1627 and 1636 respectively), although nearby Graz had a Jesuit university that also offered secondary education. The new schools continued to attract the Catholic or re-Catholicized nobility of western Hungary. From 1623, the Lutheran nobles of Vas County could send their sons to the new Lutheran grammar school (*lyceum*) of Sopron.[56]

In the seventeenth and eighteenth centuries, grammar school curricula were based on Latin and developed very slowly. This is supported by the accounts of the guardians of the orphaned boys of two fashionable noble families from Vas County, the Ostffys and the Chernels. Both families were Lutheran and attended the Lutheran school in Sopron.[57] Mihály, Miklós

Ostffy's son, studied there between 1696 and 1700; the two orphans of Jób Chernel—György, eleven, and Sándor, thirteen—studied there some ninety years later, from 1786 to 1788. Several items in the two accounts were identical: boots had to be resoled and pelisses patched up, and the scholars needed candles, stationery and writing implements. The accounts also provide insight into the differences of the noble way of life at the end of the seventeenth and eighteenth centuries. Within the ninety years, the lifestyle of nobles changed, becoming more sophisticated and more similar to the Vienna model. In 1786 the guardian of the Chernel boys purchased pomade, several pounds of hair powder and silk ribbons for his charges and even snuff and nail clippers for the older boy—items that could not be found at the end of the seventeenth century.

The curriculum, however, barely changed during this ninety-year period: Mihály Ostffy's guardian bought a songbook, a prayer-book, a Latin dictionary, a catechism and Rhenius's *Latin Grammar* at the end of the seventeenth century. These books also were used by the students of the Lutheran lyceum of Sopron ninety years later: the poet János Kis (1770–1846), who began his studies at the school in 1782, studied Latin from Rhenius's book.[58] Similarly, Ovid's poems were used to teach Latin a century earlier. The geography book, however, written by the famous geographer János Tomka-Szászky (1700–62), was a great improvement over the teaching material used a century before.[59]

Real progress in the education of nobles is illustrated even more clearly by the fact that Mihály Ostffy learned only German and Latin at the end of the seventeenth century, while a century later the landed gentry in Vas County put great emphasis on acquiring French skills as well: Voltaire's language was taught to the Chernel boys by an independent "French language master".

Schools in Vas County in Comparison to Those of Other Counties in Transdanubia

Education in Vas County at the end of the seventeenth century may be compared to the school systems in the neighboring Sopron, Győr and Moson counties and, in the second half of the eighteenth century, to Somogy County.

In 1697 there were schools only in forty-six percent of the Vas County Catholic parish districts, while in the 1696 church visitation in the Sopron archdeaconry near Vienna, there were schoolmasters active in all ten market towns and twenty village parishes, as well as in five of the six outer parishes. In other words, there was only one village without a teacher. At the same time, in the Locsmánd archdeaconry, Sopron County, there were teachers in all twelve market towns and all but one of the thirty-four parish villages. In the same district, however, only four of thirty outer parishes had a schoolmaster. In the Moson archdeaconry in Moson County, the situation was even more favorable—there were schoolmasters active in all seventeen market towns and eighteen parish villages and in eight of the twelve outer parishes.[60]

The school network, therefore, was significantly more developed in both Sopron and Moson counties at the end of the seventeenth century. The greater density of schools, already conspicuous at the end of the seventeenth century, was the reason—as the historian Kálmán Benda established during his research—there were many more literate peasants living in these two counties than in Vas around the middle of the eighteenth century. In 1769 only 6.9 percent of the Vas County village mayors and magistrates were able to sign their names, while 45.5 percent in Moson and 49.4 percent in Sopron were able to do so. In other words, seven times more village mayors could sign their names in Sopron than in Vas County.[61]

Compared to the more favorable state of affairs in Moson and Sopron counties, the circumstances in the vicinity of the town of Győr were, in many respects, similar to those in Vas. At the same time that the Catholic Church visitation was conducted in Vas in 1697–1698, the archdeacon of Győr also visited the settlements under his care. The wounds of the Turkish wars, especially the 1683 campaign, had not healed yet, and many churches were still in ruins. Due to the spread of Protestantism, sometimes it nearly required an archaeologist's examination to ascertain if a church had once been Catholic. The disintegration of the parish network was due to the same reasons; a one-time parish village could hardly be distinguished from its outer parishes. In total, the archdeacon visited forty-two villages and only found school buildings in six. In several settlements, the priest or the schoolmaster trained his pupils in his own rooms.[62]

In the majority of villages (twenty-eight) there was no education offered at all. In ten villages the schoolmaster taught children; in four, the Protestant minister; i.e. in three, the Lutheran minister and in one, a Calvinist. In general the schoolmasters had finished some grammar school, but the Lutheran rector in Rábaszentmihály, who did not teach, learned "some Latin" from his father, a Lutheran pastor, at home. The Catholic rector in Fehértó, who also did not teach, also learned his trade from his father.

What makes the 1698 visitation in the Győr archdeaconry especially relevant to the history of education in Hungary is that in seven villages, all inhabited by Hungarians, the archdeacon recorded the number of schoolchildren and the total number of children in the village (see table 1.8). Although he did not specify the definition of "child" in this case, the archdeacon undoubtedly meant those who were too young to attend confession (that is, under seven), as was customary. As with the case of Vas County, an approximation of school-age children may be calculated according to the number of children too young to go to confession.

Table 1.8

Number of Schoolchildren in the Villages of the Győr Archdeaconry
(1698)

Village	Denomination	Number of Children	Schoolchildren
Mezőörs	Calvinist	198	17
Táp	Calvinist	231	16
Felpéc	Lutheran	89	16
Kaját	Lutheran	536	11
Gyömöre	Lutheran	105	6
Gyarmat	Catholic	174	22
Tét	Lutheran	89	13

The number of children attending school as a percentage of the total number of six to nine year-old children may be calculated from the data presented in table 1.9. In seven villages of the Győr archdeaconry (one Catholic, two Calvinist and four Lutheran settlements) 14.2 percent of all school-age children attended school in 1698). In this case as well, the average is based on highly varying circumstances: in Kaját, with a population of 1,594, the Lutheran schoolmaster had merely eleven pupils (4.1 percent of all school-age children), despite the fact that the village was predominantly Lutheran. In Tét, which also was predominantly Lutheran and was inhabited by only 259 persons, the number of pupils was the same as in Kaját, which in this less populous village meant some thirty percent of all children. The number of pupils in Tét certainly was not so high because their teacher was exceptionally talented: the visitor noted that the schoolmaster was "an immature lad, Slovak by birth, who is a bell ringer and cantor in one person. He came here straight from the fourth form of the Lutheran school in Trencsény". The largest percentage, one-third of all children, studied under the schoolmaster in Felpéc, a rector and bell ringer who had studied at the Győr grammar school. Whether or not the high rate of school attendance was due to the influence of the local pastors is unknown, but even in nearby villages with the same denomination, school attendance figures showed significant differences.

Table 1.9

Percentage of School-Goers in the Győr Archdeaconry (1698)

Village	Denomination	Number of School–Age Children	Number of School–Goers	Percentage of School–Goers
Mezőörs	Calvinist	99	17	17.1
Táp	Calvinist	115	16	13.9
Felpéc	Lutheran	44	16	36.3
Kajár	Lutheran	268	11	4.1
Gyömöre	Lutheran	52	6	11.5
Gyarmat	Catholic	87	22	25.2
Tét	Lutheran	44	13	29.5
Total		709	101	14.2

On average one-seventh of the children in these seven villages were sent to school. However, of the forty-two villages that the archdeacon visited, there was no teaching whatsoever in twenty-eight. The archdeacon counted 9,271 people in thirty-eight villages; in four additional villages, the Protestant inhabitants refused to be counted, instead making "frivolous and impertinent comments" to the Catholic archdeacon. Thus one hundred one schoolchildren were among the approximately 9,500 inhabitants. Using the method established earlier, hardly more than one-tenth, or 10.6 percent, of the children were sent to school in the region of Győr.

In Vas County, there was one school building for every 1,188 inhabitants in 1698, while one school existed for every 1,583 people in the Győr archdeaconry. In other words, the number of school buildings was very low in the vicinity of Győr. Due to the ravages of war, most churches were also in ruins; in other places village quarters were scarcely populated, and the peasants apparently deemed the construction of a school as a lower priority. The region was, however, better supplied with teachers than Vas County; in the same period, there was one teacher for every 1,134 inhabitants in Vas and for every 678 in the vicinity of Győr.

The position of schools was better on average in the Győr archdeaconry than in the whole of Vas County and was largely comparable to the northeastern, developed part of Vas County. As the 1770 survey testifies, the percentage of literate persons in Győr County was significantly lower than in Sopron and Moson counties but better than in Vas: in 14.8 percent of the villages and market towns at least one magistrate was able to sign his signature.

Education in Vas in the second half of the eighteenth century can be compared to the situation in Somogy County on the basis of the national school surveys. While Vas County had 213 teachers, there were only 146 teachers in Somogy in the 1770s. The population of the county was lower, though: instead of Vas's 188 thousand, only 126 thousand individuals resided in Somogy. Therefore, the number of inhabitants per teacher was approximately the same in both: 863 in Somogy, 867 in Vas. These numbers are, however, highly misleading unless corrected. The poet Mihály Csokonai Vitéz (1773–1805), in his 1799 pamphlet entitled "Prophesy about the First School in Somogy", posed the question: "Is the peasant of Somogy good for nothing else but to be a swineherd?" Differences in terminology must be considered. The word "schoolmaster" itself is misleading, because in 1770 thirty-seven percent of the schoolmasters in Somogy County did not have a single pupil to teach, and only sixty-one percent taught at least reading. Therefore, in practice many schoolmasters were only cantors, as were the masters of the Tótság region in Vas. Despite the fact that the data tallies, the circumstances for learning were much better in Vas County than in the more backward Somogy. Therefore, Csokonai was not wrong when daydreaming about the first grammar school of Somogy. This is reflected in the fact that in 1769 barely eight (2.9 percent) of the villages and market towns in Somogy had at least one literate mayor or magistrate.[63]

Elementary Schools in the Habsburg Empire from Lower Austria to Galicia

The percentage of schoolchildren in Vas County also may be compared to that of other provinces of the Habsburg Empire. Although no detailed data from the eighteenth century has survived from villages in Styria, lying directly next to Vas County and from which several teachers came to Vas, a picture of the region still may be formed on the basis of a 1617 church visitation and an 1805 survey (see table 1.10).

This data may provide at least some indication of the development of schools in these Styrian villages between the seventeenth and the early nineteenth centuries. As emphasized in the histories of Styrian schools, putting the principles of Maria Theresa's and Joseph II's school reforms into practice was left until the early decades of the nineteenth century, under Emperor Francis (1792–1835).

Even in Graz, the capital of Styria, only a fraction of children were sent to school; in 1772, two years before Maria Theresa's Austrian educational reforms, seventeen percent of children in Graz attended elementary school, while in 1780, six years after the reforms, thirty percent did so. Although the data testify that the number of those attending school had nearly doubled in only eight years, seventy percent of the children in Graz continued to lack an elementary education—and Graz was the capital of the province.[64]

Table 1.10

School-Goers in Eastern Styria (1617 and 1805)

Settlements	Number of Pupils in 1617		Number of Pupils in 1805
	Winter	Summer	
Gnas	unknown	20	125
Sankt Margarethen an der Raab	0	0	60
Sankt Ruprecht	15	3	112
Weiz	5	0	68
Friedberg	15	4	16
Leutschach	20–24	"almost nobody"	70

In the bishopric of Passau, which extended to both Lower and Upper Austria, there was a school in every parish in 1772, but only ten to twenty percent of the children attended. Surveys indicate that the school age went up to twelve rather than nine as in Hungary, which is indicative of the difference in development between the two regions. This explains why the percentages cannot be compared directly to those of Vas County. One thing is clear: those attending school were in the minority in these provinces as well.

The data from the survey conducted in the Passau Bishopric is corroborated by a state survey, in light of which only 18,527, or sixteen percent, of the 114,105 school-age children attended school in Lower Austria in 1771. Nor was the percentage of school-goers much better in the imperial capital, Vienna, and its outer districts. In 1770, 4,665 pupils—that is, hardly more than one-third of all children—attended sixty-five schools. Maria Theresa's school reform contributed to significant progress in Vienna as well: in 1779, five years after the reforms, the number of elementary schoolchildren registered in Vienna was 8,039—their number had nearly doubled over nine years. In the same year, thirty-four percent of all children in Lower Austria attended school, as compared to sixteen percent in 1771. Although the number of school-goers practically doubled in a few years, precisely two-thirds of the children were left without an elementary education even after theoretically compulsory schooling was introduced. These averages, however, hide huge discrepancies: the proportion of children attending school in Lower Austria only exceeded one-half in the vicinity of Vienna and in the Gaming Archdeaconry. Farther from the capital, in the Weitra, Altpölla and Pottenstein districts, only fourteen to twenty percent went to school. There was still a great deal of progress to be made under the Enlightened Absolutist school policy, even in the most developed province of the Empire, the region around the imperial city of Vienna.[65]

In the archives of the Court Commission for Education (*Studienhofkommission*) in Vienna, several tables of figures have been preserved. These figures were compiled about the schools and school-age and school-going children in particular provinces by the Abbot Johann Ignaz Felbiger, father of the school reforms.[66] At first glance, these tables offer the promise that calculations can be made based on their data concerning the percentage of school-goers among school-age children in particular provinces. On closer examination, however, the sources reveal that the state bureaucracy at the end of the eighteenth century did not fully meet the demands of the administration to the effect that precise and unified data be submitted about everything. The number of pupils attending normal schools may be considered realistic, with the exception of the Trento data, which contains an obvious clerical error. However, those conducting the survey apparently lacked detailed instructions as to whom they were to consider to be "of school age" (the Abbot Felbiger counted one-eighth of the total population as being of school age in his memoirs).

This explains why 94 thousand school-aged children were registered as being of school age in Lower Austria in 1781 (see table 1.11), while in Upper Austria, which had half the population, the number of school-age children was recorded as 67 thousand. Similarly, in Moravia the figure was 118 thousand, while in Bohemia, with a population two and a half times that of Moravia, only 156 thousand school-age children were recorded (see fig.1). It is more effective to collate the numbers provided by Felbiger with the data from the census taken under Emperor Joseph II (1780–90), as in the case of Vas County.

Table 1.11

Percentage of Elementary School-Goers within
the Total Population in Provinces of the Habsburg Empire
(1781)

Province	Pupils	Population (Thousand)	Percentage
Lower Austria	37,393	1,268	2.94
Upper Austria	13,987	621	2.25
Bohemia	65,552	2,922	2.24
Moravia	22,252	1,262	1.76
Tyrol	14,572	430	3.38
Carinthia	4,297	295	1.45
Carniola	1,124	440	0.25
Galicia	5,864	3,268	0.17

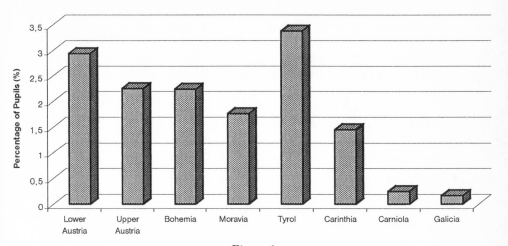

Figure 1.

Percentage of Elementary School-Goers within the Total Population
in the Provinces of the Habsburg Empire (1781)

According to our calculations in Vas County in the 1770s, 1.68 percent of the population went to school. This percentage was significantly lower than in the more developed provinces of the empire, Lower and Upper Austria and Bohemia, or in Tyrol with its confident peasantry. The standards of Vas County, at least in terms of quantitative indices, were largely the same as in Moravia and somewhat better than in Carinthia. Carniola and underdeveloped Galicia lagged behind western Hungary in education.

Elementary Schools in Western Europe:
Light Years Ahead

The following section provides a comparison of the elementary school situation in Vas County with that of two countries, Prussia and France, which were pioneers in educational affairs in the eighteenth century. The best comparison may be made between the schools in eighteenth-century western Hungary and Prussian schools. In the age of Enlightened Absolutism, Prussia was a paragon of educational policy. It is hardly accidental that Queen Maria Theresia entrusted the Abbot Felbiger, a person who had acquired experience in educational policy in Prussia and authored several surveys mentioned earlier, with carrying out school reforms in the empire.

The state devoted special attention to schooling in Prussia, and Prussian kings issued several decrees related to education. In villages farther from the central administration, however, the circumstances at the time were surprisingly similar to those in western Hungary before the introduction of *Ratio Educationis* in 1777.[67]

It is also possible to compare the salaries earned by western Hungarian schoolmasters to those of their Prussian counterparts. Teachers in the Protestant Kingdom of Prussia also worked primarily as cantors and sacristans. Accordingly, those employed in the outer parishes earned much less than their colleagues in the parish villages; at funerals it was always the schoolmaster who escorted the parish priest and who received remuneration, as in Vas County. The similarities also extend to the complaints of inhabitants in the outer parishes about their difficulties in finding suitable teachers due to meager salaries. In Prussia as well, only a portion of a schoolmaster's income (in some places one-third, but more generally, one-quarter or one-fifth) came from tuition fees. Tuition fees were sanctioned by centuries-old customs in Prussia, as in Hungary, and consequently a fee that once ensured a decent living for the schoolmaster depreciated over the course of time. Using a rate of two Hungarian forints per Prussian thaler, Prussian teachers in the second half of the eighteenth century received on average one and a half or twice as much as did their counterparts in Vas County. Those who also were cantors in parishes could earn three times as much income (forty to sixty thalers) as their colleagues in the outer parishes, who could "only" teach and did not earn more than thirteen to thirty thalers.

A comparison between incomes requires a parallel comparison of prices. Although the mainly state-salaried Prussian schoolmasters may have earned more than their church-employed counterparts in western Hungary, they still remained at the bottom of the village hierarchy. As noted, in Vas County in the late eighteenth century, teachers in the outer parishes received significantly lower salaries than gamekeepers, ox herders or farm hands. This was the same in Prussia: in 1764, the inspector of the Zossen school district compared the income of the schoolmaster (twenty-four thalers and four groschen) for teaching twenty pupils with the local farmhand's payment of sixteen to twenty thalers. In addition, a farmhand also received in kind payments—twelve bushels of rye and twenty-four fathoms of linen—so it appears that farmhands were not worse off than schoolmasters.[68]

Teachers, therefore, were compelled to look for other sources of livelihood. In western Hungary there were many schoolmasters who, in addition to acting as the cantor, sacristan or notary, engaged in another branch of craftsmanship. In Prussia, supplementary work for teachers was so common that its absence was conspicuous. The pastor of Germensdorf in 1792 wrote that "teaching seems a burdensome and unrewarding side-job". The decrees issued by King Frederick William I (1786–97) in fact encouraged rather than forbade teaching by tailors, wheelwrights, weavers, et cetera and stipulated that for schoolmasters, "such people should be employed as are industrious in their trade [crafts], so that they also earn their livelihood through some subsidiary work rather than sponge on the community".

Accordingly, between 1780 and 1806, of 232 village schoolmasters in Brandenburg, 153 (57.3 percent) were also tailors, twenty-five were weavers or had a related occupation, eight were shoemakers, three were bricklayers, and three worked as carpenters. Only eighteen (7.8 percent) lived solely on teaching. In 1770, of the 464 village teachers in Neumark, only eighty-three (17.9 percent) did not hold second jobs, and 259 teachers (55.8 percent) were also tailors. More thorough surveys in western Hungary probably would have shown more schoolmasters who were also artisans in this region, although most likely not as much as in Prussia.

In Prussia, the state established teacher-training institutions decades earlier than these institutions appeared in the Habsburg Empire, yet until the end of the eighteenth century their influence was insignificant. In 1799, of the 601 teachers in Neumark, only twenty-one (3.5 percent) were graduates of a teacher-training college. By 1805, the proportion was still not higher than 4.1 percent. Most of the teachers of the period learned their profession in practice, as in western Transdanubia, most often from their fathers who bequeathed the schoolmasters' positions to them. In eighteenth-century Prussia, those capable of reading and writing were deemed capable of teaching, just as in Hungary.

One record of a schoolmaster in Ruppin in 1798 stated that "he leaves teaching the children to his son, thereby he trains his son; a son can receive no better guidance in the profession from any other person but his father". Schoolmasters strove to leave their posts to their sons, and as a result virtual schoolmasters' dynasties emerged in Prussia. A significant portion of teachers were trained by the family; others were introduced to the profession as assistants to active teachers. As these individuals were taught only by the family, it is no surprise that many teachers in Prussia did not provide arithmetic instruction. This is evident from contracts made with teachers, which rarely prescribed teaching arithmetic as compulsory for a new teacher.[69]

In Prussia, as in the Protestant-inhabited parts of Hungary, many would-be pastors engaged in teaching until they found a parish for themselves. In

German historiography, this is cited as a negative example, arguing that teaching was in the hands of persons who were untrained for the profession and were anxious to leave their posts. In reality, though, these future pastors were obviously better qualified than the average schoolmaster.

The greatest problem for village schools in the eighteenth century in both Prussia and western Hungary and probably in the whole of Europe was that while instruction in principle lasted the whole year, in practice children attended school only for three winter months (traditionally from St. Martin's Day to Shrove Tuesday), when the fields were covered with snow. In other months, parents put their children to work. As a result, children forgot what they had learned the previous winter, and the teachers had to begin teaching the lessons anew. For the same reason, decrees on the compulsory schooling of children until the age of fourteen introduced by *Ratio Educationis* mostly were unenforced. The peasants needed their older children's labor, and therefore in Prussia and western Hungary, peasant offspring only attended school until the age of eight or ten or, at most, eleven.

In Prussia, unlike in Hungary, assistant teachers often were employed for the winter months in villages without either a teacher or school. These individuals were called "winter schoolmasters" or "line" or "row" schoolmasters (*Winterschulmeister, Reiheschulmeister, Gangschulmeister*), as they would visit one peasant home after another in the winter, teaching the children in succession.[70]

Prussian school reforms reached fruition in the nineteenth century, just as did the *Ratio Educationis* reforms in Hungary. According to a reliable national survey conducted in Prussia in 1816, sixty percent of all school-age children actually attended school.[71] In the eighteenth century, however, the circumstances of the rural schools in Prussia were not drastically different from those in western Hungary. In 1792 the illiterate wife of a tenant farmer from Neumark told the court in an account authenticated by three crosses that her children "could not learn letters for three winters in a row in school. It would have been a miracle indeed if they did learn anything by the methods their schoolmaster employed; instead of teaching the children one after another ... he would copy the full alphabet on the board and ask all the children what a particular letter was". The school fee was a waste of money for her and her husband, and for the children school was a waste of time; they should have worked instead.[72]

Based on the above, elementary schooling in Prussia was somewhat more developed than in western Hungary. If Prussian education is viewed in light of the reports describing the real situation of village schools rather than through the educational decrees that were issued earlier than those of the Habsburg Empire, there are more similarities between the two countries than differences. The discrepancies between intentions and realities were huge in both places. In both countries, the realization of the goals of Enlightened Absolutism—general compulsory schooling and instruction in reading, writing and counting—was to be implemented in the nineteenth century.

The huge gap separating Hungarian education from developed European countries in the eighteenth century can be demonstrated by comparing Hungarian schools to those in France. Louis XIV issued a detailed decree stipulating compulsory schooling as early as 1698. His successor confirmed the decree in 1724 and called upon schoolmasters to prepare detailed registers of all those children not attending school.[73] After repealing the Edict of Nantes, King Louis XIV aimed less to raise educational standards than to contain and repel the spread of Protestantism: in school, all children were required to learn the basic tenets of Catholicism. Even the Sun King failed to make schooling general and compulsory, just as Austrian Enlightened Absolutism failed seventy-five years later, although its goals were quite different.

Comparing education in various regions is never easy; in France one must also consider regions with highly varying geographical conditions and settlements. In addition, the methods employed during the various church visitations and surveys in the eighteenth century were hardly similar.

There is no comprehensive picture of the density of schools and the percentage of school attendance in France under the Ancien Régime. In 1826 Baron Charles Dupin, a mathematician and politician, prepared a national survey of school attendance in France. Although the survey was conducted long after the eighteenth century and, more importantly, a revolution, its data are still relevant. As the map was drawn before the large-scale school reforms of the nineteenth century, in many respects it reflects the situation under the Ancien Régime. The state of affairs as fixed on the map is further confirmed by research conducted on the literacy of the French based on eighteenth-century marriage registers: literacy was high in the eighteenth century wherever school attendance was high in the early nineteenth century. On both maps, the imaginary dividing line between Saint Malo, on the border of Normandy and Brittany, and Geneva is prominent. The more advanced regions of France, where both literacy and school attendance were high, were to the east and the north. In the regions lying to the west and the south and the central, mountainous part of the country, illiteracy and the low percentage of children attending school were apparent.[74]

In the early nineteenth century, there were huge differences within France: in the densely populated northern and eastern parts of the country, there was one schoolboy for every ten to fifteen inhabitants (hence, almost all school-age children went to school). In western Brittany and in the mountains of the Massif Central, this ratio was one to two hundred. Data from rural canonical visitations support the hypothesis that the regional differences as registered by Baron Dupin in 1826 were largely identical to the eighteenth-century statistics.

The church visitations reported on the bishopric of Rouen in Normandy in the early eighteenth century, between 1710 and 1717, recording that there were boys' schools in seventy-four percent of the parish villages (only boys' schools are discussed in the following sections). The findings in the bishopric of Châlons-sur-Marne, east of Paris, were the same in the 1720s. At the foot of the Pyrenees, though, in the diocese of Tarbes, only thirty-eight percent of the parishes had boys' schools in 1783; similarly, in the bishopric of Bordeaux, teaching was carried on only in twenty-four percent of the parishes in 1774. Worse, in the mountains and valleys of the Massif Central, a mere seventeen percent of the parishes of the bishopric of Rodez had schools.[75]

One must be cautious when comparing these data to western Hungary, where both the settlements and the sizes of parishes were different. In 1778, 238 teachers were registered in 119 parishes in Vas County; that is, not only was there at least one teacher in every parish but also in many of the outer parishes. However, the parishes in Vas County were large and had several, in places dozens, of affiliated outer parishes. Of the 661 settlements in Vas, therefore, only thirty-six percent had schoolmasters (only towns and larger market towns had more than one schoolmaster).

In the eighteenth century, the percentage of children attending school in Vas County was higher than in the most backward regions of France in the early nineteenth century. In the 1770s there was one schoolchild for every fifty-three inhabitants in Vas County (no data about the number of girls are available, but the figure could not have been high). In underdeveloped, Catholic western Brittany and in the similarly remote but Protestant-populated valleys of the Massif Central, there was one schoolboy for every 108 to 260 inhabitants in 1826; in the eastern part of Brittany and the hilly region around the Massif Central, the relevant ratio was one for every 91 to 150. Data for girls are unknown in France as well. In all likelihood, the figures for schoolgirls would not make a significant difference to the above ratio, for in the previously mentioned diocese of Tarbes, 61.6 percent of boys and only 2.2 percent of girls attended school.

Despite the uncertainty, these calculations make it probable that with regard to educational matters in the second half of the century, Vas County, one of the developed regions in Hungary, would have held its own with the most underdeveloped regions of France. Yet the massive difference between Hungary and the developed regions of Western Europe is well exemplified by a single comparison: 85.5 percent of school-age children attended school in the diocese of Rheims in 1774; 33.8 percent in the diocese of Tarbes in the Pyrenees in 1783 (which is frequently brought up in French historiography as a negative example); and only 14.9 percent in Vas County in the 1770s. The actual discrepancy was even greater than is suggested by the figures, as the French data are based on a period of seven years of compulsory schooling, while the Hungarian calculations, in accordance with reality and resources, are based on three years of education.

According to another method of calculation, which was employed earlier in the case of Vas County, 13.8 percent of the population in the Rheims Diocese and 5.4 percent in the bishopric of Tarbes attended school in the 1770s and the 1780s. The corresponding percentage for Lower Austria was 2.94, and for Bohemia, 2.24. In the same decades, a mere 1.8 percent of the population of Vas County attended school—one-eighth the percentage of Northern France. This is a difference that quite obviously affected the potential for literacy and the spread of written culture in the given countries.[76]

In this analysis of Vas County schools, available eighteenth-century sources, unfortunately, do not make it possible to ascertain the influence of the *Ratio Educationis* educational reform plan introduced in 1777. The last eighteenth-century survey to cover the entire county, Bishop Szily's canonical visitation, began one year earlier than the *Ratio* was issued, ended in 1781 and could not reflect any influence the Queen's decree may have exerted. After the decree of tolerance issued by Joseph II in 1781, the Catholic church visitations conducted in the early nineteenth century no longer made any mention of Protestant schools. From the findings of Bishop Szily around 1780 and the national survey of schools in 1770, it is clear that the educational reforms could not produce rapid results. It was in vain that *Projectum Budense*, a supplement to *Ratio Educationis*, stipulated compulsory schooling for all in 1778; neither were there enough teachers to teach all school-age children, nor could they have all attended school if the parents had decided to observe the royal decree for lack of room in the tiny school buildings. In addition to the teaching of reading and writing, *Ratio Educationis* also prescribed the teaching of arithmetic and, for a number of selected pupils, Latin. In the second half of the eighteenth century, the figure of the illiterate schoolmaster, who could read but not write, was a rarity, yet even then only about every fifth teacher could teach some Latin, and the portion of those knowledgeable in arithmetic was about the same. It may be stated that in the remaining two decades of the eighteenth century, newly established teacher-training schools could make up for the loss only in part. The effects of school reforms in the period of Enlightened Absolutism did not come to fruition in Hungary before the early nineteenth century. Joseph II's decree of tolerance may have exerted a more direct influence at the end of the eighteenth century than did *Ratio Educationis*: it allowed Protestants to set up schools everywhere, and thus within a couple of years the number of schools in Protestant-populated areas grew rapidly.

The majority of rural residents still remained outside the walls of schools in the second half of the eighteenth century, never acquired reading and writing skills and continued to live in the world of oral communication.

CHAPTER 2

THE SLOW ADVANCE OF LITERACY IN PEASANT CULTURE

The Advance of Literacy among the Peasantry

THE spread of literacy is one of the most important features that characterizes a society. A statistical analysis of this issue in Hungary before the advent of censuses that registered literacy (among other things) is only possible in some rare cases and areas where such sources are available. One of these areas is Vas County, on which extremely rich source material is available.

Researchers are more fortunate when it comes to examining developed Western Europe. In England, for example, from the seventeenth century on, witnesses authenticated their testimonies by putting their signatures or marks on records. In several Western European countries, from the seventeenth century spouses and their witnesses also confirmed marriages by signing or marking marriage registers. This explains why marriage registers are a major source when tracking the spread of literacy. In Hungary, however, only the minister conducting the marriage ceremony was expected to write in the register, and it was not compulsory for eyewitnesses to sign their accounts in court. There were detailed notes taken on the witnesses, their ages and the span of their memories, but they confirmed their accounts only by taking an oral oath. This in itself is indicative of the lesser role literacy and writing played in Hungary in comparison to Western Europe. When researching literacy in Hungary, therefore, one has to seek sources other than those used in French or British historiography.[1]

For the period before the census of 1870, which surveyed the literacy of the population in Hungary for the first time, literacy among the peasantry can be measured only in areas where documents authenticated by peasants in the capacities of sellers or guarantors survived in larger quantities. Such papers include promissory bills, bills of debt, deeds of sale and village mayors' accounts. Documents of this kind are found primarily in the archives of large estates. Therefore, the literacy of the peasantry can be researched in areas that used to belong to large estates.[2]

In the sixteenth century, no signature, or even putting a cross at the bottom of the page, as an authentication by an individual's own hand, was deemed necessary among the peasantry; taking an oral oath was accepted as sufficient. On seventeenth-century documents only crosses originating from the hands of the peasants of Vas appear and no signatures can be found (see table 2.1).

Table 2.1

Peasant Literacy in Vas County in the Seventeenth Century

Settlement (Number)	Method of Handwritten Authentication	
	Crosses	Signatures
The Szentgotthárd Estate		
Hungarian Villages (9)	80	0
German Villages (6)	50	0
Slovene Villages (6)	160	0
The Batthyány Estate at Körmend		
Hungarian Villages (3)	75	0
German Villages (2)	46	0
Croatian Villages (2)	17	0
Other Batthyány Estates		
Hungarian Village (1)	36	0
German Villages (4)	16	0
Croatian Villages (2)	12	0
Estates of the Middle Nobility		
Hungarian Villages (9)	119	0
Total (44 villages)	611	0

A total of six hundred eleven crosses and zero signatures were found on surviving documents from forty-four villages. Although the number of men marking documents with crosses represents merely a fraction of the county's seventeenth-century male population (an estimated fifty thousand at the end of the century, including adults and boys), the fact that no signatures were found at all in forty-four villages in different regions of the county permits the conclusion that illiteracy among the peasantry in Vas County was common. In the eighteenth century, however, there were examples, although rare, when peasants did sign papers.

The data gathered from large estates in the western and southeastern parts of the county can be compared to the data from the villages of landed lesser noblemen in northeastern Vas County, the region of Kemenesalja. Here, too, analphabetic serfs were in the majority.[3] These statistics are summarized in tables 2.2 and 2.3.

Table 2.2

Peasant Literacy in Vas County in the Eighteenth Century

Settlement (Number)	Method of Handwritten Authentication	
	Crosses	Signatures
The Szentgotthárd Estate		
Hungarian Villages (8)	196	0
German Villages (10)	260	0
Slovene Villages (6)	151	0
The Batthyány Estate at Körmend		
Hungarian Villages (5)	195	12
German Villages (2)	66	2
Croatian Villages (3)	47	2
Other Batthyány Estates		
Hungarian Villages (6)	106	1
German Villages (15)	288	19
Croatian Villages (3)	43	1
Slovene Village (1)	33	0
The Festetich Estate at Vasvár		
Hungarian Villages (5)	119	0
Estates of the Middle Nobility		
Hungarian Villages (6)	96	3
Total (70 villages)	1600	40

Table 2.3

Peasant Literacy in Eighteenth-Century Vas County by Nationality

Settlement	Method of Written Authentication			
	Crosses	Percent	Signatures	Percent
Hungarian Villages (30)	712	97.8	16	2.2
German Villages (27)	614	96.7	21	3.3
Croatian Villages (6)	90	96.8	3	3.2
Slovene Villages (7)	184	100.0	0	0
Total (70 villages)	1600	97.6	40	2.4

There were five hundred ninety-seven villages in Vas County in the second half of the eighteenth century, meaning that at least some data on literacy are available from every eighth village. The first census in Hungary, from 1784 to 1787, recorded 70,990 adult men in Vas (no women are found among those signing the papers).[4] If the noblemen, clerics and burghers are subtracted, the number of adult males within the Vas peasantry may be estimated at about sixty thousand. A total of 1,640 signatures and crosses was found from the eighteenth century. Some of the men registered during the 1784–87 census certainly put their signs on documents from the nineteenth century, while others who gave their signatures in the eighteenth century did not live to be registered by the census at the end of the century. Supposing that these two instances approximately balance each other, the sample of peasants in Vas whose literacy is being discussed comprised some 2.6 percent of adult males. Apart from territories in which sources are exceptionally rich, research conducted in Western Europe generally relies on similar representative samples. This fact should not in itself convince a researcher of the sufficiency of data indicating the level of literacy among the peasantry in Vas County. However, it may be acceptable as, apart from a few villages, illiteracy among the peasantry was general in every part of the county.

The literacy rate among the peasantry probably could be calculated as even lower if statistical data were available on all strata of peasants. The lowest stratum of peasant society, however, was not represented in the sources: they neither were asked to be village councilors or guarantors nor possessed land that could have figured in purchase deals and thus provided a subject for such documents.

No more than five villages in Vas were identified that had at least three peasants who could write. Two—Hidashollós and Molnaszecsőd, situated near the market town of Körmend—were populated by Hungarians. The other three—Némethidegkút, Királyfalva and Patafalva—had German-speaking inhabitants. The one feature common among the five villages was their geographical position: proximity to a town or a market town and location on an important trade route. This indicates that peasants made the first steps towards literacy wherever the need for it arose and they thus were urged to do so. On one hand, the nearby towns or market towns, where the population had a higher rate of literacy and inscriptions and printed products were on public display, stimulated the visiting villagers. On the other hand, peasants who regularly visited the market and were involved in purchase deals had a greater need to know how to write than their counterparts living in more secluded areas if they wanted to understand bills, agreements and costing.[5]

The overwhelming majority of peasants in Vas County were illiterate in the seventeenth and eighteenth centuries, which does not contradict findings concerning schooling in the county. Although the elementary school network, which was rather sparse in the previous century, had expanded by the mid-eighteenth century, and many children in Vas, dotted with small villages, traveled to a school in a nearby village if there was no school in their own, only roughly one-sixth of all children attended school in the second half of the eighteenth century. In addition, only a fraction of the school-going minority learned to write, and even if they did, many may have forgotten the skill by the time they reached adulthood due to a lack of practice. The number of schoolmasters in the county may have reached two hundred by the end of the period, yet their influence on village society remained modest. It would be quite surprising then if, under such circumstances, researchers found a large number of peasant signatures in the villages.

It was possible to gather more signatures and crosses from the first half of the nineteenth century alone than from the two previous centuries combined (see tables 2.4 and 2.5). Yet these data cannot be accepted as representative of the entire county.

The numbers presented, however, do not mean that ninety-five percent of the Vas peasantry still would have been illiterate as late as the first half of the nineteenth century; they only refer to the more backwards western and southeastern parts of the county. In the Slovenian and Hungarian villages on the Szentgotthárd estate and in the small villages of the Festetich estate, hidden deep among the hills, only every twentieth serf could write. However, there is no data whatsoever in the archival material from the more developed northeastern parts of Vas. At the same time, the number of literate peasants found in some villages was relatively high, so it is clear that the rather uniform picture of general illiteracy among the peasants in the seventeenth and eighteenth centuries already had changed in the first half of the nineteenth century. While some of the villages (the majority in the given area) continued to be illiterate as in earlier centuries, in others signatures—even if in a jerky hand—began to appear on charge letters and the accounts of village mayors.

Table 2.4

Peasant Literacy in Vas County in the First Half
of the Nineteenth Century

Settlement (Number)	Method of Handwritten Authentication	
	Crosses	Signatures
The Szentgotthárd Estate		
Hungarian Villages (8)	168	0
German Villages (9)	885	40
Slovene Villages (6)	365	0
The Batthyány Estate at Körmend		
Hungarian Villages (5)	362	91
German Villages (2)	26	17
Croatian Villages (3)	124	5
Other Batthyány Estates		
Hungarian Villages (4)	138	2
German Villages (4)	149	11
Croatian Villages (1)	37	2
Slovene Village (1)	12	4
The Festetich Estate at Vasvár		
Hungarian Villages (11)	827	7
Total (54 villages)	3093	179
Percent	94.5	5.5

Table 2.5

Peasant Literacy in Vas County in the First Half
of the Nineteenth Century by Nationality

Settlement	Method of Written Authentication		
	Crosses	Signatures	Percent
Hungarian Villages (28)	1495	100	6.26
German Villages (19)	1060	68	6.02
Croatian Villages (4)	161	7	4.16
Slovene Villages (7)	377	4	1.04
Total (48 villages)	3,093	179	5.47

Table 2.6

Villages in Vas County with More than Five Literate Peasants (1800–48)

Settlement	Nationality	Method of Written Authentication	
		Crosses	Signatures
Hidashollós	Hungarian	66	35
Egyházashollós	Hungarian	51	24
Molnaszecsőd	Hungarian	12	14
Nádasd	Hungarian	108	18
Nagyfalu	German	33	7
Kristyán	German	130	24
Ercsenye	German	176	8
Sámfalu	German	10	9
Total		586	139

Greater numbers of peasant signatures from the first half of the nineteenth century were found in four Hungarian and four German villages (see
table 2.6). The four Hungarian villages lay near the important market town
of Körmend, while three of the German villages were near the town of
Fürstenfeld, but all were situated along an important trade route. In three
villages, the number of peasant underwriters exceeded twenty, which signals
the spread of peasant literacy in villages that were open to international

commerce. By the 1870 census, which will be examined in greater detail later, the literate proportion of the population in the northern and north-eastern districts of the county was considerable: in the district of Celldömölk, seventy percent, and in the district of Sárvár, sixty-one percent of men over six years of age could both read and write. Analphabetism most probably was driven back in the area by the first half of the nineteenth century, although little is known about this development due to a lack of adequate sources.

The Role of Differences in Nationality and Denomination

When examining the spread of literacy among the peasantry, the disparities that are observed in standards among villages are accounted for—beyond geographical location—by nationality and denomination. In the late eighteenth and early nineteenth centuries, many more literate people were found in the Hungarian and German villages of Vas County than in the Croatian or Slovenian settlements. Slovenian villages were located in one mass in the southwestern, economically backward part of the county, in isolation and far from roads. In their case one cannot determine whether nationality or geographical, economical and social circumstances are to be blamed for general analphabetism. In the case of Croatian villages, however, whose inhabitants settled in the area in the sixteenth century after fleeing from the Turks, the differences between their standards and those of in their Hungarian and German neighbors are striking (see table 2.7). They are especially conspicuous in the villages near Körmend, where Hungarian and Croatian villages were situated only three to seven kilometers apart on the northern bank of the Rába River.

In the case of neighboring German, Hungarian and/or Croatian villages, any differences may be attributed to nationality. While German villagers spoke only broken Hungarian, the Croatians spoke Hungarian well as early as the seventeenth and eighteenth centuries. Yet the inhabitants of Croatian villages saw much fewer written texts in Croatian than the populations of neighboring German villages encountered in German or the Hungarian peasants in Hungarian. Written culture appeared for inhabitants of Croatian villages in a well-known yet foreign language.

Table 2.7

Peasant Literacy in Villages of the Körmend Estates (1600–1848)

Settlements	1600–99		1700–99		1800–48	
	Crosses	Signatures	Crosses	Signatures	Crosses	Signatures
Croatian Villages						
Berkifalu	–	–	26	0	51	2
Horvátnádalja	6	0	13	2	29	2
Harasztifalu	11	0	8	0	44	1
Hungarian Villages						
Hidashollós	16	0	36	4	66	35
Egyházashollós	11	0	25	2	51	24
Molnaszecsőd	38	0	88	6	12	14
German Villages						
Németsároslak and						
Kertes (Together)	46	0	66	2	26	17
Total	128	0	262	16	279	95

The religion of peasants who marked or signed documents is not indicated. The majority denomination of a village, however, easily can be ascertained on the basis of canonical visitations and, from the end of the eighteenth century, the diocese registers, even though one rarely can tell if an individual peasant was Catholic or Protestant. One may think that, in examining literacy among either the peasantry or the nobility, if Protestants could be distinguished from Catholics, more underwriters might be found among the former. The hypothesis, however, is refuted by another group of sources. In 1732, after the Emperor Charles VI (1711–40) issued the *Carolina Resolutio* (1731), a decree that significantly curtailed their rights, the Protestants of Vas County authorized an influential Lutheran nobleman, Károly Ostffy, to mount a protest on their behalf against the injustices meted out against their denomination. The letters of warranty giving full power to Ostffy were signed by village mayors, councilors and noblemen in the Protestant villages or were authenticated by crosses—in any case, these sheets bore marks from Protestant hands only (see table 2.8).[6]

With two exceptions, all Protestant village mayors and councilors whose marks appear on the documents were illiterate. These villages in the regions of Őrség, Tótság and Hegyhát all lie in the southwestern part of Vas, the first inhabited predominantly by Slovenes, the other two by Hungarians. The northeastern Kemenesalja region in the other half of Vas also was inhabited by Hungarians.

Table 2.8

Literacy among the Protestant Peasants in Vas County in 1732

Settlement (Number)	Denomination	Method of Authentication		
		Signatures	Crosses	Total
Hungarian Villages in Őrség (15)	Calvinist	1	26	27
Slovene Villages in Tótság (22)	Lutheran	0	85	85
Hungarian Villages in Hegyhát (8)	Lutheran	0	39	39
Hungarian Villages in Kemenesalja (3)	Lutheran	1	22	23
Total (48 villages)		2	172	174

Of the twenty-six Protestant noblemen who empowered Ostffy to represent them, only two signed their signatures; the remaining twenty-four merely left the mark of the cross on the document.

Drawing comparisons between the literacy and, in general, culture of Catholics and Protestants in the eighteenth century is not an easy task, as a dominant state religion is being compared to a persecuted denomination. Yet the almost total illiteracy of the Protestant gentility and peasants who raised their voices against religious intolerance cautions one against attributing widespread illiteracy in western Hungary in the eighteenth century to the fact that, in this region, Catholics were in the majority.

Grades of Semi-Literacy

Analphabets and literates never in fact were separated as sharply as may be suggested by rows of crosses and signatures. No clear-cut distinction can be made among the peasants between fully illiterates, who could neither read nor write, and semi-literates, who could read but not write: both groups left crosses on documents. Yet there is no greater gap in levels of education than that separating those at least able to read and to gather information from written texts from those to whom the world of letters was totally closed.

Nor did the two groups separate sharply. There were certainly many among the peasants in western Hungary who could not negotiate longer texts in any script but could decipher inscriptions and shop and road signs in capital letters. This seems logical yet is merely a hypothesis unsupported by contemporary documents. Other sources indicate that some people in the seventeenth and eighteenth centuries, although not analphabets, could read letters in print but not in hand, although it is doubtful that statistical methods ever can be applied to these resources.

In 1670, when unraveling what came to be known in Hungarian historiography as the "Wesselényi conspiracy", whose participants schemed against Habsburg rule, the equerry of one aristocrat, Péter Zrínyi, was among those arrested. In his confession, twenty-four-year-old Johann von Lahn, a German nobleman born in Cologne, said that he "knew but little how to write and can read only printed letters".[7] However, some skepticism in his words was justified, as his aim in his confession was to extricate himself from a tightening noose. He must have hoped that, if the jury believed he only could read a text in print, they would not interrogate him about the contents of the letters concerning the conspiracy, which were written in script. In any case, he could introduce this in court in his own defense only because there were many at the time who were stranded at this first stage of literacy and could indeed read printed texts only, and the court may have given credence to his statement. This was borne out by a witch trial that took place in 1727, in the course of which the witnesses in Nagymacséd, Pozsony County, heard about the witchcraft of one peasant woman. The woman, "her mind deranged", showed three notes that had miraculous powers around the village and then called to her sister-in-law "requesting that she read these very notes, upon which she replied that she could not read letters in hand, only those in print".[8]

Those who could write also were not separated sharply from illiterates—in fact, there was a broad transitional group between the two. Scrawls that appear to have been drawn rather than written are found among peasant signatures from the seventeenth, eighteenth and nineteenth centuries beside some fine, established, running handwriting. Such marks rightfully arouse suspicion as to whether or not the writers really had been lettered men, in the sense that they could have been able to write any text and not just their names. In twentieth-century American historiography, a functional illiterate is defined as one who may be able to sign his or her name with difficulty but is unable to complete a postal order or write a postcard. Very probably those peasants and landless lower nobles who signed documents in print or wrote their initials in an uncertain hand were such functional illiterates.[9]

The papers also preserved attempts made by semi-literates who tried to sign them but failed. The village mayor of Pásztorháza could not write down more than two letters of his name in scrawled script, and the clerk in a practiced hand then finished the signature. A serf from Németbük changed his mind when, after having written the words *coram me* ("in my presence") in huge, erratic print, he gave up and allowed the clerk to write his name on the document.[10]

A distinction between literates and analphabets in Hungary can be made with greater accuracy than is possible in Western Europe, where a lot of initials, handmarks and tiny signs are found alongside the crosses and signatures.[11] In Hungary it was rare that someone gave his initials because he could not learn all of the letters in his name. In addition, no such symbols were used in Hungarian documents that usually depict various occupations and may have developed from stamped signs or hallmarks, such as a ladder, scissors or barrel, which otherwise were engraved in stone or carved in wood.[12]

Individual marks or paraphs, which in Britain or France often substituted for signatures, were not used in Hungary. In Hungary people also had less of a need for individualized signatures. Those unable to write their full names, apart from a few exceptions, used a cross instead. In Western Europe, some semi-literate persons tried to avoid using the mark of the cross and replaced it with a paraph or their initials for fear of admitting their deficiency. This reflects the expectations or pressures of more advanced societies in Western Europe, where a lack of writing skills meant greater opprobrium than in Hungary.

Illiterate persons in Hungary put a cross at the end of documents. The question that this raises is whether the cross was indeed a sign of illiteracy or a religious symbol that conveyed some deeper meaning. In 1762 in a village belonging to the estate of the Cistercian abbey of Szentgotthárd, a peasant woman left her mark on her letter of dowry with the comment that she confirmed it "with the sign of the Holy Cross, in my own hand...as I am not knowledgeable in writing".[13] It may well be that this fine phrasing reflected the mentality of the cleric who had drawn up the letter rather than the thoughts of the illiterate peasant woman. Even if the mark of the cross, used instead of a signature, preserved something of the idea of taking an oath on the cross—supported by the frequent use of the finely drawn cross on a base—the reason for the spread of the cross as a mark of authenticity was more trivial: it was easy to draw. A cross substituting for a signature was actually more often an "X" rather than a cross, and for many even the drawing of this simple symbol presented an insurmountable obstacle. This is why the Hungarians in Moldavia, devout Catholics who lived among backward circumstances, endorsed their documents *apposito digito*—by thumbprints—rather than by placing their signature, seal or a cross on them. In contrast to modern fingerprinting techniques, a thumb dipped in ink left a print that gave scant grounds for identification, as it revealed hardly more than the size of the finger. Still, its use may indicate that the individual could not master the use of a pen even to the extent of tracing a cross with one. With regard to the study of literacy, a cross is testimony to ignorance, yet tracing a fine, regular cross called for a practiced hand and the use of a pen at a higher level.[14]

Most villagers who placed crosses on documents in the seventeenth and eighteenth centuries were either councilors or farmers mortgaging a plot of land—that is, they were higher in the local hierarchy. One can understand their performance and the standards of penmanship they mastered only in comparison to the marks left behind by those at the lower rungs of village society. Swineherds, cowherds, servants or roaming thieves were not elected as councilors in the village magistrate, of course, nor were they requested to make statements on behalf of the village community, and the warranty they may have given would not have been valued highly. Being landless, they could not mortgage anything. Therefore, the marks of their hands are found mostly in court records and on contract bonds, in which a condemned person would pledge to change for the better (that is, stop stealing or seeing a partner in adultery, et cetera). The seventeenth- and eighteenth-century documents of legal courts in the archives of the Vas, Zala and Somogy county courts fell victim to barbarian selection in the twentieth century. However, among the documents in other county court archives, a number of letters of bond contracts survived, and these display how difficult it may have been for someone who never took a pen in his or her hand (and thus, never attended school) to trace the mark of the cross. A thief named András Demén of Gömör County twice set about to confirm that he would change for the better by putting a cross on his pledge in 1724, yet in both cases, just a scrawled loop came from the pen in his hand. The cross Mária Boros of Lipóc traced on a paper followed the curve of the letter "U" rather than the form of a cross; an adulterer from Abaúj traced a semicircle crossed with a line instead of a proper cross, as did another licentious woman from Tiszanána; and a swineherd of Alsóravasz, caught in an act of theft, made more smudges on the paper than the lines he eventually managed to draw. The pen scratched and ink splotched as a young man, caught fornicating in the Eger baths, traced his cross; and a cowherd in Hídvég, who had stolen chests, tried more than once to draw lines that vaguely resembled a cross underneath his letters.[15] True, these crosses certainly were not drawn under peaceful circumstances: the accused, who may have learned the verdict only a few minutes earlier, had to make the effort in public under the strict, watchful eyes of the court officials. One cannot assume, however, that it was merely tension that jerked the hand of the accused—all the more so because a good number of finely drawn, regular crosses and even signatures can be found on some bonds, as demonstrated below.

In 1768, a twenty-six-year-old servant, Jankó Klement, was sentenced by the Kis-Hont district court to sixty strokes for theft. The clerk wrote the culprit's name on the sentence, but the latter did not content himself with putting a cross on it; underneath his appellation he traced his name again in fine hand: Johannes Klement.[16] Although employed in the village of Rahó, the lad was born in Besztercebánya (Banská Bystrica) and must have learned his skills in the town, although in the rural environment he was not deemed to have command of them. Miklós Provata, caught stealing when he was barely fifteen, was able to write his own name partially, though not fully, as he was from the small town of Breznóbánya. Nor was the shepherd Dániel Csuzi illiterate. An incorrigible thief who was sentenced several times for serial thefts and eventually was hung in 1781, Csuzi was skilled enough to sign his name in regular script and knew the value of writing as well. He helped himself to anything within reach— from a pair of trousers to accoutrements, and loved full purses best—but once relieved a schoolmaster of three books and later broke into the library of the Protestant minister of Klenóc. The boy was brought up on charges in the market town of Boca, Liptó County, from which he went on as a servant in the village. All three literate thieves were raised in urban environments and, having been brought to court at early ages, still remembered the letters they learned in school. Their signatures are proof enough of the fact that the crosses found in great numbers on bonds are due less to a state of excitement than to general illiteracy. Clumsy scrawls and cacography reveal that it took some practice to form a decent cross, let alone pen a signature.[17]

Crosses in Lieu of Signatures by Literate Persons

Statistical data hardly reflects the real state of affairs in literacy even with the reservations formulated earlier. Culling crosses and signatures rests tacitly on the supposition that all those persons whose signatures have been found could indeed write, while those who merely left crosses on documents could not even scrawl their names. Both suppositions are erroneous, as examples abound of illiterate persons' counterfeit signatures and of crosses made by people well trained in penmanship. This does not come to light unless more than one sample of signatures or crosses left behind by the same person exists, which in turn presupposes a recurrence of the same name, whose bearer produced his signature at one time and a cross at another.

Similar instances might be found in Western Europe as well, yet the plentious historiography has devoted little time to this problem. In developed regions, historians researching literacy usually process such a wealth of signatures and marks that it is not conducive to collating individual cases. In Hungary, however, where sources are incomparably scantier, and signatures can be located by the dozens rather than by the thousands, cases of persons alternating their modes of signing documents are more conspicuous.[18]

Forty-four people from the market town Körmend in the seventeenth and eighteenth centuries and an additional eleven in neighboring villages were found who left both their signatures and crosses. As "senior" or "junior" were widely used to distinguish between fathers and sons of the same name, alternating occurrences must be restricted to namesakes—or illiterate fathers and literate sons of the same name—only in a few exceptional cases, especially because the signatures frequently occur within a short span of time, often a few days. There is also one case in which the same person authenticated texts on both sides of a paper, placing his signature on one and a cross on the other. Similarly, in Rezi, Zala County, the headman of the winegrowers, József Németh, first used a cross and then signed his name in a jerky hand on the same sheet a month later when the text was continued a couple of lines below.[19]

Persons who first signed accounts, then placed crosses on them, and vice versa, can be found in both seventeenth- and eighteenth-century samples and even in the first half of the nineteenth century, but the explanation for this practice varies according to place and time.

In 1635 the vice captain of Körmend and his eleven companions issued a warrant endorsed "by writing in our hands and by our own seal". All of the signatures were followed by the letters "m.p.", short for *manu propria* ("with his own hand"). Yet of the vice captain András Hidassi and one underwriter, Mátyás Horváth, the landlord Ádám Batthyány clearly stated in writing that "they know not the letters"—that is, they were illiterates. Although the steward György Falusi's signature is followed by the same abbreviation, it was not written in his hand: his letters have been preserved by the hundreds, and therefore, one rightfully can deduce that this signature was not written by him. Ten of the twelve signatures are from the same single hand, and the remaining two from another; that is to say, the twelve names written "with his own hand" were committed to the document by a total of two persons.[20]

The abbreviation *manu propria* was added to signatures that were not in the underwriters' own hands, but not to create the appearance that the vice captain Hidassi or the others could pen their names. In the first half of the seventeenth century, just as in the Middle Ages, the most important method of authentication was the seal, and this document bears the stamps of all the witnesses; the names by the stamps merely indicate the persons to whom the seals belonged.

Another document, drawn up in a similar vein, was issued by the mayor and the council of Körmend in 1715. The mayor's authentic signature, well known from several other papers, is followed by the names of the nine councilors, all in the same hand as the text (obviously the clerk's). Four names are followed by seals, four others by crosses, and one by neither.[21]

The names of five of the nine councilors were found on other documents. One went on to serve as the mayor of the market town, whose signature later was drawn in various hands. This man also did not deny his lack of literacy, adding to a certificate of pledge: "I issued this writ and confirm it with my seal, not knowing letters." In other words, the (future, at the time) mayor of Körmend was illiterate, in contrast to another councilor who was a fine calligrapher and whose signature is displayed on several other documents, yet he only placed a cross on the deed dating from 1715. The idiosyncratic, scrolled paraph of a third councilor, which could not have derived from the previous underwriters, was identified on another deed. This same person certified a document as a witness by putting a distinctive cross on it in an ink of a different color than the others, indicating that both the signature and the cross came from his own hand in the same year.[22]

The contradiction is ostensible only in that a signature did not count as the primary mode of authenticating documents during a period in which even the mayor of a sizable market town like Körmend lacked writing skills. Although not exclusive, the first and foremost means of certification was a seal. Whoever stamped his seal on a document generally would not also use a cross, while those who used a cross had the clerk write their names as well: "not knowing letters, not having a seal, by drawing a cross in my own hand [I confirm this]."[23] In 1650 a surety bond was made out for the steward of the Batthyány estate in this manner: "those possessing a seal stamped it; those not possessing a seal drew a cross."[24] This explains the frequent instances of providing authentic signatures, adding *"manu propria"* and then a cross again—the latter obviously in place of the missing seal.

From the mid-eighteenth century on, the attitude towards literacy changed, particularly in market towns. With the majority of councilors knowledgeable about writing, those members of administrative bodies who were elected despite being analphabets were ashamed of their ignorance. This is borne out by the emerging use of pairs of signatures, which are found everywhere; source materials are ample enough to allow the observation of repeated occurrences of names. On the steadily growing number of documents, the names of two councilors very often figured one under the other in the same hand; that is to say, one of the pair was obviously illiterate. It took a great deal of research to find additional signatures by both persons to establish the identity of the illiterate one—his signature showed up in another "pair". These pairs are fairly constant, though; the unlettered councilors obviously relied more or less on the help of the same colleagues. In the village of Kukmér, for instance, the signatures of two councilors from 1774 showed conspicuous similarity; one of them may have been illiterate. However, the literate one of the pair may not have provided help to only one analphabet. In another village in Vas County, the 1753 final accounts bore the following signatures: two councilors each signed for another colleague, and two other councilors left signatures for a total of an additional nine members of the village administrative body. In the following year, the accounts of the village of Királyfalva bore three pairs of signatures by the same hand, and two sets of four names were penned by the same hand.[25]

These cases have two flagrantly different explanations. According to one, underwriting documents by signature did not have and could not have had any power of authentication in a predominantly illiterate society, as the majority of individuals was unable to sign anything. It is, therefore, all the same whether they left their names or just crosses on documents. According to the other view, with the number of literate persons rapidly increasing, those who could not write were ashamed of their ignorance and tried to create at least an appearance of scholarship.

In the villages, the two views continued to coexist as late as the early nineteenth century. In the village of Nádasd, situated in a less-developed part of Vas County, all heads of families certified agreements made with the landlord on the redemption of lands in 1845. Alongside sixty-nine crosses, the number of proper signatures was fifteen. Five of the peasants who signed in 1845 also had authenticated a previous agreement on the lands in 1830 by putting crosses on the sheet because, at that time, all one hundred five peasants, with a single exception, signed using such marks. In the same year, the peasants in the neighboring village of Halogy also entered into an agreement with the estate owner. All fifty-four family heads put crosses on the paper, as did József Mihályka, whose cross is found on other documents from subsequent years. However, he was certainly a literate man, as he left a number of identical—that is, authentic—signatures and was the village notary.[26]

In places where no one could write, even the village notary did not take the trouble of underwriting documents. The same peasants who put crosses on a paper in Nádasd in 1830 deemed it necessary to set about the difficult task of signing their signatures fifteen years later, when almost one-fifth (17.9 percent) of the village family heads were able to write their names.

József Mihályka of Nádasd was not the only village notary to have traced crosses on agreements instead of signing them. In Tótfalu, a Slovene-populated village on the Szentgotthárd estate, the notary certified documents with crosses in 1834 and again in 1838, as did the rest of the "underwriting" serfs.[27] From 1819 onward, papers created in Döbörhegy display crosses left by Ferenc Vörös, councilor and head of the winegrowers. In one 1834 petition, however, he not only gave his signature but also penned the whole document in a fine ornamental scrolled hand, as though he wanted to flaunt his skills. Later Ferenc Vörös also drew up last wills for the villagers. On one of these he made a point of advertising the skills he apparently boasted exclusively in his village, stating on behalf of the testator that "this last will and testament...is confirmed by the marks of the cross drawn by the five sworn councilors of the village in attendance and audition thereof, all but one knowing not the art of writing". So the serf, who earlier placed crosses on documents, not only attended to the duties of a notary but also, as is evident from his signature on another document, was the notary *pro forma* of the village of Döbörhegy.[28] However, had this research only known about him from the crosses he earlier used, he may have been classified among the illiterate. This is an example of the extremely approximate nature of calculations concerning the real proportion of the literate during this period. A full portrait can be gained only if the roles of literacy and of signatures in a particular community are examined.

It was not overnight that formerly analphabetic peasants became literate. It took a protracted period of uncertainty and occasional relapses before the use of signatures in one's own hand seemed important enough for consistent use.

In German-populated Nagyfalu on the Szentgotthárd estate, a serf traced his singular cross under village accounts in a shaky hand in the 1830s. In 1838, however, when he took the post of village mayor, he used his signature, though it was in an uncertain hand. The following year he was still mayor but reverted to making the mark of the cross. What may have urged him to write his signature on the document in 1838 was that the peasant authenticating it before him, Joseph Dax, also scrawled the letters of his name on it. Mathias Dax, who may have been a kinsman of Joseph, traced a cross in 1841, but when he became village mayor two years later he signed papers, complete with a paraph; hence, he was a penman, although he had written crosses as well.[29]

No one, with the exception of a serf called József Csatsits, knew how to write in Harasztifalu in the first half of the nineteenth century. While a councilor, Csatsits himself pressed just a cross on the documents he had to certify. In 1836, however, he was elected village mayor, from which time onward he felt the proper thing to do was to sign the documents of his village and went on to draw his clumsy, ill-formed letters for the next ten years.[30]

Serfs who reached the borderline between illiteracy and literacy, who once learned the skill in school but never practiced it enough, drew crosses or put signatures according to the expectations of the given community. In 1815, when not one member of the village council of Hollós could write, councilors György Bogár and György Tóth the Elder also drew crosses; these often are displayed on documents from the early years of the nineteenth century. With the passing of time, however, increasing numbers of councilors could sign such papers, and from 1832—the year when the number of councilors signing their signatures reached half the total—the honorable aldermen began putting their names on them as well. The two signatures were invariably from the same hand. Collating them with other autographs by the two persons, it appears that it was György Bogár who supplied the signatures; he was genuinely literate, although earlier he had not deemed it important enough to practice his skill. As for György Tóth the Elder, he was an analphabet who by that time felt the need to have his name written on documents rather than a cross.[31] If only one paper had come down from the village, these two easily might have been counted either among the literate or the illiterate group. This example of the Hollós councilors serves as a warning that bare statistical data are insufficient in drawing up a true picture of literacy in a community; attitudes and the ideas behind them also must be considered.

The findings at Kristyán, a German-populated village, confirm this. From 1813 to 1815, the village accounts did not even display crosses; attestation was performed by the clerk who wrote all names in his hand. Between 1816 and 1824, the local serfs still used crosses in authentication. In 1825, however, three councilors, who until then had drawn crosses, scrawled their signatures in clumsy handwriting. The ice was broken: the peasants developed the need for endorsement by signature, and the next year no fewer than twelve hands produced signatures in the village. The actual number of signatures found is higher, but only twelve individuals had the ability to commit them to paper. Literacy came into fashion and gained prestige, as illustrated by the fact that six of the names are not from the clerk's hand, as are the names of the undeniably illiterate persons at the end of the list, but from a literate colleague or friend: twice from the same hand, creating the illusion that the bearers of the second names also could have commanded the skill of writing. Such pairs of signatures are clear indications that a number of serfs had extricated themselves from the world of illiteracy and that scholarship and literacy had gained respect.[32]

Even individuals who lived during this period were intrigued by the question why lettered people reverted to using the mark of the cross. The last will and testament of the serf Ferenc Dobronovits was contested in 1802 on the grounds that it bore crosses by witnesses who knew how to write. "Who is to believe a man", the defense of the manorial estate stated, "who as well versed in calligraphy as was...János Kis, who even could speak Latin, would have taken the quill in his hand and, rather than noting down his own name, merely drew some cross. Verily, all they could have said in wisdom was that whoever was ashamed of or forgot the knowledge of writing, or else his hand was already shaky, had others to write his name, he himself merely putting a cross on it all. Those, however, who were better writers would themselves draw their name, adding their *manu propria* also...and whilst documents of lesser import, letters of purchase of cleared lands for instance, amongst many other things, were prepared at the village mayor's house, the notary often wrote the names of those absent on them, also adding the cross."[33]

The representative of the Calvinist Church, the beneficiary of the last will and testament, argued that the two serfs who appeared as witnesses were widely known to command the skill of writing, yet the letters and testaments that were presented in court bore only crosses from their hands. The case of the serf Farkas Joó of Hollós served as another piece of evidence for the lawyer: "drawing the cross was customary even among those serfs who were scholars." Although he was an "elder mayor, first magistrate of the village and a literate man,...he availed himself of drawing a cross by way of testimony...If a scholar put a cross after his name, indeed a very common practice amongst peasants, especially when a notary stylized, attested and certified the documents...In peasant communities the official attestation by a sworn-in notary would have served as authentication", not the signature.

In the course of lengthy indictments, two views clashed—the old and the new. The lawyer for the estate represented the attitude of the literate world: a signature has its weight and may be conclusive evidence; should all literates put crosses on documents, these would be too easy to forge, for anybody "could sign the names of those making their wills and the attestors and could also make the cross". The plea of the Calvinist Church displayed the attitude of a traditional peasant society: a last will was rendered authentic not by the witnesses' signatures—there were far too few literate persons for that—but by the seals and signature of the notary and, not admittedly, collective memory. The witnesses listed at the end of the document could have been summoned later if necessary, even if they only left crosses. In contrast, the lawyer represented the view that is potent to this day: namely that a unique signature is the single most important means of authentication and the adept forgery of which on an account may cause great damage.

On the Esterházy estate in Sopron County, which had a developed administration, the two mentalities came into conflict a good half-century earlier. The clerk and the caretaker from the village of Schwarzenbach, who forged the Frakno steward's signature on letters, were arrested in 1745. In the course of the interrogation, the clerk was called upon to account for his imitation of the signature. He pleaded that he had altered his handwriting with no ill intent: he used a different quill and was standing, not sitting, while tracing the steward's name—hence the different letters. Besides, he said, he was not aware that writing another person's name could have counted as a sinful act, for he knew the steward would soon return. "How did you dare to imitate another person's signature?" the judges bellowed at the caretaker, upon which he replied in fright that "he did not mean so, he did not think it was the wrong thing to do". As in the earlier case, according to the old mentality, still prevalent in the lower classes in which both the clerk and the caretaker belonged, signing the name of a person who was absent was no crime, for in a predominantly illiterate society it had no significance at all. The castellan who led the interrogation held a more advanced, modern view: he was outraged at the forgery of a signature, for whoever was capable of forging signatures was a dangerous impostor, a fraud who could have claimed anything in the name of the steward.[34]

Genuine signatures already had some weight in the eighteenth century among the landed gentry and their stewards. In 1760 the chief magistrates and a councilor of Vas County had to certify the authenticity of the signature of the estate steward of the Count Szapáry, János Kuzma, when a conflict developed with his landlord. The magistrates stated that it was "his veritable own handwriting indeed, for the said steward, having dwelt in our midst for the duration of circa thirty-five years, we have seen and read his handwriting on countless occasions". For the same reason, a nobleman from Kisunyom gave testimony in the case of the sale of a vineyard in 1716 that "it is fresh in his memory...that it was his own handwriting",—that is, it was to be regarded as authentic.[35] Among the peasants, though, who were mostly illiterate, signatures still bore no significance, as is best testified by the case mentioned earlier of the village councilors who used the cross even though they knew letters.

Literacy is a social phenomenon that can be examined by means of statistical analysis. However, the tables can be used correctly only if the role literacy played in the life of the community also is examined. Dozens of signatures and crosses could have been copied from archival documents without finding a solution, were it not for the Horváth family of Nagynarda, Vas County, the family of a friend of mine.

Part of the family lives in the United States. The grandfather maintained contact with them, sending them at least a picture postcard or a short letter for Christmas each year. This was indeed the expectation in the village community they live in. The grandmother never wrote a word on the cards, and she even had her husband sign them for her, as in her view writing was the task of the head of the family. In addition, the poorly schooled peasant woman was ashamed of her ignorance and feared that she would be ridiculed for her clumsy handwriting and bad spelling. However, upon the grandfather's death, the grandmother, considering maintaining family ties and fulfilling communal expectations important, set herself to the immensely difficult task, although she had hardly written anything before. As a result, she let her kinsfolk in the New World know about births and deaths in the extended family in scrawled letters, with no heed to orthography. She could write, then, even if poorly, and it depended on the concrete situation whether someone else wrote her name at her request or she took the pen herself.[36]

The statistical data concerning crosses and signatures, therefore, reveal the attitudes of a community toward literacy rather than the concrete spread of literacy: they speak about community expectations regarding literacy and the pressure on semi-literate persons to sign documents themselves as well as on genuine analphabets to forge signatures. This mentality, as illustrated above, only emerges if literacy spread in a village. In their totality, therefore, statistics more or less do mirror the advance of literacy.

Prayer-books in the Hands of the Illiterate

When examining the spread of literacy among the peasants in Vas County in the seventeenth and eighteenth centuries, it may be stated that the over-whelming majority were illiterate. There must have been quite a few, though, who held only a passive knowledge of letters—that is, they could not write, but were able to read them, even if with difficulty.[37]

The percentage of those able to read in Vas County in the late eighteenth century can only be approximated. However, at least one estimate should be attempted. When researching the elementary schools in Vas County, it was established that roughly one-sixth of the children attended them in the second half of the century. There was not one school at the time in Vas where the tuition of at least reading was neglected. These children, therefore, must have learned to interpret the written word, even if they only attended school in the winter and intermittently. Yet the skill of reading can be acquired outside school. If we take into consideration half the number of children who could have picked up the skill outside the classroom—although no data is available to support this surmise—it seems probable that by the time the schoolchildren registered in 1770 had grown up, roughly every fifth peasant in the villages of Vas County was a reader. This probably meant that the proportion among men was higher, and among women, much lower. All this is but mere surmise. Yet there are specific data from Vas County concerning semi-literates who could read books but were unable to reproduce the letters in handwriting.

A cabinetmaker from the village Kisunyom, Vas County, died in 1786. Among his personal effects, which were put up for auction, were "one large book and a small one"—this constituted his entire library. The records unfortunately reveal nothing about the content of the books. Although the deceased had always put a cross on the papers he had to sign—hence, he could not write—he still kept two books at home and could read.[38]

Mrs. Szajkovics, a widow, was one such semi-literate person who bought books although she could not write. In 1796 she attended an auction in Szombathely, where the chattels of a county warden were put up for sale. The widow purchased the deceased's prayer-book, apparently the only book to be found in his house, for three forints. Accordingly, she may have been able to read, even if in concluding the deal she put a cross in place of her signature on the account. So did a Lutheran woman from Körmend in her last will and testament in 1788, even though among the personal effects itemized therein, abounding in dresses and utensils, a book of hymns also was listed.[39]

Semi-literates most easily could do justice to prayer-books, which served as the classic example of intensive reading. The reader repeatedly peruses a single, highly appreciated text, which he or she probably knows by heart, as opposed to scanning large quantities of constantly changing texts, as one reads newspapers today. Even those who had lesser reading abilities must have been able to negotiate the prayers they knew half or fully by heart, less reading the text than glancing at it from time to time to refresh their memories—much as if reciting a poem.[40]

Prayer-books also serviced praying or singing in chorus, when a better scholar could assist the poorer one. This clarifies the words found in an undated, probably early nineteenth-century book of prayers entitled *Hét Mennyei Szent Zárok Imádsága* (Prayers of the Seven Heavenly Saint Locks), addressing the analphabet reader thus: "And those not being able to read shall say their prayers to the five wounds of the Man of Sorrows", followed by the titles of the prayers. Since this instruction could have been understood only by someone who could read, the book obviously was meant for common praying aloud.[41]

"Saying prayers from the book" must have been quite common among the peasants; however, they only found it worthy of mention in connection with an important event, such as when describing the last hours of a dying man. In 1741, for instance, a serf's wife in the village of Homok, Sopron County, held vivid memories of the death of a local woman. She was present when the dying person, "a good pious woman, was saying prayers from the book, together with the witnessing woman", after which she proceeded to put a curse on one of the women standing by her bed, claiming she was responsible for her demise.[42]

The last hours of a serf's wife from Nagybesse were recalled in court in Bars County. Seriously ill, she sent her son for the witness saying that he must "bring his own Papist book and come to say prayers together with her...upon his coming into her presence, the sick woman demanded at once if he had the prayer-book with him, which he had left at home...She instantly gave him her own prayer-book, which she had acquired for herself earlier, a good year before, when still in good health...from some Papist man, and having sought out the prayer appointed to be said on receiving the Holy Communion, asked the witness if he were willing to recite it with her" until the priest's arrival. In other words, the serf's wife did keep a Catholic prayer-book at home (which was to prove a point of importance in the case, since her family was Lutheran), but more importantly, she found a suitable prayer in it without difficulty. She obviously thumbed it frequently; therefore, she must have had some reading skills. In the village of Harsány, Borsod County, after the Catholic priest left the house of a dying Calvinist man, the latter's sister sent for a local Calvinist peasant to say prayers with the sick man "from my dear mother's book"—she had inherited that prayer-book from her mother.[43]

In 1757, another serf's wife in Felsőbár, the husband of whom had "mightily wronged" her by almost beating her to death, took her prayer-book to escape from her troubles. A day laborer found her by the haystack, "saying her prayers from the book". Her husband had broken her arm, and she "rested that afflicted arm on her leg and, taking the book in her other hand, she was turning the sheets [pages] only with her thumb" because she could not move her arm properly.[44]

The percentage of peasant men and women who would mark documents with a cross and say their prayers from a book can never be ascertained precisely. The scattered data available show that, among the eighteenth-century Hungarian peasantry, the prayer-book was by far the most common type of book. Moreover, reading and praying were associated so strongly that the two words were used as synonyms. An early eighteenth-century court case in Gömör County serves as a good example as to how peasants at the time associated the concept of books mostly with books of prayer. The nobleman Pál Szőcs was found dead along the road near Putnok, and his brother-in-law was suspected to have murdered him, probably rightly so. However, there were no eyewitnesses, the crime having been committed in the open land. It was therefore decisive that the last hours of the victim be reconstructed in great detail. The last man to have seen Pál Szőcs alive was a fifty-year-old servant who in the course of the investigation said that he saw "a man clad in a red cloak, riding a gray horse on the high road, advancing slowly and also praying from a book while riding, with his high cap off his head".

This sentence subsequently was deleted, as the judges must have asked the witness how he knew the victim was saying prayers, upon which he qualified his statement in the following fashion: "Since the red-cloaked man was holding a book in his hand, the witness deems that he must have been saying his prayers; therefore, he kept the distance of a gunshot between the two of them, not wishing to disturb him in his prayers." For the servant at the hearing, reading a book and praying were one and the same.[45] This was the kind of reading he primarily, if not exclusively, must have seen in his environment. Reading and praying also were blended together for the tailor of Sajószeged, who was taken into custody as a suspicious vagabond. He claimed in court that he was no thief, but that he was a good Catholic who, widowed and homeless, as his house had burnt down, was preparing for a pilgrimage to Rome and eventually wanted to become a hermit. "If thou be a true Papist Christian soul, where is thy book of prayers or rosary?" he thus was interrogated. He replied that he had lost his rosary and could not "read from a book". What he meant was not that he could read printed letters less than handwriting—the latter was, for an inexperienced reader, a much greater challenge. He intended to say he could not "pray from the book" but rather only with a rosary, so he was fully illiterate.[46]

Nor was the distinction made between reading and praying at Ácsteszér, the birthplace of Mihály Táncsics (1799–1884), around 1815, when the writer was still a child. In his autobiography, he described how "I would spend long winter evenings reading all that was available in a village like ours, which the people called praying, not reading."[47] Such fragmented sources as these reveal that peasants in the eighteenth century mostly took a book of prayers in their hands, if they could read at all.

Calendars and the Concept of Time

No data exists on the availability of calendars, another possible source of reading matter among the peasantry, in western Transdanubia in the seventeenth and eighteenth centuries. It is known that calendars were for sale at fairs, as this is mentioned in a letter written by the estate steward of Körmend: "The *compactor* [bookbinder], having attended the fair the other day, gave Your Honor two items of the Calendar for the coming year of 1690", he wrote to his landlord, Count Ádám Batthyány, in December 1689. The rest of the copies obviously were sold at the fair. Imre Beythe, Calvinist pastor from Németújvár, remarked that the printer Matthaeus Berhardi, protégé of the Batthyánys, was not printing at that time, as "he was out selling his calendars". No comment was found, however, as to who the buyers of these calendars were in and around Németújvár.[48]

Parish priests must have had calendars, as they needed them for the events and feasts of the ecclesiastical year. In 1756, one item on the list of the thirty-five books the parish priest of Pinkamiske possessed was the calendar for that year. The priest at Sitke, also in Vas County, made his last will and testament in 1736, from which we learn that records of lesser importance concerning his household were entered in the calendar. "Should I decide to grant some further payment to my servant maid" in addition to that incorporated in the will, the testator wrote, "it will be recorded in the calendar". The testator bequeathed his books to his executor and trustee, the parish priest of Csény, with the exception of his books in Hungarian, which he left to his servant. "Of the books, those that are written in Hungarian shall be given unto her together with the other household articles, for she was not only my servant but also my mother", he wrote. These Hungarian-language books must have been prayer-books, pious readings, and, as is clear from the will, the servant-maid commanded the ability to read them.[49]

The first mention of a calendar in a peasant's possession in western Hungary was from the mid-nineteenth century. Even then it was not a personal possession, for it was purchased on behalf of the village community. In addition to sealing wax and ink, the villagers of Zalaszántó bought a calendar for their mayor in 1844.[50]

Nor does the mode of specifying the date, as was common among the peasants in the eighteenth century, indicate the use of a calendar. At court hearings they never stated which year it was and held imprecise notions about their own ages. It was customary for them to give a date in terms of ecclesiastical feasts, which they were likely to hear from their priests or ministers in church, or in terms of their agricultural duties, rather than specifying the names of the months—either in their Latinate form (for example, *február*) or according to the contemporary Hungarian usage (*Böjtelő hava*, "the month when Lent begins")—or the days of the week.

Court clerks committed the words of witnesses to paper. Many affidavits have survived in draft and final copy alike, which allow one to conclude that they faithfully mirror the witnesses' accounts. Often the clerks would interpret some phrases the witnesses used, adding, for instance, "that is to say, the fifth of May" after "the Sunday after Holy Thursday"—the former is, naturally, not to be looked upon as a phrase the peasant may have used at the hearing. Nor do the highly precise dates and times, that figure at the beginning of the accounts mirror the peasant way of thinking; these are simply repetitions of the phrases used in questions that were put to witnesses who began what they had to say about the case with something to the effect of "at the time in question".

Table 2.9 shows how peasants acting as witnesses in witchcraft trials in Sopron and Zala Counties in the eighteenth century indicated time.[51] Furthermore, an examination of the dates specified by peasants acting as witnesses in fornication trials in the eighteenth century leads to similar results (see table 2.10). Data from the eighteenth-century manorial court records that have come down from western Transdanubia were compared with records found in Nagykőrös, a Great Plain market town in eastern Hungary, where the culprits from the neighboring villages were called to account for their deeds.[52] In both tables the figures confirm that in the eighteenth century, peasants primarily associated dates with ecclesiastical feasts and, to a smaller degree, activities of the agricultural cycle, such as the harvest of certain crops.

There is no data about the number of calendars purchased by peasants in the eighteenth century. One fact, however, is certain—their traditional concept of time was based on church feasts and recurrent agricultural activities rather than the numerical articulation of time as fixed in calendars.

Although indirectly, but in the last analysis inevitably, the skill of writing is as crucial in the transformation of the concept of time as it is in the spread of literacy. Acquiring the skill alone did not necessarily involve a change in mentality. Owing to the gradual spread of literacy in society, however, more and more people were able to read dates in writing, and this affected the way of thinking in the entire society. People knew what the date was, how old they were, and tied events to specific days, months and years in addition to epidemics and wars, the melting of snow or the harvest. The traditional concept of time resting on oral tradition and memory slowly gave way to a new concept based on literacy, supported by available documents.

The skill of writing and the precise determination of dates and times were associated in people's minds as well. In 1755, a forty-year-old charcoal burner appeared in the manorial court of the Festetich family in Keszthely. He tried to deny that he had been living in left-handed matrimony with a woman. The judges, however, succeeded in getting him mixed up in his story, for at one time he said they had been married for three years and at another that he had been discharged from the army two years before, after he was wounded in the fight against the Turks near Belgrade. When confronted, he lashed out angrily, stating he had said that because "I am no literate man who could have noted it down; I merely kept it in memory."[53]

Table 2.9

Dates Specified by Witnesses in Eighteenth-Century Witchcraft Trials
(Sopron and Zala Counties)

Reference	Number of Instances	
	Sopron County	Zala County
Month and Day	0	0
Ecclesiastical Feast	39	23
Event of the Agricultural Year	2	5
Day of Fair	3	0
Total	44	28

Table 2.10

Dates Specified by Witnesses in Eighteenth-Century Criminal Trials
(Western Transdanubia and Nagykőrös)

Reference	Number of Instances	
	Western Transdanubia	Nagykőrös
Month and Day	3	0
Ecclesiastical Feast	32	23
Event of the Agricultural Year	7	9
Day of Fair	0	2
Total	42	34

Peasants mostly kept prayer-books at home, and they would turn to them frequently; this explains why in their minds the concepts of reading and praying overlapped. No evidence is available on the reading of calendars by peasants. An examination of the concept of time they held reveals that they specified times and dates in a traditional fashion, and they did not rely on calendars. The picture of the peasant turning the pages of a calendar in winter evenings would have been a rare sight indeed in Hungarian villages in the seventeenth and eighteenth centuries.

In the eighteenth century small, unbound books were easily accessible even for peasants. Bequest inventories of the lower nobility indicate that a prayer-book or a hymnbook cost ten to fifteen *kreutzers*—the price of a broom, a sieve or a churn; a peasant could have afforded to buy them at the fair. It was not the expense but the low literacy rate that prevented the advance of written culture among the peasantry.

Analphabets also could benefit from readings or recitals offered by their more educated fellows. In 1769, in the village of Harsány, Borsod County, an eighteen-year-old servant-maid, Maris Vadászy, read aloud from a book by Péter Pázmány, Archbishop of Esztergom, "before her dear mother and kinsmen". She also read from a book containing "diverse hymns on the Blessed Virgin Mary and the Holy Sacrament". She served in Miskolc and must have purchased Pázmány's book in the town—it obviously cost several times the price of a prayer-book. Maris was a member of the local congregation and saw it fit to strengthen her Catholic kin in their faith, living as they were in the midst of Calvinists. Her father obviously had a great need for it, too, for he "could not read", as he said. Meanwhile István Szilvássy, a man from the village, entered the house and, on looking at the book the girl was holding in her hand, stated: "'Tis but all the priests' very own concoctions; whatever they may have dreamt up they would hastily hold up and record."

Szilvássy, forty years of age, had converted from the Lutheran to the Catholic faith twenty years earlier. Yet he kept censuring Catholicism to whomever cared to listen, praising the teachings of Calvin rather than Luther according to the accounts given by all the witnesses: the peasant, the former serviceman, the vinedresser and the village smith's apprentice. Szilvássy owned a "Calvinist Bible" from which he read aloud at his Calvinist brethren's homes in the village. He also acted as the local exegete, explicating the scriptures to his fellows, with special emphasis on the futility of faith in the Virgin and the saints. "He brought forth the Wedding of Canaan [sic!] in Galilee, saying that Christ Our Lord hath denied the Blessed Virgin Mary there when she asketh Him to turn the water to wine, scolding her mightily thus: Hearest Thou woman, what hath you common with me or with this matter?"

Szilvássy was one of the few literate people in his village; therefore, the local Catholic priests were glad to entrust to him any number of prayer-books, catechisms, missionary writings, "congregational books on the

Eucharist...for to read thereof". As the Eger Bishop's Court established, Szilvássy "as a literate person, having kept himself above the other local paupers in wisdom...set himself up as *praedicator*, reciting from heretic books to those lying on their sickbed", for which he was duly sentenced to six months of imprisonment and two hundred fifty strokes. The literate peasant was punished strictly for not being able to keep his knowledge to himself, posing as a self-taught pastor, a pseudo-intellectual.[54]

The case of Maris Vadászy, who read hymns and pious texts to her illiterate relatives in the evenings, probably was not rare in Hungarian villages in the eighteenth century, as is supported by the sentence quoted from the prayer-book addressed to nonreaders mentioned earlier. István Szilvássy, on the other hand, who read passages from the Bible to the local peasants and explicated the text, too, broke through the confines of the peasant world, at least with regard to intellectual standards. Having read through thousands of court records, there appear to be only exceptional references made by peasants to information they gained through dictations from books. One such exception was the case of a nobleman, György Gönczi, of the village of Fony, Abaúj County, who converted the wife of the local butcher from Catholicism to Calvinism. Before the Decree of Tolerance was issued by Emperor Joseph II (1780–90) in 1781 granting the freedom of worship to Protestants, this counted as a grave criminal act. Therefore, in 1751 the county authorities started an investigation. After a lapse of some fifteen years, the peasants of Fony still had vivid memories of what this nobleman read to them. "It was some fifteen or sixteen years ago that the Honorable György Gönczi, having read from a book before this witness, reading therein also that a certain Holy Roman Pope would have kept seven concubines, upon which the witness became incensed, exclaiming that devils should plough the soul of such man, damn him, as would have printed a book like that", so the serf thought it fit to emphasize in court. While other locals gave similar accounts, it emerges clearly from their words that it never even occurred to them that they too could look into the book and read its contents. The wife of the estate purser, however, apparently possessed some reading ability, as she confessed that some fifteen years before György Gönczi told her, "amongst many other rumors, chatting about the Papist faith and the Calvinist religion" that "...the Popes keep some six or seven servant-maids for cleaning the palace, upon which the witness stated that it was impossible, my dear Master Gönczi; thereupon he added to this witness, my dear lady, aye 'tis so, as I will show it to you in the very book in which it is said"—unlike the peasants, this woman could read. Written culture was spreading by word of mouth in this example. The Calvinist nobleman from Abaúj County apparently conceived of the Pope as some well-to-do provincial parish priest. The fact, however, that his words lived on so vividly in the memory of the village serfs after fifteen years indicates that the incidence of a literate nobleman reading to the serfs must have been rare.[55]

Analphabets in Correspondence

General illiteracy made it difficult for the peasantry to maintain contacts with the world outside the village in the sixteenth, seventeenth and even eighteenth centuries. In the late twentieth century, it is natural for a literate man to write a letter and read a notice or a brochure. For analphabets though, these caused grave difficulties and were activities left to the assistance of others.

Until the widespread use of the telephone, broad sections of society practiced their writing abilities mainly through letters sent to relatives. Among the peasantry, however, the single most important subjective criterion of letter writing—the skill of writing—was missing. In addition, of the required materials, it was only the quill that was easily available; ink and paper, expensive and rare as they were, and writing sand were as scare as was a well-lit, quiet nook in which to set about the slow and laborious work of tracing letters. Nevertheless they tried to maintain contact with their distant kinsfolk through correspondence.

Even illiterates tried to exchange letters, which meant sharing their innermost thoughts with those who offered to commit these to paper for them. In 1598, Count György Thurzó, the would-be palatine, wrote to his wife about a love letter written by one of his men: "János Trombitás dictated a letter to his wife in Slovak; it was taken down as he told, couched in fine Slovak words. I have sent it to you, but do not pass it on to his wife until you have it read to yourself; at least you will have something to laugh about." Illiterate János Trombitás had no choice but to confess his love for his wife in front of another. Some two hundred years later, in 1780, a woman from Keszthely who was charged with incest told the manorial court that her brother-in-law—at the same time, her lover—"hath sent me a letter from Hahót, which must have been noted down by the publican, I think". Her words reveal that her lover, a German carpenter aged forty-eight and a resident of Keszthely who originally came from Regensburg, could not have written the letter by himself.[56] An eighteen-year-old maid had an extraordinary and no less important letter written in Báhony, Pozsony County, in 1763. She left her illegitimate baby on the steps leading to the entrance of the Nagyszombat Seminary, with an amulet around its neck and a short letter addressed to whoever happened to find the child. She could not prepare the letter herself, and therefore she availed herself of the services of the parish priest's servant, a guest of her landlord. Another eighteen-year-old illiterate servant from Pozsony County, Anna Klukan, also wanted to leave her newborn baby in Nagyszombat. She had to ask the parish priest of the village to pen a letter on her behalf to the father of her baby, even though it was about a matter of the most intimate nature.[57]

Peasants recruited to be soldiers and sent to distant battlefields tried their best to let their loved ones know they were alive, begging them to wait for them. These letters usually were committed to paper by the clerk of the regiment or the army chaplain. A further difficulty was for the women to read the letters, as recorded in the case of one fifty-year-old peasant woman in Csongrád County who frequently received letters from her son and each time had to find someone to read them to her.[58]

The number of illiterate persons who wanted to have letters or petitions written must have been high. Walking the streets of Istanbul, even now tourists may see the modern-day colleagues of scribes sitting on street corners with their typing machines, waiting for assignments from analphabets for a modest fee. Similarly, occasional scribes were active in public squares in eighteenth-century Hungary; they were usually schoolmasters or students earning a few *denarii* for their work. In Pozsony (Bratislava) in 1770, the wife of a knife grinder had a petition drawn up for her by a schoolmaster on the main square, saying when questioned that "I myself dictated to him what to put down." In 1786 a certificate was forged in the name of the chief magistrate for the mother of a steward in Szikszó. It turned out, though, that the forged document was written in the wrong name. The woman confessed, "I requested a student at the lodge of the Franciscans at Kassa…who hath adjusted the characters." In Eger in 1766 a discharged soldier was caught: the word "married" was scratched from his discharge letter, which enabled him to marry again. "Who hath inscribed in it a different word…since thou knoweth no writing?" the judges asked, upon which the soldier confessed that it was a student from the town of Pápa who adulterated it.[59]

In villages, the local notary and schoolmaster usually drew up letters and documents for the locals, and the estate archives preserve peasants' petitions by the hundreds.

Illiteracy among peasants obstructed the reading of not only private letters but also circulars, the forerunners of leaflets. In 1765, the period of the
great peasant movements, inflammatory circulars spread from village to
village in Vas County; however, they could not be read everywhere. A
thirty-three-year-old serf from Nagymedves, who was also the village
mayor, could not read. Thus when the circular arrived to his village, it had
to be sent to the nearby vineyard in order to be read. It was often the case
that the serf who brought the circular showed it to the villagers for the sake
of authenticity; however, he did not actually read it as he was not able to do
so. Instead the messenger told the villagers what was written in it; in other
words, the written document was only the material proof of authenticity of
the orally transmitted text.[60]

In 1673 in Gönc, a market town, the forty-eight-year-old mayor also received a circular "mobilizing" the peasants. "As he himself could not read",
he handed it over to his deputy. One could suppose that the reason the
mayor said he could not read was because he wanted to shrug off responsi-
bility regarding the dangerous piece of writing. However, this supposition
can be contradicted: the other witnesses easily could have disclosed the fact
that the mayor was able to read. In addition, the mayor never denied in-
citement, the subject of the litigation. As soon as the deputy read the letter,
the mayor urged the villagers to engage in action.[61]

The illiteracy of the mayor of Gönc is plausible: in 1778 it was revealed
that the tax collector of Csongrád was illiterate, and thus he always had to
be accompanied by the notary. In 1760 the mayor of the big market town
Hódmezővásárhely and his deputy could only put crosses instead of their
names on documents. In 1719 the mayor of Körmend market town, "being
an illiterate", as he wrote himself, issued charters by putting only his seal on
them.[62]

Wide-scale illiteracy created an obstacle to the spread of leaflets. These
statements do not contradict data from which it transpires that peasants
often used prayer-books. When putting peasants' signatures under close
scrutiny, one can see that if society is divided into literate and illiterate
people, the major point remains concealed: the semi-illiterate layer of society that did learn the alphabet and later, in accordance with the community's wishes, either put crosses or wrote down their names on official
documents. The same applied to reading as well: those who were taught
letters at school but hardly ever read could profit from the text of printed
prayer-books, which text they knew by heart. However, they quickly became
embarrassed when they had to read a handwritten circular, the contents of

which were unknown to them. It also follows that few people had the advantage of being able to read in this era, and it was only natural for the illiterate to obtain the help of their literate fellows just as if they had borrowed a tool from them.

Forged Documents and Peasant Forgers

As literacy gained ground little by little, the forgery of documents, an inseparable companion, appeared in the countryside. In 1762 one György Spaics from the village Nádalja, Vas County, who was nicknamed "the deaf scribe", submitted various papers to the steward. The surveyors' suspicion was aroused merely while consulting those dated 1605 and 1657, noting that the documents may have been drawn up much later. However, on seeing one supposedly prepared twenty-seven years earlier, they had no doubt that it was spurious. In this case, oral testimony won over falsified writing: the village mayor and those councilors old enough to remember the year of the paper's alleged creation had no knowledge whatsoever of the document that was drawn up on their behalf. Spaics, a former clerk who had to give up his post due to his deafness and returned to tilling the land, faced no difficult task when employing his skills: he merely had to imitate the crosses the magistrates would have placed on the document.[63]

Despite having been exposed, Spaics continued to employ his skills in performing dubious activities. Although his adversaries maintained that "both the office bearers of the estate and the villagers at large were fully aware that he was a man who made forged documents and sold them at a price", sixteen years later he contested the ownership rights of a peasant woman with a document dated 1685. The defendant first said she had "no document of any hue" of the land under dispute, then claimed that the document submitted by Spaics in fact verified her rights—that is to say, she hardly could have been able to read it. When her son, a cleric, returned to the village, he did not content himself with tearing up the documents produced by the deaf scribe; he retorted with another document, allegedly from 1693: "God Almighty only knows from whose hand it may have come", Spaics wrote "in righteous indignation". In view of the obsolescent and suspicious writings, the jury could do nothing else but return to oral testimony and carry on the examination under oath. Due to the repeated forgery of relevant documents, the judges turned to hearing witnesses rather than relying on written evidence.[64]

In 1792 another serf from the same village, István Marancsics, initiated court proceedings against Spaics for occupying one of his meadows. Marancsics verified his statement by bringing in two witnesses—that is, through oral testimony. György Spaics, in contrast, claimed "his inheritance in the guise of some bogus letter" and refused to give up his claim on the meadow. György Puskarits, in all probability the only other lettered person in the village, went through all the documents held by Spaics and found only letters of mortgage, not of purchase. Nine months later György Spaics still presented the certificate allegedly made out one hundred fourteen years earlier, according to which the meadow under dispute was sold to Spaics's forbears in perpetuity. No better evidence of the great advance literacy made in thirty years could be presented than the deaf scribe's success in having the document, however false, accepted by both the manorial court and the county court. Marancsics's case was turned down because it was supported by oral testimony rather than written evidence.[65]

Nor was the "deaf scribe" the only person in eighteenth-century Vas County's semi-analphabetic village society who profited from forging documents. In 1771, two serfs from the Németújvár estate, an environment of more advanced literacy, prepared bogus seals of the estate officeholders and placed them on documents certifying socage services performed. "They hath drawn up such notes, sealing them with the stamp they had fabricated, and distributed these between themselves as well as to other serfs on soc-age", the charge against them read. The prosecutor for the estate owner proposed that the court cut off the right hands of the forgers and chase them from the estate. The verdict is unknown, but the serfs under the duty of socage, as a precious working force, supposedly were sentenced to corporeal punishment and monetary compensation rather than amputation and expulsion.[66]

General illiteracy may have encouraged a Szentgotthárd schoolmaster to commit an extraordinary crime of forgery in 1738.[67] Upon his lover's request, he pilfered a document from the archives of the Szentgotthárd Abbey and drew up a death certificate for her husband on the paper, which thus must have looked very official. Needless to say, the man was alive. To what use the lovers put the paper is unknown—it may have been an insipid prank. It is true, though, that a woman from Felsőbár remarried with the help of a similar forged document: in 1778 she abandoned her syphilitic husband and married a titled man. When the bigamist was brought to court, it turned out that "last year she had sought a good scribe for the purpose of commissioning him to draw up a testimonial letter [certificate] for her about her husband's death". The document that served as the model stated that "one man clad in blue pelisse lined with black fur" had been interred, but this ought to have been reworded so as to include the adulteress's husband's name. However, the local notary refused to cooperate, so she sent for a student from Magyaróvár. He also turned down her request, and the person who eventually prepared the forged document is unknown. It is clear from the court records that the two peasant women could not even read the documents, let alone copy them; they were illiterate and could understand what was in them only when a schoolboy dictated them. Their illiteracy, however, did not prevent them from committing forgery.[68]

A peasant from Korlát, Abaúj County, resorted to forgery in an attempt to cover his adultery. Having lived in matrimony for twenty-two years, he impregnated his servant-maid. He bought some concoction at the fair that was supposed to abort the fetus, but the phial broke, and its expensive contents were lost. The peasant then sent the pregnant woman away from the village to have an abortion far from her village. For this purpose, he drew up a forged passport for her in his own hand and sealed it with the village seal on behalf of another village elder. He gave this document to his servant-maid, warning her to set out in any direction but toward Tokaj, where his handwriting was likely to be recognized. It can be inferred that the peasant was courageous enough on this occasion to commit forgery because literate men were few and far between in the village, and he may have been the only one able to fabricate an "official" document.[69]

Documents: Carefully Preserved and Little Understood

Literacy made considerable advances in the eighteenth century among the peasantry, even though the number of serfs able to write in the villages was low. Owing to general illiteracy, however, many were not aware of the types of documents they held. In 1733, one Anna Szabó presented a document in court in Körmend, "a certain useless letter" concerning a plot of land she held, which she said was about a mortgage of eight forints, "albeit the letter does not say the sum".[70] In the same year in Lövő, another peasant submitted papers that he believed justified his claim concerning certain clearings. The estate officeholders, however, informed him that "in these same letters presented, no mention is made as to the mode of possession he has over the lands". Therefore, the serf most probably could not read. Dániel Kis of Kér, who also could not read, nevertheless claimed he could not present the relevant document concerning the same land as "he could not find it among the numerous letters he possessed".[71] In 1762 in Berkifalu a serf tried to justify his claim to have purchased the piece of land under dispute in perpetuity by presenting a document that concerned another plot. He hardly could have known the content of his document. Similarly in 1812 a serf's wife from the next village wanted to certify possession of a plot of land by a document concerning a different piece of land. The peasants who presented the wrong documents in support of their claims obviously were unable to read the carefully preserved writings.[72]

For an illiterate peasant, the many documents governing his fate held by the estate administration must have been alien indeed. To what extent is exemplified by the case of a serf from Selyeb, Abaúj County. This peasant, age ninety, stated in 1737 that the plot in question at one time belonged to the family of the princes of Transylvania, the Rákóczi family, although "this witness, not being able to read, has never seen this in writing". However, "numerous years ago, one steward of the House of Rákóczi, Vilhelm by name…visited him in his home, bringing with him a big book consisting of writing [not printed], which they said was the village book; he took it and read therefrom", telling them which plot of land should belong to which serf.[73] Exposed to abuse and helpless on account of illiteracy, the witness and many others hardly could have verified what the "big book" said about their possessions.

Not only official documents of land possession were held by peasants who were unable to decipher them, but also some sort of certification of identity, which they carried with them.

In the second half of the eighteenth century, with the advance of literacy and the increase in writing services, travelers were expected to produce passes or permits about their missions and itineraries, in which the issuing county or town administration warranted that the holder was neither a thief nor afflicted by an epidemic disease. Many were unable to read these and were, therefore, ill-informed about the documents they used for credentials. "I cannot read", admitted a brandy maker from Nógrád County in 1781, when it turned out that the passport he held contained data quite different from his own specifics. "A poor peasant man as I am, I would not know about it", a serf from Torna County pleaded in 1785 when his pass was found wanting.[74] A peasant from Encs thought his pass was from the notary in Tállya, but it was from the hand of a trader. Had he been able to read, he surely would have looked into it, if only to tell a more clever lie.[75] One soldier was self-assured enough to state that his discharge letter said how long he had served—eight years and four months. When the judges informed him that the document said something entirely different, he said, in helpless indignation, "I would not know what they had written and what not; I myself know not writing and reading, and they wrote as they liked to." The same frustration over being illiterate is heard in the words of Péter Óváry, a foot soldier from Ráckeve. His mother died in 1790, and his brother-in-law tricked him out of his due inheritance. Having served in the war against the French, he received leave, and on arriving home his brother-in-law thrust a false settlement of accounts under his nose. "Amid abundant deceitful cackle and babble, he hath tricked me into putting the mark of a cross underneath a writing (when I myself know not writing or reading, and therefore can fall into this trap set up by soulless people most easily)…which was drawn up as though he had settled accounts with me." The duped soldier went on to say his brother-in-law, "having blinded him, hath elicited and extorted his handmark of a cross", which he then and there ceremonially withdrew together with the letter "underneath which my good brother-in-law had me put the mark of a cross in my hand by connivance". What the magistrates of Ráckeve decided with regard to Óváry's letter is not known; however, the bitter tone of the petition reveals the fear and suspicion illiterates felt concerning written documents.[76]

Illiterate persons usually hold special respect for official papers; they cannot themselves check their content but are well aware that the indecipherable documents might prove very important. For analphabets, it was the appearance of a document rather than its contents that aroused awe. One peasant in Haraszti recounted before the manorial court in 1768 how a Vas County juror tried to persuade him to give a false witness's statement: "My good Lord Svastics hath invited him to testify in court, on behalf of a judge of the venerable county, brandishing before him a letter with a mighty seal."[77] In other words, this serf knew nothing of the contents of the letter or of the person who issued the orders, but he was deeply impressed with its large seal. It was also the huge seal, "the size of a plate", on an *armalis* (certificate of nobility) that aroused respect in peasants and lower nobles who were questioned in cases examining letters patent and lineage. From the fact that the councilor was "brandishing" the document, it emerges that he never handed it to the serf, who was in all probability illiterate and urged by the mere spectacle of the official paper to comply—it exerted the same effect on him as summoning seals and badges in the Middle Ages did—without really knowing the letter's contents.

The Gradual Recession of Peasant Orality

As discussed earlier, few peasants could read in the seventeenth and eighteenth centuries. Their fate, however, largely was determined by written material produced by the state and manorial administration, most of which they could not read. For peasants it was almost exclusively collective memory that retained knowledge and information in the eighteenth century. This orality, on the other hand, was not a separate world isolated from written culture; the culture of the society's dominant minority penetrated the peasants' oral culture. Manorial and county officials often put into writing what was retained by the peasants' collective memory about long-since vanished written documents: the contents of lost documents were passed down by word of mouth. In 1718 in Papkeszi in Veszprém County one of the witnesses heard from his father what was written in a document defining the boundaries that previously had been read to his father.[78] The memory of witnesses spanned approximately seventy to eighty, and sometimes ninety, years. Naturally, this meant that even the elders could remember events in their childhood through orality.

The passing on of information was a conscious activity; the reason witnesses remembered the trees marking the village boundaries, old traditions, et cetera was because the elderly consciously tried to pass on this body of knowledge. The eldest members of the community knew perfectly well that on their deaths, a large chunk of this collective knowledge could disappear. "Lo, brother, I am an old man and I am afraid I am going to die soon", said a peasant from Taszár to his brother-in-law, carefully pointing out the boundary markings to him. A witness from Bácspuszta stated that an old man from the village pointed out the markings so that the young men would learn them as soon as possible. This old man who taught the younger ones was at least one hundred fifty years old according to the witness, which constituted the oldest recorded age in sources dating from the sixteenth century to the eighteenth century. Characteristically, this witness attributed this "biblical age" to a villager who had long been dead.[79]

The memory of the old spanned approximately seventy years. Beyond these seven decades the uncharted territory of word of mouth began: a strip of land in question had been in the possession of the witness's father for about ninety years, as stated unanimously by the peasants at Nádalja in 1762. However, how much he paid for it or from whom he bought it, they could not recall. Another peasant's land had been in the possession of his father, grandfather, great-grandfather, great-great-grandfather, et cetera for a long time, undisturbed, as the village community attested to this by word of mouth. They knew that the land was bought by his ancestors; however, they could not remember when or from whom it was purchased. The expression 'for three generations' became synonymous with 'for a very, very long time'. When in 1762 a serf in Berkifalu presented a letter about his land dating from 1630, the judge wrote, "*ultra memoriam hominum possidet*" (it belongs to the family beyond human memory).[80]

The collective memory of the village spanned a period of centuries in matters affecting the entire community. In 1762 the villagers of Berkifalu told officials the story of their community that was transmitted from generation to generation since their arrival. According to this account, they fled from Bosnia and first settled near Nádalja, where they were expelled. Then they settled by the Csörnöc creek but moved back to the north of the Rába River as a result of the constant pillaging by Turks from the Kanizsa castle.

The peasants of Berkifalva were illiterate in the eighteenth century. Village documents from this period only appear to include crosses instead of people's signatures. Stories were passed on by word of mouth generation by generation. The village's story was verified step by step with the help of charters dating back two centuries kept in the archives. As far as the date was concerned, the villagers missed the mark by some years: according to the register their village by the Csörnöc creek was already deserted in 1589, and Kanizsa was captured by the Turks only in 1600; thus, they could not have fled the Turks coming from the castle. Except for this minor mistake, every other aspect of the story of their finding a new home and the route of their migration was retained perfectly by their collective memory. The sixteenth-century Latin charters that record the conflicts between the migrating Croatians and their landlords perfectly verify the itinerary that was passed on by word of mouth. Even if the story is authentic, it is somewhat abstract: except for the name of a balk, there is not anything concrete in it that could be held onto by human memory. Contrary to peasants acting as witnesses when determining village boundaries, the storytellers of this Croatian village were unable to relate their story to any familiar person or event. The story, although a bit staggering, was on its way to becoming a legend.[81]

The legend of the Mályinka village in Borsod County also was passed on by word of mouth, according to which the villagers once entertained King Matthias Corvinus (1458–1490), who in return granted them freedom. In 1638, at a court deposition, some witnesses claimed to be over one hundred years old, and the serf who was only eighty was quite young in comparison.

The latter heard from his father that King Matthias once visited the village and granted its inhabitants freedom. A charter or other document attesting to this did not survive, but the legend persisted among the villagers. Ninety years later, in 1728, the inhabitants of Mályinka refused to pay tithe because of the legend: two noblemen said that they had heard from the people in Mályinka that King Matthias once stayed there overnight, and the villagers served him such delicious food and wine that he immediately granted them freedom. In order to prove this, the trunk of the pear tree under which this charter was written still existed. Although the people of Mályinka had no charter granting the village's freedom, the authenticity of the story was reinforced by a visible object, the old pear tree, and by oral tradition. Beyond seventy to eighty years, the 'days of yore' dominated the peasants' collective memory based on orality. As opposed to the educated and literate noblemen, who could relate the events of the ancient past in their statements to concrete years through reading (even if not without mistakes), the illiterate peasants' perception of the past remained unsystematic, and legendary kings from different centuries could live next to one another in collective human memory.[82]

This was demonstrated clearly by the people of Mályinka, who 'remembered' King Matthias, who had by then been dead for two hundred thirty-eight years, and by a statement of the village mayor of Gyöngyöspata. Marino Ibrishimovich, a Franciscan missionary bishop from Belgrade, visited his bishopric that consisted of the Hungarian territories under Turkish occupation in 1649. At Gyöngyöspata he stated that no Catholic bishop had visited the place for at least one hundred thirty years. The mayor of Gyöngyöspata told the bishop that "his father had been to Buda three times to attend the crowning of three kings"—John, Matthias and Louis—"the latter who was killed by the Turkish Sultan Suleyman at Mohács. Furthermore, all of these kings visited Gyöngyöspata, but no bishop has done so". John Szapolyai was crowned king one hundred twenty-three years before, in 1526, and King Louis II was crowned one hundred thirty-three years prior to the mayor's statement, in 1516. King Matthias was elected in 1458, precisely one hundred ninety-one years before the visit by the bishop of Belgrade. No matter how old the father of the mayor of Gyöngyöspata may have been, it seems very unlikely that he attended the election of all three kings, especially that of Matthias, as is the allegation that all three kings visited the market town.[83]

The names of kings were retained by collective memory going back hundreds of years, but they occupied their places beyond the times of oral culture, in the region of an ancient past filled with legendary heroes.

Knowledge of village boundaries was one of the most solid bases of peasant orality. From the Middle Ages the village boundaries were remembered for centuries as a result of repeated inspections. On such occasions, a host of witnesses went to the fields and, after having sworn an oath, pointed out to the officials where those trees, rocks and other landmarks were that would allow the officials to define the boundaries and put them into writing. Scores of written Latin charters would have been of no use if they had not coincided with the landmarks vivid in the villagers' collective memory, which often happened in the case of deserted villages.

In the third part of the eighteenth century, at least in the most developed regions of the country, orality was overtaken by written records and a developing administration. Large estates employed professional surveyors who charted the village boundaries with mathematical precision and made maps and land registers to keep an account of the lands owned by the landlord and the peasants' plots. As the uncertain concept of time linked to illiteracy gradually was replaced by measured time and was expressed by means of numbers (year, month, day, hour, minute) and written records, the conception of space in the villages also changed. The bailiffs went to inspect the boundaries not with the gray-bearded elderly but with surveyors and maps. Knowledge passed on by word of mouth was replaced by written records.

Illiterate Witches and the Devil's Book

Respect for writing and its inscrutable power on the part of an analphabet sometimes assumed magical dimensions. Mention often is made of the Devil's book in witchcraft trials: the investigating judges, influenced by "advanced" West European practices, questioned suspects as to whether they were registered in it or not. The level of literacy, however, was no higher among witches in the seventeenth and eighteenth centuries than it was among other peasant women: however depraved they may have been, they generally could not write. In 1742 Mrs. András Hegedüs, charged with committing acts of witchcraft, was tortured in Kaposvár. The unfortunate woman "confessed" that she was in league with the Devil, who had appeared before her in human shape, dressed in a blue Hungarian-style garment, high boots and a hat. He had "entered her name [in the book] with her approval with a pen dipped in blood from her little finger". When confirming her statement the next day, she modified it, obviously in reply to questions probing for further detail, inasmuch as she said "the Devil noted down her name in her own blood not in the book but on another paper, on which occasion the Devil asketh her what her name was". The supernatural content suggested by the interrogators was mixed in the peasant woman's statement with meticulously precise, realistic details. Apparently, the judges only could give credence to the appearance of the Devil by the inn of Dőr and his control over the woman if it was not she but the obviously literate Evil One himself who registered her name in the book.[84]

In nearby Csorna, Éva Katona, a sixteen-year-old servant to a serf, confessed in 1733 that a host of witches had seized her and employed diverse methods of torture on her, until "a tall man having come before her, book in hand, in which she was to be registered, hath urged this 'ere witness with the following words: Though she should not believe in the black writing, for Hell is black all through, you believe much rather in the red and yellow writing, for heaven is red and yellow, and those who doubt the veracity of the book will not see Heaven, so the Devil wanted to beguile her,'" the girl confessed. A fortnight later the "tall man" tempted her again "with a big book in his hand...to cut her finger and write her name in it, which she refused to do". It is unknown if Éva Katona could write her name, but it seems highly improbable; nor is it known if she tried to read the black, red and yellow writings, for the devil contented himself with merely showing her his book. In any case, the witness's landlady said that the devil attempted to persuade her maid to "cut her own finger and drop her blood on the books"—no mention is made of any signature in the landlady's statement.[85]

The maid maintained that she saw the devil holding a *big* book. The wife of András Takács of Ebergőc, Sopron County, confessed under torture in 1746 to having been in league with Satan for four years and "saw how a man in a blue caftan hit her in the nose, with the blood issuing from there he entered her name in a book that looked like an almanac". In this case as well, the Devil used a witch's blood, yet registered her name *in his own hand* rather than leaving the peasant woman to sign. The devil's book was small and looked like an almanac: in villages, the only book they knew apart from the prayer-book (which could hardly be mistaken for the Devil's book) was the almanac, so Mrs. Takács used it for comparison under torture.[86]

Another witch already had been sentenced to death when in 1701 she was again interrogated under torture in the Bazin castle. On that occasion she said that eight years before, the devil, in human shape, had taken blood from her right hand and written down her name—again the act of entering the name was left to the devil. Judit Jászberényi, a witch from Szeged who eventually was executed, appeared before the Komárom County court in

1728. The Evil Soul, she confessed, had come to her in human shape and in a black garment, but with a horse's legs, and fornicated with her several times, she lying "now upon her back, now on her side, even though the nature of the Devil's virile member was cold". In response to the sheriff's question regarding whether she had entered in league with the Devil "in word or by way of writing", Judit Jászberényi said "she hath given him her hand and denied God, whilst the Devil branding her forthwith, noted down her name on a sheet"—once again it was not the witch who wrote the name.[87]

In 1730 Mrs. István Vecseri admitted in the Csongrád County court that "she hath given a bond about herself to the Devil...which He hath taken down himself"—again, the act of writing was performed by the Devil. The jury accepted the making of a contract with the Devil but would have found it dubious if the peasant woman had written the document in question herself.[88]

Nor did Mrs. Ferenc Bodnár of Vadász, subsequently burnt at the stake, enter her name into the Devil's book herself. She confessed under torture in 1756 that "the Devil having arrived, hath brought forth his roster, and another woman hath taken me to Nagy-Zerind and put my name down in it in her house, knowing the scholars' language well". Jerky and obscure as her confession was, one thing was made clear: it was neither one nor another witch entering the name in the register; it was the Devil himself who knew the language of clerics and judges—Latin—well.[89]

In the eyes of the illiterate, books and writing in general had miraculous power. Not only witches but also priests and monks made use of the supernatural power attributed to writing, thereby eliciting disapproval from the official Catholic Church.

In the mid-seventeenth century, Bosnian Franciscan missionaries used writing and books of preternatural power among their illiterate flocks in the southern part of Turkish-occupied Hungary, which raised strong objections from their adversaries, the lay priests in the mission's bishopric in Belgrade. The friars, the lay parish priest wrote, "perform marriages so as dispatching only a small book [that is, instead of going there themselves], should it be of any kind, which the spouses are to put underneath their pillow on the wedding night, this serving as testimony for the ceremony having been performed, in case the Turks start an inquiry". In other words, a book itself, as an object and irrespective of its content, substituted for the priest and his power to administer the sacraments when he was reluctant to venture into dangerous territory.

At other times, the Bosnian Franciscan friars "composed certain writings against weapons, saying that whoever carry these with themselves would go unharmed thereby". These prodigious notes must have been prayers in

Latin, which the Franciscans, missionaries of the Catholic Church, distributed. Yet the promise of protection from weapons was not tied to the prayer itself, that is, the content of the writing. The protection issued from the outer form of the prayer, the piece of paper; the supernatural powers attributed to the writing is why this custom qualified as "abuse" and elicited censure on the part of the lay priests.[90]

Writing, therefore, as attested to by the above examples, had a magic power in itself—at least for those who could not read. In 1727 a peasant woman in Pozsony County charged with witchcraft held up three notes to another peasant woman; the latter, however, could not read them. Upon this, she declared that they were "notes such as those carrying it should have a large amount of butter".[91] In this instance, the writing itself held positive power, allowing the carrier to gain advantage over others. No cases were discovered in which the accused attributed harmful intent to any writing; in the witchcraft trials no one was debauched, corrupted or driven into illness through use of writing. On the contrary, the letters in themselves had a healing power through their sheer magic force. As witnesses claimed in 1770 in Szerdica, a Slovene-populated village in Vas, a peasant held "such a writing as should be attached to the neck of a person who had been bitten by a mad dog, upon performance of which the bite would harm him no more". In the entire region of Tótság, not a single literate peasant was found from the eighteenth century, and as evidenced by the nationwide school survey conducted in 1770, a couple of children attending school only could be found with difficulty in the whole region. General illiteracy was largely responsible for the respect shown toward "magic" writings and toward the peasants who distributed them.[92]

In Peresznye, Sopron County, witnesses told the court in 1743 that János Somogyi had "diabolical writings" on him, and as Mr. Somogyi himself had often said, these "demoniacal writings were so miraculous...as could be read neither by priests nor friars". It is suspected that Somogyi was illiterate, yet from the sentence he flung at the bailiff of Peresznye, it seems clear that he may have envied the scholarship of the priests and friars and was proud to own such writing that even they could not decipher. Nor did Somogyi's bragging leave the village untouched. His mother-in-law, with whom he apparently was not on good terms, gave her testimony in court, stating that her daughter, Somogyi's wife, once had opened her husband's secret casket. Somogyi usually carried this box with him everywhere, but on this occasion he left it at home, for he had been summoned to the bailiff and was afraid it might be found on him. Taking advantage of the opportunity, his wife opened the box and, as the mother-in-law related, they glimpsed the Devil himself. The peasant woman stated under oath that she had seen the Devil clearly perched among the writings that were worn as amulets and proffered a description: "The box having been opened, she saw the Devil in the midst of the writings, in human shape and in a white pointed cap." It is virtually certain that Mr. Somogyi's mother-in-law was illiterate and held an instinctive awe for the incomprehensible and indecipherable writings, an awe that may have grown to frightening proportions.[93]

The peasant woman's confession exemplifies the attitude the peasantry generally had towards literacy in the eighteenth century. At the time, the presence of written texts was common in the villages, but the majority of the inhabitants were illiterate and could not decipher the content of the writings. Thus, the mysterious writing preserved in a box may have appeared to be diabolical to the analphabetic peasants.

CHAPTER 3

LITERACY AMONG THE NOBILITY

W HEN examining the attitudes of the Hungarian nobility concerning literacy, attention should be directed toward two social groups. The gentry ranking under the aristocracy was divided into two markedly different groups—the landed and the lower (or lesser) nobility. The financial positions, lifestyles and cultural possibilities of these two strata differed substantially. This was obvious to their contemporaries but has received less than due emphasis in Hungarian historiography. In 1728 in Rogasóc, Vas County, two old noblemen insisted that the Bozókis were "genuine and true gentry" and "not just run-of-the-mill nobles—they counted among the gentlefolk, too". Their account continued to explain why the Bozókis were "not just run of the mill" in the witnesses' eyes: these "gentlefolk" not only owned lands but also serfs. Similarly, in 1719 witnesses verified in the county court that Gottfried Klein, a nobleman though his credentials may have been lost, "was accounted for in the county at all times as a man of importance and considerable means"; that is, he was not just an ordinary member of the lower nobility, but one of the landed gentry—a *portalist*.[1]

Landed gentry who owned estates exceeding one hundred Hungarian *iugerum* (a contemporary land measure equaling approximately 1.4 English acres) and/or possessed serfs or cottars were distinguished from the lower-ranking noblemen of the title *nobilis* with the more fashionable titles of *generosus ac perillustris*. There were about two hundred fifty families in Vas County in the mid-eighteenth century that belonged to the landed nobility. They were called *portalists* because their estates were registered by the *porta* (serfs' house) they owned. The lower ranks of the nobility, those possessing less than one hundred *iugerum* of land or none at all, numbered some two thousand five hundred in this county. They were called *taxalists*, as they did not have serfs and, hence, no one paid tax on their behalf. Therefore, from the end of the seventeenth century they paid *taxa* (taxes) into the county purse; in other words, even their legal status differed from that of the landed nobles.

Literacy and written culture revealed substantial differences between the two strata, which calls for a separate examination of both. The method used here, however, is the same as that employed in the examination of the peasantry. The findings then will be compared to data on the nobility of neighboring Transdanubian counties (Veszprém, Sopron, Moson, Győr and Zala) and of the control group in Upper Hungary, in what is now Slovakia (Abaúj, Torna and Borsod counties).

Literacy among the Nobility in the Sixteenth and Seventeenth Centuries

There were a significant number of noble families in Vas County in the Early Modern Age. According to data from the census conducted under Emperor Joseph II from 1784 to 1787, 6.75 percent of the inhabitants professed to be of noble descent. The rich sources that have been preserved in the archives of the Vasvár chapter, by the county and by some families offer the researcher ample information for the study of their culture. Crosses and signatures, refined or scrawled, reveal the literacy rate within the leading elite of the county: the *portalists* and the more numerous *taxalists* of the lower nobility of poorer means. The letters and last wills and testaments written by these nobles also provide insight into the changes in their attitudes towards literacy and the prestige that it was accorded.

Charters and deeds from sixteenth-century Transdanubia reveal that the practice of authentication by signature did not yet exist at the time, primarily due to general illiteracy among nobles. As in the Middle Ages, the primary means of authentication was the seal. Some nobles also would place their signatures underneath their seals, while others used crosses in substitution for their names. In any case, the lack of signatures on sixteenth-century documents did not necessarily mean a lack of writing skills; often the clerk wrote the names of those who were known to be able to write—another indication that signatures were seen as less important than seals.

Indeed, many sixteenth-century documents contain only seals and no signatures, names or crosses at all. In a culture of general illiteracy, signatures did not yet have a legal role as a means of authentication.

This situation changed during the seventeenth century. Signatures as a required means of authentication slowly emerged and strengthened within the nobility. This is depicted clearly by a mortgage letter concerning a meadow that Pál and Mátyás Sibrik, two landed nobles from Vas, issued in 1610. Only Pál could write of the two: his fine signature is found next to his seal. Mátyás was illiterate and embarrassed by this, for he had the following postscript added to the document: "P.S. For I myself, Mátyás Sibrik, cannot write with my own hand, wherefore I have drawn three crosses instead, to command as much power as it were my own name in my own hand."[2]

Six years later Gáspár Cziráky, a nobleman, mortgaged a plot of land to his brother-in-law, the notary of Vas and Sopron counties. Since the latter was obviously a literate person, Cziráky, like Mátyás Sibrik, must have been embarrassed by his ignorance—at the bottom of the letter he addressed the witnesses, stating: "therefore I request these honorable gentlemen that since I myself have no knowledge of letters, their Mercies confirm this letter also with their handwriting and seal." The mortgage certificate eventually was signed only by one of the two witnesses. The other county councilor, Miklós Mesterházy, merely placed his seal upon it; he may not have had the writing skills with which Master Cziráky credited him.[3]

The modern view that holds a signature to be of great importance was slow to spread among the nobility. The literacy of the nobles of western Hungary in the seventeenth century still defies examination through statistical means as there are an inadequate number of signatures for numerical analysis. However, this fact in itself reveals a great deal about the nobility of the seventeenth century: they excelled in wielding swords rather than pens, which explains the scarcity of written texts that have come down from them.

Boldizsár Kisfaludy, from a western Hungarian noble family, served in the insurgent army in the war led by the prince of Transylvania, Francis Rákóczi II, against the Habsburgs (1703–11). After the defeat of the freedom fighters, he emigrated to France and served in that country's army. In a letter he looked back on the seventeenth-century history of his family, stating: "true enough, I know not of a single lawyer in our family, for they were all men-at-arms. Not that soldiery was of much use to them." Having recognized that the age of warfare had passed after centuries of battles with the Turks, he recommended that his mother put his brothers "in the hands of advocates and judges. Once my brother had learnt German law, he also should learn Hungarian law; not many weapons and horses are needed for that".[4]

In the eyes of the nobles living along the marches dividing the Habsburg and Turkish parts of Hungary in the sixteenth and seventeenth centuries, proficiency in handling "weapons and horses" was more prestigious than "Hungarian law." This is supported also by Captain-General and Count Ádám Batthyány's comments on his officers: "take no heed of his illiteracy", the aristocrat defended his nominee for the post of army justice of the Körmend garrison in 1650, "for poor András Hidasi [a former captain in Körmend] too could not write at all; however, he could make good of his post with distinction—for it often happens that a man is well versed in writing yet knows nothing of military matters". Clearly the land-owning aristocrat, himself an educated man and a book collector, thought it more important for a military man to know about military matters than to be able to write.[5]

The nobility of western Hungary also participated in the noblemen's *insurrectio* and the wars of the Habsburg Empire in the eighteenth century. By that time, however, they increasingly recognized the importance of legal knowledge. The three last wills of György Bogyay, a wealthy nobleman who owned lands in several counties, were written between 1702 and 1711, during the same period from which Boldizsár Kisfaludy's quoted letter originated.

György Bogyay intended to provide for his children because he was afraid that his wife would disown them after his death in favor of her daughters from an earlier marriage. In his 1702 testament he declared that he hoped his wife would not swindle his sons and would "raise them, put them to school...and thereupon have them tutored in the legal practice" with the fortune they would inherit. His wife, he maintained, should not remarry after his death except to a man "of fine repute, who should have his sons taught arithmetic and legal matters". In 1710 György Bogyay drew up a new testament in which he requested his brother-in-law "to force my sons into the legal profession". Bogyay's anguish was in vain, as he survived his wife. He made out a third will after her death, again insisting that his sons study law. Both he and Kisfaludy clearly saw that a new period had begun in western Hungary, from which the land of marches became the province of a peaceful country removed from any borders. During this period jurisprudence promised a better future than did the use of arms.[6]

In the seventeenth century the skill of writing was not yet common among the landed nobility in western Hungary. Although impossible to illustrate through statistics, this is supported by the fact that although the tasks of county officials required writing skills, the county administration did not employ only literate individuals. While the majority of councilors in the Vas County administration left proof of their literacy by placing their practiced signatures on documents in the seventeenth century, at least fifteen only could draw crosses.

Ferenc Tánczos, a councilor of Vas County, was honest enough when he put his cross on a document in 1655, adding: "since writing I know not".[7] Another Vas County councilor, Gáspár Nagy, did the same in the 1620s and 1630s and wrote "not being knowledgeable about handwriting".[8] Others, especially in the second half of the seventeenth century, did not advertise their illiteracy and can be identified only by comparing the signatures they left behind, from which it appears that several different people's signatures came from the same hand. In 1653 Deputy District Magistrate György Horváth traced his name in jerky script. He also committed another councilor's name to paper as is proven by the similarity of the characters in common—the latter obviously could not write. After Councilor Tamás Pochkay's name, his colleague even added "m.p." (*manu propria*, "with his own hand"), although he could not write and both his signature and the abbreviation were written by his friend. Similarly, Deputy District Magistrate Ádám Gaiger regularly signed documents for another county councilor.[9] Among the many signatures found in pairs, the one that allegedly was written by Boldizsár Tulok (i.e. Balthasar Bullock) is particularly conspicuous. This illiterate nobleman must have asked Boldizsár Bozzay, a fellow councilor, to sign the paper for him. Mislead by the identical given names, Bozzay automatically wrote his own family name again in lieu of Tulok. After noticing the error, he crossed it out and completed his friend's name.[10]

There were councilors with some writing skills who were at a loss when it came to writing the Latinate form of their Christian names. The Latin language played an important role in the county administration at this time, so they must have had a difficult job—not unlike the analphabets. A district magistrate could write but only with difficulty: it was not just his scrawled hand that revealed his lack of experience but also his attempts at penning the Latin version of his Christian name. While he should have written Georgio, he wrote "Görgio", mixing in a Hungarian accented vowel. At another point he wrote "Gurgius" instead of Georgius.[11] In 1699 another county councilor had difficulty writing the Latinate form of his Christian name, Georgius; he first wrote "György" in the Latin text, then "corrected" it to "Gyorgyus" in a different ink.[12] His colleague, György Dese, otherwise an excellent writer, came up with another version—"Gerorgio", a combination of the Latin and Hungarian versions of his Christian name. Benedek Börsöny, a Vas County councilor and no calligrapher, committed another mistake to paper in 1701: instead of Benedicto, he wrote "Benedekct." It is small wonder then that the rest of the Latin text is found wanting as well.[13]

In 1668 a district magistrate in Vas was capable of writing down his own name, though in uncertain hand, but after his signature he tried to add those of his two fellow councilors, who loathed to admit to their illiteracy by drawing crosses. He made a minor mistake in the Latin name of the first one, doubling a consonant, but in the name of the second he committed a much more serious error, writing "Griorus" instead of Gregorius.[14]

A typical representative of the semi-literate county councilors, János Bodis, a squire from Meszlény, could make only a sizable cross underneath his name. He was not a full analphabet, however, for five years earlier he had issued a letter "under writing with his own hand"—although this actually meant that the semi-literate nobleman merely scrawled his initials beside his seal.[15]

Putting a cross on a document did not necessarily signal illiteracy, as the mark may have served as a substitute for a seal beside a name. A cross after a name only indicated illiteracy beyond doubt if the name itself was written in a hand identical to that of another name—that is to say, if the name was written by a hand other than that of the "owner" of the cross.

The poor writing skills displayed by county councilors were not only typical of Vas. There was a councilor in neighboring Zala County who as late as the mid-eighteenth century scrawled his name on documents, committing great errors, yet held the post for twenty years.[16] Other Zala County councilors were baffled by Latin. After a hearing in 1727, the first underwriter, a county councilor, still deemed it proper to write his name and title in Hungarian rather than in Latin. The next one to sign, however, penned his title in Latin, and this prompted the third councilor, Márton Kelemen, to try writing in Latin as well. He may have been a literate county councilor, but he obviously had not gotten past elementary school, since he did not know a word of Latin. He was unable to copy the Latin words for his own administrative unit, *inclyti comitatus* (honorable county); he apparently only understood the curlicues and flourishes visually, eventually tracing the nonsensical "Neloctj Camitajus" instead.[17] Another councilor from Somogy County put his name and title on documents incorrectly, and moreover, the word *originale* (original document) appeared under his pen as both "orgenare" and "organale."[18]

A similar incident could not have occurred in the more developed Vas County during the eighteenth century. In the seventeenth century, however, there are instances in which Vas councilors committed similarly serious mistakes in their titles. When grappling with the Latin words for their own county, *comitatus Castriferrei*, one wrote "Castraferrei", and another, "Crastriferey". These are no less erroneous than the signature of the Zala councilor, although for a different reason. The Vas councilors, rather than copying something they had not understood for lack of education, must have learned at least some Latin and, remembering their undoubtedly short-lived "scholarly" studies, may have identified part of the county name with common Latin words they found familiar (*cras* means tomorrow, and *castra* means camp).[19]

Illiteracy among the county leadership was common in other counties as well. In 1754 in Gömör County, Upper Hungary, an advocate in a lineage case argued that it would be wrong to accept any old documents as evidence of noble descent, as there must have been a significant number of people who had given titles to themselves, posing as nobility in court "at some time in the previous century, before some simpleton, an unlettered magistrate, for in that dark century [that is, the seventeenth] some county councilors who could not even write their own names properly were truly found".[20]

In the middle of the eighteenth century the advocate already spoke of the ignorant county officeholders of the previous century with reprehension; by then it was unheard of that an analphabet should hold an office of this rank. In Sopron County, near Vienna, which was more developed than Vas in many respects, literacy was a precondition of qualifying for a councilor's post as early as the late seventeenth century. When the Horváths sought their nobility, a sixty-nine-year-old nobleman recalled their grandfather, Gergely Horváth, who had fought once against the Turks during the siege of Buda (1686). He was a well-to-do nobleman, the witness from Dőr maintained, "on his very own manor house in noble liberty". Moreover, he heard people say that "had he been a man able to read and write, he would have made a chief magistrate or a councilor, for he was one who commanded respect".[21] Thus, in the late seventeenth century in Sopron County even a respectable squire was not elected councilor unless he could read and write.

Crosses and Signatures from Noble Hands in the Eighteenth Century

In general, all county councilors and the landed gentry could write in eighteenth-century western Hungary. A significant number of signatures have survived, preserved in family archives, and not one cross is found among them. It is also possible to examine the writing skills possessed by the middle and lesser nobility in this century. This is largely facilitated by Act No. 27 of 1715, which stipulated that nobles could make their last wills and testaments only in the presence of five witnesses who authenticated them with their signatures. This act also prescribed that if the testator was illiterate, a sixth witness had to sign the will.[22]

In his work *Tripartitum Juris Hungarici Tyrocinium*, used by advocates of the period as a handbook, the Jesuit jurist János Szegedy further clarified the stipulations of the law. Witnesses to the will had to be adult male nobles, he wrote, and had to number at least five in order to validate the testament. Testaments that have come down from the eighteenth century in Vas show that these stipulations, unlike a number of other legal articles, were strictly observed. This is not surprising, as it served the interest of the testators to ensure that their testaments could not be contested on formal grounds after their deaths.[23]

Testaments are excellent sources for the study of literacy, since they contain a wealth of information about the testators, their domiciles and their possessions. Moreover, they provide information about the position the testator occupied in not only the geographical and chronological but also the social sense. Witnesses generally came from the ranks of like-minded and similarly positioned people—friends and more distant relatives (family members were barred). During the course of researching this publication, witnesses were treated as though they belonged to the same social group as the testators. The samples are most probably not fully representative in this respect. It may be assumed that these individuals were somewhat wealthier than the dying person himself, just as was typical when selecting godparents. In any case, the categories of financial position are broad enough to protect against possible distortions. Rab Houston, the author of a definitive work on literacy in Scotland, suggested that those asked to witness last wills and testaments were primarily literate persons. Therefore research based on testimonies may distort facts "upwards", he writes. The testaments left behind by the Vas noblemen, however, display a large number of crosses, indicating that literacy was not the primary reason for selecting particular witnesses in western Hungary.

The shortcomings of testaments as source material on literacy are also obvious. One may think that only the nobles of greater means made testaments, since they had abundant enough possessions to dispose of after their deaths. An examination of the testaments, however, shows that this supposition is groundless: many in the lowest ranks of the nobility also had their wills drawn up even if they had only a small plot of land, a pig or a carriage to leave behind.[24]

The credibility of a last will and testament as a source on literacy also may be questioned on the grounds that the majority of those writing one did so when old and ill. This was not true for all wills, as young and healthy persons also decided to make bequests in case they feared to die young, including young men leaving for battle or women before giving birth. The testament of István Kelédy, a descendent of an old noble family in Vas, illustrates that it was not necessarily a feverish, weak and bedridden man who scrawled a testament. In 1583 Kelédy made out a will for his goods, chattels and a casket full of gold jewels—he was definitely a man of considerable means. Although not illiterate, the wealthy squire jotted down the characters of his name in an unpracticed hand, each letter separated from the next, leaving one out or randomly replacing a letter with an odd one. It was semi-literacy, rather than senility, weighing down his hand, because he emphasized that he was drawing up his will while "being of a healthy disposition in my person". Countess Borbála Esterházy, from one of the most prominent aristocratic families, also enjoyed good health when drafting her testament: "though God hath blessed me with good and fresh health…nevertheless giving thought to Man's mortality especially in this my pregnant and expectant state", she wrote in 1690. Luckily, the countess survived giving birth to her child, and her will was opened only centuries later. Anna Gosztonyi, a gentlewoman, was also healthy, although "gravid in my body and expecting the birth of my child any day now" when she had her will drawn up in 1692. Setting out to fight the Turks, Sándor Keczer, age twenty-eight, made a testament in a military camp, "albeit not in my advanced years…with respect to my state of warfare". Other nobles aimed to make bequests while healthy, fearing sudden death. Both of György Bogyay's wills from 1702 and 1710, for example, emphasized that "now I feel no disease whatsoever" and "I am of a healthy and sound disposition", but the threat of war and pestilence led him to plan for his death and the future of his possessions.[25]

The majority of bequests, however, were dictated from sickbeds. This casts doubt on the legitimacy of our entire research method, as a person who could write in childhood may have forgotten the skill in his or her senility, and a weak and afflicted individual, even though literate, may have been unable to grasp a pen, requiring the document to be written by another person.

Legal practice at the time, however, refused to accept "guided" signatures as, although by a person's own hand, they did not display the testator's real intention. If the testator's hand was led by someone else, the signature and the document as a whole was null and void. Although not regulated by law, the handbook of the Jesuit jurist János Szegedy stressed that it followed clearly that a signature was spurious if the writer's hand was led by another person. Pressure on the testator in shaping not only the letters but also the content of the will was justifiably suspicious in cases of "assisted" signatures.[26]

Signatures made through the agency of another person were not considered authentic in legal practice. In 1696 Ferenc Babocsay, a rich nobleman and captain-general from Vas County, made his bequest in the office of the chapter of Vasvár. Five years later the testament was contested by the family of his first wife. During the hearing, noblemen stated that the captain's second wife often had signed "diverse papers of lesser import" on behalf of her husband. In cases involving more important documents, "the lady commonly took his hand, on account of his tremor, and thus led him to subscribe these". His secretary did the same: "His *secretarius*, having drawn up the letter, took my Lord Babocsay's hand and thereby had him subscribe the letter." This is also how the squire's last will and testament was made—and for the same reason, was not deemed authentic by the court.[27] The rate of signatures and crosses figuring in this investigation is not distorted, therefore, by "assisted signatures".

A number of noblemen attended school and learned to write but later forgot the skill for lack of practice. Subsequently, they used crosses for signatures on testaments. They can be regarded rightfully as functional analphabets who were unable to use their writing skills, so sources do not distort the real situation in these instances either.[28]

The inability of older gentlefolk to write was counterbalanced by the role social prestige played. Literacy came to be respected by this period; anyone who could write his or her own name could not afford to be thought of as uneducated and illiterate, even on the deathbed.

In 1661, Judit Pongrácz, the wife of a rich nobleman, made her bequest at their Bozsók mansion. "For some days now I have felt mighty powerlessness in my body", she wrote in her will, but she emphasized that she signed her will "in my very own hand even in my great sickness". Made up of small disconnected letters without any capitalization, her signature indicated that she was not much of a scholar, and she was also sick, but she made the effort not to be taken for illiterate. It was extraordinary when a literate person did not sign his or her testament, no matter how sick he or she was.[29] This explains why witnesses were asked to provide detailed accounts of the last hours of Countess Antónia Königshegg's life in Trencsén County in 1743. The countess was sitting in her bed, unable to speak but nodding her head, they stated in court. Her testament lay on a small table in front of her, and she "kept a pen with her fingers but could not move her hand, for she was unable to sign her name because of the apoplexy". She merely nodded in affirmation when asked if the testament was her last will. When asked if she could sign the paper, she shook her head. "Would she sign it in case she could", they asked, and she nodded again, replying merely with "aye, aye". Again they asked her if she wanted the witnesses to sign it for her and "upon this she merely nodded—when the steward read out the testament and they all signed it there and then".

The nobility strove to put their signatures on testaments in whatever shaky and scrawled writing they were capable of. József Laky, a lower nobleman from Hollós, who must have been Lutheran judging from the books listed in his bequest, signed his own testament. The jerky hand and crabbed letters, repeatedly retraced, mirrored the challenge the task presented him. Nor did the parish priest of Hídvég rely on a cross to authenticate his last will and testament in 1783—he signed it, as he wrote, "with my own trembling hand". A prebendary of the Vasvár Chapter put his signature on the paper with such a trembling hand that it was barely legible; however, he insisted on signing his own will.[30]

Those literate persons who were too weak to sign their wills found it important to stress that infirmity and not illiteracy prevented them from supplying their signatures. "In my sickness of body because of the grave diseases God hath released upon me", János Hódosi, a nobleman, wrote in his testament in 1754, "herewith I confirm it by the mark of my own hand, before the persons listed hereunder, as I am unfit to subscribe on account of my trembling hand". He pointed out that he was not illiterate, even if he could not write at that time. [31]

A lower noble from Vönöck made his bequest in 1757. "Unable in my powerlessness to write my name, putting the sign of the cross after my name", he wrote to authenticate his testament. It was apparently important for him to point out that he did not use the cross due to a lack of writing skills. A lower noble from Kolta had the same reason in 1728 when he stressed in his testament that he used the cross only "for the gravity of my affliction and my great powerlessness prevents me from subscribing" the testament.[32] The gentry also found it important to emphasize existing but unmanifested literacy in documents other than testaments. In 1716, when a register of the Batthyány counts' estate was made, one steward of noble lineage signed it by writing "I, István Taba, hereby confirm it with my seal, though in alien hand, on account of the affliction of my right hand."[33]

The ability to write commanded ever greater respect in the eighteenth century. In 1701, next to a witness's cross on a testament from Hodász, Vas County, *manu aliena propter ignorantiam scripturae* (in alien hand on account of the underwriter's ignorance) was written.[34] In later periods nobles refrained from admitting illiteracy in public. In the second half of the eighteenth century, the number of lower nobles who could write grew, which presented a challenge for the semi-literate. The lower nobility certainly did not make the transition from illiteracy to literacy overnight: the process was full of hardships, as well reflected in the jerky, ill-shaped letters. Between 1758 and 1781, eight lower nobles in three neighboring villages used crosses at one time and their signatures at others. The reason for this alternating usage is clear: if the majority of witnesses contented themselves with crosses, they too followed suit. If, however, the witnesses produced their signatures, they tried not to lag behind.[35]

In Kisfalud in 1773 György Gombás witnessed the testament of a noblewoman and signed his name on the document in huge, clumsy letters, misspelt as "Görgörg" (sic!) Gombás. Six days later the lady changed her mind and made a new bequest, on which Gombás put a cross, just as he did two years later on another testament. The identity of the witness is certainly the same in both cases, as each time it was specified that he was György Gombás, Junior, and each time the document displayed the senior's cross as well. Gombás knew letters, although his writing skills were rather poor. Two other gentlefolk from the village also scrawled their names in block letters when the rest of the witnesses used writing, but in other cases they used crosses. Attestation by one's own hand grew in importance in this period, which is further supported by an investigation conducted by Vas County authorities in 1703. The inquiry aimed to ascertain if, on a document drawn up four years before, all the witnesses had placed the crosses after their names themselves. This document from the beginning of the eighteenth century mirrors the transitional period of literacy: none of the four rather poor noble witnesses could write. While in the seventeenth century it would have sufficed if the clerk wrote down their names without any assistance, a century later all four illiterate noblemen found it important to stress that they at least drew their own crosses.[36]

The increasing prestige of literacy is exemplified by cases in which literate nobles refused to let the notary—who was expected to deal with analphabets—sign papers on their behalf. In 1771 in Mizdó, the notary listed the names of noble witnesses on a document, who then put crosses by their names except for one who wrote "m.p.", although only these two letters were written in his own hand.[37] On a document drafted in Boba in 1772, one nobleman crossed out his own name, which the clerk had written, and replaced it with his autograph in clumsy script, adding a cross in lieu of his seal. He was the only literate person among the witnesses and obviously did not want to be taken for an analphabet.[38] In 1749 the notary of Kispöse signed a document for a nobleman, but he made a mistake in the name of the gentleman testator. The latter, Ádám Benda, crossed out the wrong Christian name, László, and replaced it with his own in an uncertain hand. He too could write in an emergency.[39]

In view of the above one may state that wills are legitimate, appropriate sources for an examination of literacy. True, the majority of testators were advanced in their years, or at least middle-aged, and it may be asserted rightfully that the younger generation of the gentility was better educated. Most signatures on the testaments are, however, from witnesses and not the testators. The former undoubtedly represented the gentlefolk as a whole, for there was no reason that only old people would have been requested to act as witnesses.

Respectable landed gentry preserved testaments in family archives, in chests for documents that often figure in manorial inventories. The lower nobility, on the other hand, handed over their testaments to the county archives. Five hundred seventy-six signatures or crosses from members of the lower nobility, testators and witnesses were found on eighteenth-century testaments. According to the 1754 register of the county nobility, there were some 2,500 heads of families who were *taxalists* in Vas County. The sample, which contains testaments from the beginning through the end of the century, represents about twenty-three percent of the lower nobility of Vas—a rate that is comparable to international literacy research.[40]

It is clear from the figures in table 3.1 that illiteracy was fairly common among the lower nobility in Vas as late as the eighteenth century. However, the figures also attest to positive developments: while in the first half of the century four-fifths of the Vas lower nobles could not write their own names, the rate decreased to two-thirds by the end of the century.

Table 3.1

Literacy of the Lower Nobility in Vas County in the Eighteenth Century
(Males Only)

| | Method of Authentication | | | |
Years	Crosses	Signatures	Total	Literacy Rate
1701–1720	1	5	6	–
1721–1740	101	28	129	21.7
1741–1760	80	20	100	20.0
1761–1780	165	55	220	25.0
1781–1800	74	47	121	38.8
Total	421	155	576	26.9

Only a few testaments reveal the religion of the testator. On the basis of the scanty data available, which are insufficient for making statistical calculations, no conspicuous differences between denominations can be determined. The majority of testators and witnesses left behind crosses whether bequeathing money to a Lutheran school or having a mass celebrated in a Catholic church.

The testaments also facilitate grouping the lower nobility according to their financial positions and evaluating whether or not there were any differences in literacy in the various groups.

The law prescribed the order of the escheatage of hereditary estates, so testators were not entitled to dispose of these possessions. In the case of large estate owners, a testament did not provide as true a picture of their fortunes as an estate inventory did. When reading the testament of a large estate holder, one has the impression that it belonged to a jeweler rather than a landowner. The lower nobles, however, could be divided into two groups on the basis of their purchased or mortgaged lands: those owning a maximum of ten *iugerum* and those owning between eleven and twenty-five *iugerum* of plough land. These groupings have been confirmed both by research on the social characteristics of the eighteenth-century Zala and Vas nobility and by data concerning their chattels. All lead to a clear distinction between a poor group and a midlevel group.[41]

It is obvious from the figures in table 3.2 that the literacy rate of those bequeathing over ten *iugerum* of land and their witnesses was, in fact, even lower than for the poorest lower nobles. The size of the estate, therefore, was not a determining factor in the literacy rate of the gentry. Within the wide margins set by social and financial position, the individual's attitude toward learning was decisive.

Table 3.2

Literacy of the Lower Nobility in Vas County According to Size of Estate Mentioned in Testaments (1721–1800)

Size of Estate (*Iugerum*)	Method of Authentication		Literacy Rate (Percent)
	Crosses	Signatures	
0–10	321	125	28.0
11–25	88	20	18.5

In the eighteenth century, some three-fourths of Vas County's lower nobles were illiterate; those using crosses to sign documents were in the majority as late as the end of the century. However great the backwardness reflected through these figures, the Vas lower nobility still boasted much more literate persons than the peasantry, of whom only every fiftieth could write his name. The offspring of both strata attended the same elementary schools, but the children of the gentry considered the skill of writing more important than did the peasants' offspring. Although the advantage of nobles in literacy was very relative, the explanation for the higher literacy rate lies in the greater prestige that reading and writing skills were accorded by the gentry.

No suitable sources were identified for an examination of literacy among the nobility in Vas County in the first half of the nineteenth century. Research was conducted on this issue on neighboring Veszprém County nobility on the basis of a variety of sources, however. In 1797, of the 258 insurgents of lower noble descent, fifty percent (129 persons) could read and write. Seventeen percent (44 persons) were able to read only, and thirty-three percent (85 persons) were completely illiterate. Although the majority of those participating in the insurrection were in their twenties and, therefore, represented the youth, their high literacy rate was remarkable nevertheless.

Twenty-two men in the lower nobility could write and thirty-two were analphabets in the village of Vámos, Veszprém County, in the last decades of the eighteenth century. Only one woman of the same social standing knew letters in the same period, and forty drew crosses. Between 1831 and 1840, four-fifths of the male lower nobles, 137 out of 175 (78.29 percent), could write, while among the women the rate was the opposite: four-fifths were analphabets (sixty out of seventy-one, or 81 percent). In the same period, in the village of Henye, Veszprém County, north of Lake Balaton, 52.38 percent of the male lower nobles knew how to write; in Őrs the rate was 63.46 percent; in Kál, 77.58 percent; and in Monoszló, 73.46 percent. In sharp contrast, only six to eighteen percent of the women in this county were literate.

Literacy advanced slowly among the lower nobility in secluded villages and more rapidly in more populous places; women again followed suit but in great arrears. The rate of increase in literacy may have varied from village to village, but one factor was significant: in Veszprém County, about one-half to three-quarters of the lower nobles already could write their signatures in the first half of the nineteenth century. This was a veritable cultural revolution in the making compared to the situation in the eighteenth century in neighboring Vas County.[42]

Reading Skills among the Lower Nobility

Reading leaves no traces behind, and literacy researchers almost invariably examine writing abilities (more precisely, producing signatures) and renounce attempting to gauge reading abilities. In several European countries, however, an extraordinary source lends scope for the examination of reading skills *en masse*: Lutheran pastors in several areas conducted an annual survey of reading skills in their flocks.

Sweden (including Finland and Latvia, which still belonged to Sweden at the time), Zurich and its surrounds and particular regions in northern Germany where the Lutheran faith thrived hold eminent places in the history of European literacy. In the course of Lutheran church visitations in these territories, records were made regarding the reading skills of all adults, even indicating grades. In other words, an otherwise unmanifested skill can be examined on the basis of a large sample. The Lutheran Church attributed great importance to believers being able to read the catechism and the Bible. Those reluctant to learn to read were easily denied taking the Easter Holy Communion.[43]

There was, however, a piece of writing that was at least as precious as the Bible in the eyes of the Hungarian gentility: the *armalis*—letters patent of nobility. Once a letters patent was lost or burnt (which was not uncommon in times of war), the county administration instituted investigations in order to evaluate claims to nobility.

Ancestry investigations offer a complex picture of the lowest, poorest and populous ranks of the village gentry. In the case of the landed gentry, no doubt was raised as to their entitlement to noble privileges. It was, therefore, members of the lower nobility, the ranks of which numbered about ten times more, who figured in the records. The land-owning squires (*generosus*) rarely acted as witnesses in these cases, and thus there is no account of them (all knew how to write all the same). Among the lower nobles are the *curialists*, who owned ancestral land the size of serf plots (*curia*), and *armalists*, whose only possession of worth was the *armalis* (the letters patent of nobility) and who served other nobles or even peasants, made a living out of crafts or leased plough land. Their reading abilities are depicted in the witnesses' accounts in ancestry cases, in which members of the lower nobility sought to establish their claims to title after having lost their letters patent. In cases of this nature, the county leadership, magistrates and councilors summoned neighbors, often of noble descent, and questioned them under oath as to whether they had *read* or at least *seen* the missing letters patent.

The county officials who conducted ancestry cases interrogated the witnesses in great detail, and the latter had to reply to the questions under oath. They were asked if they had seen the letters patent in question; if so, where and when they had seen it; where it might be found; who else had seen it; who had read it; who had heard it being read; which king had granted it; to whom exactly he had granted it; and in which county it had been made public. The detailed replies reveal whether the witnesses could read or not.[44]

Examining reading abilities is also important because the available sources in analyzing writing abilities were *indirect*. It was exceptional when someone wrote that a document had been authenticated "by alien hand, not knowing letters"; in most cases, a cross or some characters suspiciously identical to those in other signatures showed that a serf or a gentleman was literate. In witness depositions of ancestry cases, however, hundreds of lower nobles, freemen, market town burghers and serfs declared that they could not read. Statistics can be formulated on the basis of these depositions only with great reservation; nevertheless, the picture that emerged from them convincingly confirmed findings concerning general widespread illiteracy.

There are two arguments against the use of witness depositions. One is that letters patent were invariably written in Latin; a gentleman able to read in Hungarian but not versed in Latin might, therefore, seem to be illiterate. The other is that many of those bearing testimony were elderly people who may have had decent reading abilities but could no longer decipher the deeds due to their weakened eyesight.

Both arguments can be refuted by examining an original letters patent. These were usually large-format, ornamental documents written in eminently legible, large calligraphy; the most important names on it—those of the king and the ennobled person—were usually written in gold. Even if no Latin scholar, a person who knew how to read could have identified at least these names. In 1766, for example, a boot maker from Szentpéter stated that he had read the letters patent in question, which had been pawned for two bushels of wheat and subsequently disappeared. It had been granted by Emperor Ferdinand and had "the name Hercsik written in it in gold letters". That much he remembered, but nothing more: apparently he could read only the great gold letters and not the Latin text. Another witness could read that much from his master's letters patent, too. In 1771 the octogenarian related how Germans had besieged the home of his master, István Hosszú, where he had lived at the age of twenty, and the soldiers tore the letters patent from his hand in the scuffle. In the document, "especially at the beginning, there were large letters in golden writing", he recalled, "and he also remembered that the name Hosszú was written in that letter of nobility".[45] A witness from Luc could decipher the names of the grantor king, Ferdinand, and the beneficiary family, Kovács, in a letters patent, "the witness having fairly known letters", even if he did not understand the Latin text. Similarly, Mihály Kovács of Miskolc read only the name of a titled person, a cobbler, and "he read from it the family name of Czakó, though as to the Christian name he could not observe that, for he has no knowledge of the Latin language"; Christian names were always in Latin in the letters patent.

A nobleman from Csát testified on more than one occasion that "though the letters patent was laid out before him, he did not read it in full, but having examined it, he clearly saw the name Frona written in it". In 1793 a nobleman from Győr, very much from the lower ranks of the nobility, as he lived by trading wash tubs as a young man, said that he had read the letters patent and "in it the name Czeglédi, though I did not understand anything else"—in other words, he could read but not understand Latin. The noble János Poroszlai was still a small schoolboy and "was therefore himself a little versed in writing" when he saw a letters patent in which he could read the name of Emperor Leopold and of the recipient. Others also could read the grantor's and recipient's names but not the rest of the text, such as a nobleman from Jászó who read the names of Emperor Ferdinand and of the noble family in the document, "but what else was in it, he did not know for the writing was ancient, thus he could not decipher" when the letters patent was made public.[46]

Even elderly gentlemen were able to read the large golden letters. In any case, this can be inferred from the fact that old age is not brought up as an excuse for not being able to read, except in one incident among the hundreds of ancestry cases reviewed. When interrogated in 1745, András Medgyessy from Tállya, age seventy-four, said that he had seen and read the letters patent Emperor Leopold I had granted János Pap, which subsequently was stolen from Mihály Gál's cellar. The testimony was found questionable, and eighteen months later he was interrogated again. On this occasion he maintained that he had not only seen but also read the deed issued by Emperor Leopold, which he claimed was written in Latin and Hungarian. As no Hungarian text ever appeared on letters patent issued by the Habsburgs, it was obvious he had never read the one in question. As a result, the jury sought to test Medgyessy's reading ability, upon which he declared in embarrassment that he was "for the time being incapable of reading on account of senescence" (*se autem pro nunc ob senilem statum suum lectionis incapacem fateretur*). This was an obvious lie, just as was his claim to have read the letters patent, which may not have existed at all. The son of Mihály Gál, from whose cellar the document allegedly had been stolen, said they had not kept a letters patent in the cellar. It also turned out that János Medgyessy was a cousin of the person who sought ennoblement, János Pap; thus, his impartiality was strongly dubious. All in all, old András Medgyessy was unable to read the letters patent in question because he was illiterate and it never existed rather than because of his advanced years.[47]

Eyeglasses and Spectacles

Spectacles were an important prerequisite for reading in old age. However, few peasants owned glasses—even at the end of the eighteenth century—and the common ignorance of their function is illustrated in the following story that was printed in the 1785 Győr calendar: "A certain peasant who could not read but, noticing that numerous men and old gents put glasses on their noses when reading, thought that whoever put on those glasses would be able to read, too." So he went to the eyeglass vendor and tried several pairs of glasses to no avail. "Ultimately the vendor suggested that his customer did not even know the alphabet, upon which the peasant ex-claimed: 'Damn it, if I could read I would not buy glasses at all!'"[48] Appar-ently, the use of eyeglasses was spreading at the end of the eighteenth cen-tury, at least in higher circles, and thus the peasant may have seen people read while wearing them. The illiterate peasant, however, had no idea what the eyeglasses were good for, and his ignorance no doubt proved hilarious for the almanac's readers. This anecdote illustrates the social position of spectacles in the second half of the eighteenth century: educated, urban people used them, and although they were sold in shops, they were largely unknown to the peasants.[49]

Eyeglasses were well known in the upper echelons of society in the six-teenth and seventeenth centuries. "I have sent thee some spectacles for your eyes, and I wonder if they may have given them unto thee", Count Tamás Nádasdy wrote to his wife, Orsolya Kanizsai. Count Miklós Bethlen had eyeglasses as well; in his autobiography he wrote that he began using spec-tacles in 1696 at the age of fifty-four "not for need of them, though, but because I heard that our eyes lasted longer this way. In my ancient state now, I can follow no writing or reading without them, though with them I do, especially in the light of the day, be it in whatever small hand; otherwise I am, with my sight, as I was twenty years ago or even more."

It was no rare occurrence for spectacles to be registered in estate inven-tories in the eighteenth century. These included glasses designed to protect eyes from dust when driving or sitting on a carriage, the equivalent of mod-ern motoring goggles. Such "leathered glasses serving to protect the eye from dust" appear in the inventory of György Hertelendi, chief magistrate of Vas. On the other hand, in the Söpte manor house of a nobleman, Zsig-mond Botka, spectacles "for reading" were itemized in 1758.

No longer considered a luxury, spectacles were known to the gentry of lesser means as well. József Laky, a Lutheran lower nobleman, was a rela-tively poor man who tilled his small plot of plough land with a pair of super-annuated horses. When an inventory of his home was taken in 1797, three pairs of spectacles were itemized alongside the seven books he owned: he had one pair in a black case, another in a red case and a third "in bare", that is, uncased.

Eyeglasses were not personalized, made-to-order items at the time—they resembled today's cheap, ready-made reading glasses sold in supermarkets rather than the expensive lenses prescribed by an optician. Very popular items, they were handed down or else auctioned upon the death of the owner as were those of the wealthy nobleman and the lower noble mentioned above. Furthermore, they were not expensive, costing three or four *kreutzer* (the small change of the day)—the price of a drinking glass, a pair of horseshoes or a kitchen grater. Since they were not custom-made, they were within reach of even the poorer lower nobles.[50]

Balázs Rusa, a lower nobleman who was a schoolmaster in Ság, Sopron County, in the early eighteenth century, was familiar with spectacles as well. In his advanced years he bragged about his excellent eyesight, saying repeatedly how, "though I have lived a long time as I am a man of one hundred ten years, yet I can sing in church without spectacles".[51] From the words of the old gent, who had filled both the schoolmaster and cantor posts of this small village, it is clear that he knew what spectacles were for and would have used them if he needed them. Needless to say, the number of lower nobles in Vas who used glasses when reading cannot be ascertained. A large portion of them never did, at least not in the first half of the century, not because their eyesight was that good, but because they had no need for them due to a lack of reading skills. However, from the depositions it is clear that reading ability commanded respect, just as writing did. Those who were unable to sign a document because their sight was poor or their hands afflicted rather than due to illiteracy made a point of saying so in their testimonies. Obviously the lower nobles would have emphasized as well that they could indeed read when their eyesight was yet good if this has been the case. However, apart from the false testimony of András Meggyessy of Tállya mentioned earlier, no examples of this have been found. Those who learned how to read could decipher the fine, large calligraphy of letters patent even in their old age. Witness depositions of ancestry cases, therefore, are very reliable sources for the examination of the reading abilities of the nobility.

Apart from Vas County, which is again the focus of this study, data on Zala and, in Upper Hungary, Abaúj and Borsod counties are sufficient for analyzing the reading ability of nobles. As a large number of lower nobles lived in all four counties (according to the census taken under Joseph II from 1784 to 1787, in Vas County 6.7 percent of the inhabitants were titled; in Zala, 6.9 percent; in Abaúj, 7.9 percent; and in Borsod, as high as 14.9 percent). While the figures on noblemen and their reading skills naturally are not appropriate for representative statistical calculations, the picture presented through hundreds of witness depositions may well be characteristic of the lower nobility's attitudes toward reading and writing. It would be wrong to gauge data on seventeenth- and eighteenth-century literacy with the measures of the age of statistics in the nineteenth and twentieth centuries. However important the gathering of data is, figures show trends and proportions at best and cannot substitute for full surveys.

The reading ability of 119 members of the lower nobility in eighteenth-century Vas County can be identified unambiguously from the witnesses' testimonies. This represents 4.8 percent of the 2,500 *taxalist* lower noblemen registered in 1754. This rate is unsuitable for representative statistical calculations yet can provide a strong indication of the lower nobility's knowledge of reading; important findings have been made in international literacy research with smaller samples.[52]

Of the 119 Vas lower noblemen, thirty-four could read (28.6 percent) and eighty-five (71.4 percent) were illiterate. Of the nobles born in the seventeenth century, eighteen could and seventy could not read. Of those born in the eighteenth century, far fewer gentlemen were asked to bear witness—eleven could read and ten could not. The dates of birth of ten noblemen are unknown. The progress is clear—a greater number of young lower nobles could read in the eighteenth century.

Fifty-nine lower nobles were witnesses in eighteenth-century ancestry investigations in Zala County, and from their accounts one can determine whether or not they could read with a good degree of certainty. Three-quarters of these (forty-four, or 74.6 percent) could not negotiate characters; only fifteen could read. This portion is, therefore, similar to that of Vas County.[53]

It is clear from the ancestry cases that reading, just as writing, evoked great social prestige. Those able to read were proud of their skills and ready to advertise them, while those lacking the ability were ashamed and attempted to hide their illiteracy.

Nobles openly admitting that they could not read were, in general, more advanced in years. In 1718, Mihály Salamon of Zala County was an old man indeed—he claimed to have lived one hundred ten years. Understandably, the ancient man was not reluctant to admit to illiteracy. He had known the nobleman under investigation, he said, but "not being able to read, the witness did not heed his letters and deeds".[54]

Imre Petruss, a nobleman from Vas County, was also open about his lack of literacy. He began his testimony by admitting that he could not read and went on to relate how he often heard from those who could that they read the letters patent of certain noblemen.[55] In 1727 Petruss admitted to being eighty-eight; therefore, he was born in the middle of the seventeenth century and thus was unashamed of being illiterate. A petty nobleman in Hollós, Vas County, made no secret of his illiteracy in 1727 when he confessed to be eighty years old. He said he did not know whose name was written in the letters patent since he could not read. Eighty-one-year-old József Lévai of Pápa did not pretend to be able to read the letters patent that he said he had held in his hand.[56] All these witnesses were elderly gentlemen; moreover, the two from Vas County gave their testimonies in the early eighteenth century when they would not have felt the social pressure that later made literacy—or the appearance of literacy—a matter of prestige.

In 1754 six noblemen from the Őrség region were questioned; none could read, but only the oldest three, between the ages of sixty-eight and seventy, said so openly. The last witness to be summoned in the case was a seventy-year-old serf of the Batthyány family; he was the only one of the witnesses to have read the letters patent in question; that is to say, the only literate witness was a serf in the company of noblemen.[57]

A literate nobleman was always ready to highlight how educated he was. One relative confessed to the nobility of the Vajda family, having heard this from his family and "from other ancients many a time, also, the witness himself being a literate man read and learned from the letter itself accordingly".[58] Péter Töreky, a nobleman from Zala, emphasized that "he read the letters patent of the said family, as he himself is able to read".[59] Reading ability was not common among the lower nobles of Vas and Zala counties in the eighteenth century, so whoever was literate could duly draw special attention to it.

Witnessing nobles were especially likely to emphasize their reading abilities if they did not actually read the document in question. The motivation was similar to the cases of those people who could write but were impeded by sickness and drew crosses for signatures, and they protested against being taken as illiterate. They peremptorily stated they did not read the letters patent, but not because they could not do so. In 1726 a nobleman from Lendva said that he heard about the letters patent a man from this village procured for himself, and "which this witness also heard others had read, and though he himself is a literate man, he did not read it because he never had it in his hand". A peasant of Jánosháza also articulated his literacy even though he was a serf and not a nobleman. Once he was drinking wine with a lower nobleman who took a letter out of his chest and said: "this is my letters patent. This witness, although able to, did not read the said letter; he only saw it as it was all folded up."[60]

Illiterate Lower Nobles in Upper Hungary

The findings in western Hungary may be compared with the state of affairs in the counties of Borsod, Torna and Abaúj in Upper Hungary for control purposes. The denominational composition of the nobility was different in these counties: the lower nobles who lived in the villages of Vas, west of the Rába, were predominantly Catholic; those living in Sopron County and in the villages east of the river were mostly Lutheran; and those in the Őrség region were Calvinist, although they rarely turned up as witnesses. In Upper Hungary, the majority of lower nobles followed the Calvinist faith. Here, as evident from the depositions, literacy enjoyed greater prestige than in western Hungary. It is difficult to justify this statement with figures, although it is clear from the sources, as witnesses occasionally spoke about analphabets in derogatory and disparaging terms. In 1744, the lieutenant of the noblemen of Bénye and his fellow witnesses stated that "the deceased Pál Balog was left behind by his father very early in infancy"—that is, he was orphaned. His mother then remarried twice, but "his stepfathers unwilling to keep Pál Balog", he grew up living in various locales. "As he had been raised an orphan, he was illiterate" and became the village swineherd. An exiled noble offspring, he did not attend school, nobody cared to tutor him and he was thus left an illiterate. This fact never would have elicited such astonishment from the nobles living in Vas or Zala counties.[61]

The Abaúj ancestry investigation offers a wealth of interesting data and descriptions of the lower nobles' literacy and lack thereof. Yet such information does not lend itself to statistical analysis, as the number of those whose reading ability can be ascertained with a sufficient degree of certainty is small. In Borsod County, on the other hand, the depositions of 174 lower noblemen unambiguously reveal their literacy or illiteracy. Some nobles appeared as witnesses several times over the years, which facilitates the verification of data, yet in these cases the individuals are included only once in the statistics. Of the 174 lower nobles of Borsod, seventy-eight, or 44.8 percent, could read; ninety-six, or 55.1 percent, could not. These rates are significantly better than that in Vas and Zala. Although the strongly relative nature of the figures must be emphasized, the higher literacy rate confirms what the sources suggested: in Upper Hungary, literacy had more prestige than in western Hungary. Whether this relative advantage—relative because the majority of the Borsod lower nobles could only hold letters patent in their hands and not read the words—may be explained by their Calvinist religion or by the denser network of developed market towns with prestigious schools will have to be determined by further research.

It took more than just living in a busy and populous market town for a member of the lower nobility to learn how to read. One-quarter of the 174 witnesses were from the market town of Miskolc, but only eighteen (forty percent) could read; twenty-seven (sixty percent) "knew no writing". In other words, the literacy rate in the largest market town in Borsod County was actually lower than in the whole of the county. A somewhat better rate was found in Csát, another market town. Of the twenty-five lower nobles who bore witness, twelve of them did read the letters patent in question.

In the eighteenth-century Borsod County ancestry cases, fifteen wives of lower nobles also testified, none of whom could read the letters patent. The words of two elderly ladies between the ages of seventy and eighty and several middle-aged noblewomen in their forties revealed that they could not read a word of the letter. One woman from Ónod, the sixty-one-year-old wife of a titleless market town burgher, emphasized that she had seen the letter, and since she could read, she saw the names of the noblemen in question. Her account also reveals that literacy among women was something of which she could be proud.[62]

The gentry of Abaúj and Borsod counties, as in western Hungary, were reluctant to admit to illiteracy. A serf could more readily confess that—"on account of his illiteracy" or because "he does not know letters" or "is an ignoramus" or "is no scholar"—he did not read the document. Social expectations of the nobility were greater than of serfs. Some serfs were even proud of their ignorance, such as a peasant in Szántó, who in 1743 declared with a degree of defiance: "Nobleman Balogh did show his letters patent to this 'ere witness, though he did not read it as he cannot read at all."[63]

Those of noble descent tried to conceal that the world of letters was unknown territory to them. In cases when nobles and peasants testified together, the nobles said only that they had seen the letters patent under discussion and did not disclose their illiteracy, while the peasants, especially the elderly, readily admitted to their lack of reading skills. The witness "observed the letter many times, yet he is an ignoramus with regard to letters", a ninety-year-old serf from Bőcs said. "On some occasions, having seen this letters patent, even holding it in his hand, this witness did not read it, as he cannot read", the records say in 1745 of a seventy-six-year-old freeman from Gönc.[64]

One year later a freeman from Dobsza testified. He said that he was eighty-six and thus could remember General Caraffa's campaign of 1687–

88, when he had seen the letters patent, but "not knowing letters", others read it for him.[65] A sixty-two-year-old day laborer from Onga saw the letters patent in question on more than one occasion, but "the witness, being *illiteratus*, did not read it". Nor was he ashamed of his ignorance, which was far from exceptional for day laborers, and certainly the fine Latin formulation was not in his own words.[66]

Nobles, unlike day laborers, attempted to conceal their ignorance. One noble from Szikszó tried to avoid revealing his illiteracy when a decisive question was asked about the Kornis family's letters patent. He stated that he had seen it and that it had been issued by King Sigismund as far as he could remember. He may have been urged to be more explicit, as he added that he knew this because the letters patent was read to him on several occasions.[67] A gentleman from Csécse testified in 1742 that he had been in the service of the Pap family for a long time and had seen their letters patent. Since the point was whether or not the missing letters patent indeed belonged to the Pap family, this witness could not avoid admitting that he could not be sure of that on account of his illiteracy.[68]

Although some Abaúj County noblemen seemed to have been proud to be ignorant, they were all children of the seventeenth century and were elderly when they appeared before the jury in the first half of the eighteenth century.

A nobleman from Szikszó pronounced himself an *illiteratus* in 1743 when he was eighty-nine; another nobleman, also of Szikszó, was seventy-nine when he informed the jury that although he had seen the letters patent, he "knew not by which king and in what year it had been published" as he was "completely" illiterate. A third nobleman from the village of Görgő was eighty-eight, another from Gönc was eighty-six, and a fifth nobleman from Tállya was seventy-six when they admitted they could not read the letters patent in question.[69]

As the prestige of being able to read increased in the second half of the eighteenth-century parallel to the advance of literacy, even elderly nobles wanted to mask their ignorance. In 1773 three noblemen in the Hegyalja region—seventy-six, seventy-four and supposedly one-hundred-three years old—stressed that they had seen the document but did not state that they could not read it. Similarly, a nobleman from Fony testified that he had kept the letters patent of the Vitelky family in his own chest but did not read it— obviously because he could not, although he did not say so explicitly.[70]

Towards the middle of the eighteenth century, the reluctance of the gentry to admit to illiteracy led to the use of euphemisms and circumlocution under questioning. In 1742 one nobleman from Bőcs said that he had seen the document and had it read by the notary—obviously because he himself could not have done so, although he omitted saying this. The testimonies given by two men from Szepsi, both seventy years old, about a letters patent in 1743 presents a typical example of the different attitudes peasants and nobles displayed regarding their own ignorance. The serf bluntly stated that he had not read it because he was illiterate, while the nobleman merely imparted that he had seen but not read it, although he obviously did not know how to read. In a similar fashion, a seventy-eight-year-old serf openly said in court that he could not have known the contents of the letters patent, while two noblewomen said before the same court that they had "seen but not read it", despite the lower social expectations for women's literacy.[71]

In 1766 in Szántó, two elderly nobles, seventy and seventy-eight years old, did not make a secret of their illiteracy, while a younger witness, fifty-four-year-old János Kardos, merely declared that he had seen the document in question, though he could not have read it any better than his wife, a woman who readily disclosed the reason she was ignorant of its contents.[72]

There were some among the illiterates who hastened to conceal their ignorance and who had to confess to their illiteracy when the witnesses' accounts were being authenticated. When the tax collector appeared at his neighbor's home, a nobleman from Pálháza said in 1766, "he displayed his letters patent on the table and had his master read it, thus proving his gentility". When verifying the testimony a second time, the members of the jury did not content themselves with the original statement, and the witness was forced to admit that "although the letters patent was written in the name of the neighbor, the witness himself could not read it because he was ignorant of reading".[73]

Analphabets were ready to agree with the words of their more educated fellows in hope of avoiding the exposure of their ignorance. In 1749 a nobleman of Telkibánya said he concurred with the previous witness's opinion. When the document had to be authenticated, he avowed that although he knew the nobles as did the previous witness, he could not read their names in the letters patent.[74]

In 1753 a nobleman from Kér testified in court that all he had to say was exactly the same as what other two gentlemen, who had read the document, had stated previously. When the document was to be attested, however, the good gentleman had to back down and admit that although he had indeed seen the certificate issued by the county administration on this man's nobility, he had no idea if it was written in Latin or Hungarian, as he did not speak Latin. In fact he could hardly have read it at all; what he could do at best, in another witness's words, was "hold and feel it with his fingers".[75]

In Borsod County, as in Abaúj County, illiteracy was increasingly regarded among the lower nobility as something of which to be ashamed. In their efforts to avoid openly admitting to looking at "the fine golden calligraphy" uncomprehendingly, they chose to emphasize "having seen the letters patent with their very own eyes". A nobleman from Csát averred in 1774 that "he had seen the letters patent, although he did not read it, and observed nevertheless that it had some golden characters in it". All a nobleman from Gelej had to say was that he saw the letters patent because it was kept in the same case as his own; had he known how to read, he would have taken a closer look. According to the draft records, a sixty-year-old gentleman from Kondó told the county committee that although he had seen the letters patent of the Lukáts family, he had not read it because he could not read, and it had not been read to him. In the final version, however, the reference to illiteracy was omitted, obviously at the request of the noble witness. Otherwise the rest of the text is identical. [76]

Nobles and non-nobles in Borsod County frequently acted together as witnesses, and non-nobles were much more willing to admit to their ignorance. In addition, the older the witness, the quicker he was to admit to "not knowing reading". Eighty-year-old János Szabó admitted his illiteracy in 1740, while his two peers, who were sixty and sixty-five years old, tried to dodge the question, and the last noble to testify proudly emphasized that he not only had seen but also read the letters patent.[77]

It was exceptional when someone could read the document in question but did not because he was not in a position to do so. A nobleman from Szikszó recalled in 1752 that he once saw the letters patent being dried on top of the oven in the home of another nobleman; "the witness aimed to read it too, but having drunk an excessive amount of wine, his host did not allow him, saying to the witness that it was no time for him to read it; should he sober up he would indeed give to him that letter of nobility to read". This occasion never was to happen though, and the testimony the once-drunk witness had to offer on the precious document was no better than that of an analphabet.[78]

These cases offer a somewhat dire picture of the literacy of the lowest ranks of the nobility. More than seventy percent of the Vas and Zala nobles could not demonstrate a passive knowledge of letters, nor could more than half of the Borsod nobles. True, the majority in Vas and Zala and almost all in Borsod were born in the seventeenth century, and the literacy rate among the nobility must have risen in the first half of the eighteenth century. Unfortunately, there is no data whatsoever as to the reading capacity of the lower nobility from the mid-eighteenth century on. In light of their signatures and crosses on their last wills, it is certain, however, that by the end of the eighteenth century those able to write certainly still were in the minority, even if presumably those able to read were already in the majority.

Noblewomen with the Quill: Literacy among the Fair Sex

The gap between male and female literacy first presented itself in the sixteenth century. While aristocratic men were literate almost without exception, women had great difficulties in this area. In contrast to the Middle Ages when women's illiteracy was taken for granted, in the sixteenth century—although not natural then either—it was already a cause for apology, and literacy was a reason for great pride. "Your Lordship has asked me if I knew how to write in Hungarian", Borbála Kerhen, the widow of nobleman András Tarnóczy, wrote to Palatine Tamás Nádasdy on 18 August 1556. "In the country in which I grew up [Croatia] I did not hear that girls or women learned how to write in this way... My poor mother indeed would have had me tutored, had others been tutored, too, but we did not even hear about it."[79]

The good lady must have been at a loss with writing, in general, rather than only in Hungarian, because she had her letters always written by somebody else. Her noble husband, a captain in the army, was a literate person who mostly wrote his letters with his own practiced hand.[80] Count Nádasdy, a man of humanist erudition, wanted to know whether the landlady of the neighboring estate was literate or not. The letter he wrote to her was lost, but her reply to it apologizes for her not being able to write, since in Croatia women were not expected to do so at the time she was raised; had it been socially common, she would have been schooled, since she was from a good family.

Orsolya Kanizsai, wife of the previously mentioned Count and Palatine Tamás Nádasdy, squire of Sárvár, was a literate woman; the letters she exchanged with her husband are among the finest aristocratic correspondence in Hungary from the sixteenth and seventeenth centuries.[81] She wrote many of the letters in her own hand, even though this posed a serious problem for her. "My beloved Orsolya, you have done well not to write with your own hand. You are not to do so henceforth either, because it is common knowledge that whereas three fingers are writing, the whole body is at work", the loving husband wrote to his ailing wife in 1552. A month later she wrote: "Why I cannot write myself, Your Honor, You must forgive me, for I dare not exert myself in bed, not even with writing." So writing proved a physical exertion for Orsolya Kanizsai. "My handwriting is proof enough, a sick person cannot write this much", she reassured her worried husband in 1560. The next day Count Nádasdy replied to her thus: "Do give me a reply to my letters, I beseech you. When you write you are in good health and I can learn about this, seeing your letters in your own hand, in that I believe you and I also rejoice because of your healthy state...I have also written to you more with my two hands in these days." It is clear from these lines that the palatine, who generally dictated his letters to several clerks, thought it important to write his letters to his wife himself if possible: the holographic letter, the content of which was known to no one except the sender and the addressee, was intimate. "I have this written to Your Honor by someone else, as Your Honor had wished me to [spare her the effort]. Indeed I now have difficulties in writing, yet when I can get around to it I shall not forbear to write to you with my own hand too", Orsolya Kanizsai wrote in 1555, and again a couple of months later: "This I have had somebody to write, for I cannot as yet bend down well to write myself."

"Write to me every day, I beseech you, about your condition", the palatine urged her on another occasion, "but do not tire yourself, for whatever you may entrust either the estate steward or the castellan to write" she should have them do for her. But, "whatever is not becoming to be written about by them [such as women's maladies] You should have my woman sister take down when she has no headache". His "woman sister", a relative of Nádasdy (and the widow of István Majláth, a famous aristocrat who died while imprisoned in the Seven Towers in Istanbul), also evidently could write, although with just as much difficulty as Orsolya if she was prone to get headaches when doing so. A century later in 1643, Count István Csáky feared for his bride, later to become his third wife, "lest you should tire yourself with so much writing, for whoever is not accustomed to it can hardly avoid a headache".[82]

Writing was both laborious and slow for Countess Nádasdy, who was unaccustomed to it and would rather dictate her letters to the clerk when in haste. "And Your Honor should forgive me for having this letter written in another hand, for I could not perform it myself, owing to the urgent departure of the post", she apologized in 1553. When pressed by duty, the palatine would often dictate his letters too: "Forgive me, therefore, my beloved kinswoman, for not writing this letter in my own hand, for the many activities I conduct."[83]

It is a mistake to believe that every woman in Nádasdy's court could write as well as the lady of the house or her sister. In 1559 a young well-off noble asked for the hand of a young aristocratic lady, Anna Frangepán, who lived in this court. The palatine sent this letter to his wife for fear of its content becoming public knowledge before the proper time and because of the girl's possible reluctance. He described in detail how his wife should bring the confidential news to the girl's notice. "When you give the letter to Anna, tell her, if you like, to get her brother to read it for her, pretending that you are disinclined, and send for him, and whilst he is reading the letter, look at Anna's face and watch how she keeps herself." That is to say, the letter had to be read for the aristocratic young lady, although reading a letter out loud would have posed a problem for the countess as well, as she would not have been able to observe Anna's reaction to it while doing so. [84]

The finest example of an aristocratic lady becoming literate in adulthood was Erzsébet Czobor, the second wife of Count György Thurzó, the richest aristocrat of his time and later a palatine. She was still illiterate when she married him in 1592. Two months before the wedding her fiancé chided her, saying: "That I have nothing to my letter by way of a reply from you, I may attribute to nothing else but your anger out of your love for me. You could perhaps find one excuse for you, I might think, that you cannot write yourself; so be it, but then you have a brother, to whom you could most trustingly present your task and your intention, and his honor shall, I know, take up the work and reply to my letter according to your wish. I beseech you, therefore, dearest heart, to write to me about your health and how you are."[85] Hardly had two years passed when Erzsébet Czobor herself penned a few words in her letter, and it is clear from her delighted husband's reply that he had taught her the art. "You have traced some words with your own hand, my sweetheart, that I see much to my liking and I was much gratified by you as my beloved and sweet disciple, that you study so diligently. And I shall bring you some fine Turkish goods as presents, for you to see that you should study even better." Count Thurzó mockingly threatened his wife, saying that upon his return home "should you commit any error in your writing I shall punish you with nothing else but some fine kisses". Three days later, on receiving a letter written entirely in his wife's hand, the loving husband enthused: "The valet has given me the letter that you wrote in your own hand...which I read with great pleasure and love indeed, especially because I have never seen a letter from you in your own handwriting. May the Almighty Lord give, my sweetheart, my soul, that you oft write to me for many years coming, about your good health."

The surprise of seeing a letter written in his wife's hand had not faded a year later: "I have received your letter, my beloved sweet soul, which you wrote in your own hand. The Almighty God only knows with how much love I looked at it and read it, especially because I had a good student in you, who could learn to write so finely." György Thurzó continued exchanging letters with his wife for several years, but references like these were no longer found in them—his wife's writing skills were taken for granted. Erzsébet Czobor developed a practiced hand but still did not write all her letters herself, rather dictating some on occasion as was the practice among the aristocracy. In 1596 three couriers arrived at once at the military camp of the army besieging the Turkish castle of Esztergom, all bearing letters to Count Thurzó from his wife: one was in his wife's hand, and the other two were committed to paper by a clerk.[86]

Not all high-ranking men could persuade their spouses to learn to write. Borbála Bánffy, an aristocrat, refused to comply with the request of her husband, Ferenc Zay, captain-general of Kassa: "My sweet beloved husband, when Your Honor requests me to learn how to write, indeed I would be glad to oblige, but it is difficult for me to learn, my beloved lord, for I have troubles and sorrows, and as long as Your Honor holds that office in Kassa, truly my heart's sorrow will not abate, my sweet lord... And also, my beloved husband, it is difficult for an old person to learn." Borbála Bánffy's exact age is unknown, but as she died the following year and she was married to Ferenc Zay for thirty years, she could not have been too young. Understandably enough, György Thurzó had an easier job convincing his young wife of the usefulness of writing than did Zay, whose wife must have been at least middle-aged.[87]

Around 1600 another Hungarian aristocrat, Pál Telegdy, often chided his wife, Kata Várday, for not writing more often: "Truly you are slothful enough, to deny writing me even a small note, though you would not tire yourself with that. Abandon your sloth and write to me at any time when you can send a man to me, for I deserve that much from you, and you have also time to spare for that in the midst of all your other tasks, for you do neither ploughing or hoeing, not cooking or washing." Writing was apparently a physical exertion for the lady: had she been illiterate and merely dictated her letters, Telegdy would not have reprimanded her in such a stern fashion. Kata Várday was literate indeed, only she wrote her letters with difficulty and none too readily.[88]

From the mid-seventeenth century on, almost all aristocratic ladies in western Hungary could write, even though their signatures were childish, unschooled and unpracticed (see table 3.3). Both daughters-in-law of Count Ádám Batthyány, Anna Palóczay and Kata Illésházy, wrote in cursive, however unpracticed.[89] Before giving birth to her child in 1690, Borbála Esterházy, the wife of Count Ferenc Kéry, had her last will and testament drafted in Tömörd, Vas County. Her signature was especially unpracticed, like the scrawl of a small child just learning to write. Countess Zsuzsanna Balassa made a bequest in front of the chapter of Vasvár in 1695, leaving her jewels to Éva Thököly, the wife of Prince Pál Esterházy, who was tending her during her sickness. The high-ranking woman wrote her will in its entirety, although in a clumsy hand and using phonetic spelling. Sickness may render a person unable to use a pen, but correct orthography, once acquired, is not easily forgotten—Countess Zsuzsanna Balassa obviously was not given to writing even when healthy.[90]

Table 3.3

Literacy among Lower Noblewomen in Vas County as Mirrored in Their Testaments (1721–1880)

Land Possessed (*Iugerum*)	Method of Authentication	
	Crosses	Signatures
0–10	96	0
11–20	28	0
26–100	6	1
Total	130	1

In Transylvania, Judit Veér, the second wife of Count Mihály Teleki, who was later to become chancellor, was able to write, although it proved difficult for her. Understandably enough, she traced the letters more poorly when sick: "God commanded great grace that now He gave me the strength to write this little letter, for indeed I would not have thought I could write today, but this morning the great hotness ceased in me", she informed her husband in 1662. Two days later she assured him: "My sweet husband, I would indeed write at greater length, had not this little writing tired me enough." However, she also had difficulty with writing when healthy. When the courier was in a hurry on another occasion, she started writing but did not get far: "this little I wrote while he was waiting here; I wanted to write, nevertheless be it short".

In January 1661 Mihály Teleki, while still engaged to Judit Veér, wrote in a love letter: "Rest assured that I want to share a bed with you as soon as possible, and that death only will depart me from my love for you." He asked his intended to write often: "When you write to me, you can speak about anything with abandon." Should she find the act of writing too laborious, she should dictate her letters: "In case Mathias from my court is with you, do write through him, when you need to write at all."[91]

Count Miklós Bethlen, the famous writer and the most educated aristocrat in Transylvania in the second half of the seventeenth century, urged his bride, Ilona Kun, not to write to him about how much embroidery or spinning she had done: "Read the Scriptures diligently, and write to me also very finely, and let me know about your health, about how much you wrote, and for how long you read the Bible." In a letter written three days later she replied thus: "I have understood Your Honor's commands about both writing and reading, which, as time and expediency allowed, I have not till now omitted and will not henceforth omit to follow." Ilona, barely fourteen at the time, must have been very diligent, for some forty years later Bethlen often recalled in his autobiography his long dead wife's fine features and figure and "her scholarly bent and fine speedy writing". This demonstrates that it was still exceptional for aristocratic women to have "fine speedy writing" in Transylvania in the second half of the seventeenth century. The wife of Bálint Szilvássy, the Transylvanian envoy to the sultan and an influential nobleman (although not an aristocrat), was illiterate: in 1667 she could only ask "well-meaning noble persons" to write for her.[92]

In the mid-seventeenth century, the gender gap, which was typical of the aristocracy and large estate owners in the previous century, divided the middle gentility: it was still natural for a husband to sign wills or agreements for his wife.

Éva Palásti, the wife of a well-to-do nobleman, put a cross underneath a letter in 1683 in Vas County. One might think she was an analphabet. Two years later, however, after she was widowed, she did write her own name with uncertain letters. In other words, she could write but did not like to, and attestation "with her own hand" was something she regarded as her husband's job.[93] In the early eighteenth century, the signature of Katalin Tevely, a gentlewoman from Vas, invariably was supplied by her husband: "Katica Tevely *manu aliena* [with an alien hand]." After her husband's death, though, she had to perform the task herself, which she did with oversized, uncertain letters.[94]

In the late seventeenth and early eighteenth century, daughters and women of the landed gentry in western Hungary could, with few exceptions, write, although in uncertain, childish hand. They drew rather than wrote their names, and examples abound, including Borbála Nicky (1690), Magdolna Niczky (1710), Kata Sibrik (1659), Mária Kisfaludy (1699), Erzsébet Svastics (1701), Mária Káldy (1734), Rozália Szelestey (1739) and Zsuzsanna Szegedy of Mezőszeged (1740), to name but a few—all from distinguished titled families.[95]

Prosperous and respectable noblemen's wives were analphabets as late as the mid-eighteenth century in the less developed parts of Hungary. In his memoirs the well-to-do nobleman Ferenc Kazinczy (1759–1831), writer, literary organizer and language reformer, offered fine portraits of his grandparents. His grandfather, Ferenc Bossányi, was an honorable estate owner in Bihar County, where he also held the post of chief county notary and later chief county magistrate and envoy to the diet. The lord often sat in front of his house, "taking delight in reading German books like *Gespräche im Reich der Todten* and *Febronius*...the German newspapers of Erlangen and Latin papers of Leipzig were his special favorites". In his youth, the Bihar chief notary used to have "pretty handwriting, the lines flowing even, as though written after the leaden print". In his old age, however, his hands trembled, and "he could write but with great exertion. For this very reason he hired a valet who was literate, and he would dictate his letters. Accustomed to excellence, he paced around the room and would press his nail onto the paper the scribe held to show him where to position the salutation, where to begin the first line and where to put the date and the name". The chief notary's wife, Julianna Komáromy, the daughter of the deputy chief magistrate of Békés County, was less educated than her husband: "She was bustling around in her own world, which consisted of her courtyard, kitchen and pantry filled to the brim with mugs and pots. She could read but could not write", Kazinczy wrote about his grandmother.[96]

As true of the majority of the women of well-to-do landed gentry families in the early eighteenth century, Zsuzsanna Pongrácz, the widow of a well-off nobleman, Mózes Kisfaludy, was a literate person. Her clumsy characters, however, indicate that she was not very practiced in the art of writing. Her son, Boldizsár, exiled to France after the 1711 defeat of Prince Rákóczi's freedom fighters, wrote home to his brother: "May I request Your Honor to express my humblest services to my dear mother, as for that slight matter she would not tire herself by writing to me about it... She should not exert herself and should therefore ask you, Your Honor, to write for her, while I shall be consoled by seeing her signature." That "slight matter", however, did indeed call for his mother's signature, as the son had forwarded a bill of exchange for a small sum. The significance of a signature already usual in Western Europe was thus introduced to a manor house in the Hungarian countryside with the bill, which was to be exchanged in Vienna. Gentlewomen like Kisfaludy's mother rarely signed papers—generally a man in the family signed for them—yet the bill of exchange was valid only if bearing her signature. Boldizsár, therefore, wrote his mother an explanation: "Should Your Grace have a quittance in German written on the back, and sign your name underneath", the banker in Vienna would promptly give him one hundred forints for it, Boldizsár wrote from faraway Alsace.[97]

The gap between the literacy among aristocratic men and women in the sixteenth century and among the landed gentry in the seventeenth century was reopened among the lower nobility in the second half of the eighteenth century. By that time practically all of the women in the landed gentry could write. In the course of the eighteenth century, the male members of the landless lower nobility were advancing slowly towards literacy, while their wives were almost exclusively illiterate. This is borne out by the last wills left behind by the lower nobility from the eighteenth century.[98]

Literacy was slowly advancing in the social hierarchy, reaching lower and lower ranks. In accordance with society's views about the differing male and female social roles, reading and writing became common among men more quickly than among women of all social groups. This is clear from the sixteenth-century correspondence of the most aristocratic women, just as it is two centuries later from the last wills and testaments of the poorest ranks of the lower nobility.

Beyond Literacy: Latin as a Spoken Language

Resources provide researchers with conflicting information on the speaking of Latin in Hungary. Missionaries and travelers who visited the country stated firmly that even coach drivers and shepherds spoke the language in Hungary, whereas county officials made ghastly mistakes with the simplest Latin words.

While the efficiency of elementary education in villages and market towns was indicated by the literacy rate, proficiency in Latin provides insight into the secondary level of education since the culture of the period was based on a Latinate body of knowledge.

Latin was the official language in Hungary as late as 1844. It was the language of the law and the state, and an active knowledge of it was indispensable in the higher echelons of the public administration. Yet, as there were no compulsory levels of written literacy in this period (for instance, a man could become a county councilor in the seventeenth century or a schoolmaster in the eighteenth century without even being able to write his own name), there is a confusing picture of the next level of education, which included the study of Latin.

Those who were unable to write or those who could scrawl their own signatures only with great difficulty did everything to create the impression that they knew how to do so, because literacy and learning in general had great prestige. This was the case with Latin, too; there were many who, although they did learn how to read and write at school, concluded their studies without learning Latin. This fact is demonstrated by mistakes in documents written in Latin made by seventeenth-century county officials who were often hardly able to wrestle with the Latin forms of their own Christian names.

The Latin forms of even the most common Christian names posed an insurmountable problem for many seventeenth- and eighteenth-century noblemen in Hungary. In 1657, for example, a vice lieutenant and nobleman from Vönöck wrote "Juhanes" instead of Johannes.[99] Distorted forms of almost every Christian name are found among the signatures of the seventeenth and eighteenth centuries, including those of some of the county councilors quoted previously. The translation of György (Georgius) proved especially difficult, as the Latin word was very similar to the Hungarian form. In lieu of Georgius they wrote "Giorgius",[100] and instead of Georgio they wrote "Geörgiö", "Giorgio" or "Gyeorgyio". On the other hand, the name Sándor was problematic because the Latin Alexander was wholly different from the Hungarian Christian name. This explains why a nobleman from Vas County, Sándor Koltay, signed his name "Alex Sander Koltay".[101] Many noblemen seem not to have advanced further in their studies than reading and writing; they could not have studied much Latin if they were unable to write down their own names in the language.

In the sixteenth century a lieutenant in the service of Palatine Tamás Nádasdy did not know Latin, although he wrote with a practiced hand. The lieutenant admitted this in a letter he wrote in 1554, in which he requested: "Your Mercy, write me in Hungarian because I have no knowledge of Latin, nor have I a scribe knowing Latin." He repeated his request a year later in a humorous manner. Awaiting the letter from his lord, he wrote: "Your Mercy, do not write in Latin because a rabbit ran off with my knowledge of Latin and they cannot expect it back." Although the lieutenant emphasized that he did not understand Latin, he could not refrain from decorating a letter written to Nádasdy in 1555 with a Latin phrase he had overheard: "Your Mercy, I serve you *ex toto korde*" (he used "korde" instead of *corde*).[102]

Similar Latin phrases (which were the simplest and most often used) such as *coram me* (before me), *manu propria* (with one's own hand), et cetera, defeated those who, although literate, did not have even the most basic knowledge of Latin. In 1634 Pál Dóczi, a nobleman from Vas County, confused the word *manu* (hand) with *malum* (apple) and, writing with large, beautifully formed letters, proceeded to describe his own incompetence: "Pál Dóczi *malum propria*"—roughly translated as "with his own apple".[103]

In 1674 a magistrate's clerk in Vas County wrote "idem guyry szupra" instead of *idem qui supra*, thus demonstrating that he had no understanding of the meaning of one of the most common phrases. The fact that the magistrate signed the document without bothering to correct this monstrous error reveals the extent of his education. The same expression became "idem quis upra" in Rábahídvég in 1635; the erroneous division shows that such men copied words without knowing their meanings.[104]

György Kelemen was an officer in the infantry of Körmend in the middle of the seventeenth century. He was literate and wrote his signature and letters with his own hand. It seems that he was a diligent primary school pupil at one time. However, he obviously only heard Latin from others and had no visual record of the words. Yet he did not want to replace Latin words with Hungarian, since he thought it more grand to use the Latin expressions employed by his more distinguished fellows. December first in Latin is "die prima Decembris", while the Latin *decem* (ten) was often replaced with a Roman numeral, *Xbris*. This soldier distorted the date, which became *die pirima Xbrys*. Furthermore, misunderstanding the significance of the "X", Kelemen drew a big upright cross in its place. Expressions that were often used but not understood were adapted to provide them with some kind of meaning. The expression *includálva* (appended) was written by this officer as "inkurudálván", which closely resembled the Hungarian word *kuruttyolva* (croaking)—thus a term that he had heard but not seen became distorted.[105]

A century later, in 1782, a lower nobleman made out a will in Vas County. In this case the notary misunderstood perhaps the most commonly

1 Hungarian noble boy with his primer (17th century)
Georg Metzner: Five-Year-Old Boy (1771)
(Private collection, Budapest)

67. A Roman Catholick Student in Siculia

2 A Roman Catholick student in Siculia (17th century).
The True and Exact Dresses and Fashions of all the Nations in Transylvania 67
(Régi erdélyi viseletek. Viseletkódex a XVII. századból.
Ed. József Jankovics–Géza Galavics. Budapest 1990. no. 67)

3 School-children learning to write.
Johann Stephan Bojack: Apotheosis of Saint Joseph Calasantius
(Church Altar, Prievidza, Slovakia, 18th century)

4 Difficult signatures from documents of the Eger and Miskolc Country Archives
(18th century)

5 A Hungarian Calvinist student (17th century).
The True and Exact Dresses and Fashions all the Nations in Transylvania. 23
(Régi erdélyi viseletek. Viseletkódex a XVII. századból.
Ed. József Jankovics–Géza Galavics. Budapest 1990. no. 23)

a)

b)

6*a*. Letters patent of Stephen Bocskay, prince of Hungary and Transylvania
(1606, Hungarian National Archives, Budapest),
b. Hungarian peasant of noble origin reading the letters patent of his ancestors.
1943 (Désháza, then Hungary, now: Deja, Romania)
(Ethnographic Museum, Budapest, F 91225, photo by Sándor Gönyei)

7 Hungarian noble and aristocrat girls and boy learning to read and write. *a*. Daniel Schmidelli: Countess Sarolta Pálffy. 1956 (oil painting, Castle Museum, Červeny Kameň), *b*. Karl W. Brand, Baron Ferenc Révay. 1756 (oil painting, Turcianské Museum, Martin), *c*. Daniel Schmidelli: Josefina Post. 1757 (oil painting, Castle Museum, Červeny Kameň), *d*. Young boy learning his first letters. Unknown master (Upper Hungray): Saint Joseph Calasantius, around 1767 (oil painting, Slovak National Gallery, Bratislava)

8 Hungarian documents deposited in the Central State Archives in Vienna (1686)

used Latin phrase, *coram me* (in front of me), which used to be written prior to signatures, and it was from this phrase that the Hungarian-Latin word *coramizált* (authenticating) originated. The writer of the will, however, was unaware of this and seeking to give some meaning to the phrase incorporated the word *corona*. Thus, the notary labeled the witnesses in the small village "crowned gentlemen" (*coronisált uraimék*).[106]

In 1834 a man in Kozmafa added *agilis* (a special legal category used by those whose mothers were of noble origin) to his name using curlicue letters. It did not mean much to him, but he did recognize the name of Prince Argirus, a hero of folktales and a popular narrative poem and the interjection derived from it, *az árgyélusát!*, as well as the folksong about the little *árgyélus* bird. As a result, he wrote the title in the form of "árgyillis", and he did so twice, as he signed the document on behalf of an illiterate friend as well. This was not a rare blunder or a slip of the pen: in the 1980s, anthropologists carrying out research work in this area noticed that older people still referred to the descendants of the *agilis* as *árgyélus*.[107]

Local village notaries, schoolmasters and lesser noblemen were often at war when it came to the use of Latin—even though they were the official representatives of knowledge and learning in the village—and attempted to keep their deficiencies in the language secret. At the end of the seventeenth century the schoolmaster of Egervár in Zala County was witness to the purchase of a vineyard. Instead of signing his name, he simply wrote his title in Latin: "Coram me, ludirectorae Egervariensis m.p." (this should have read: *ludirectore Egervariensi*).[108] The schoolmaster used round curlicue letters with enormous initials at the beginning of each word, but he still committed two serious grammatical mistakes in the four Latin words. The schoolmaster of Szentivánfa, Pál Büki, was no more practiced in the use of Latin. In 1673 he issued a debenture written with extremely decorative curlicue letters, while both the advancers of the bond and the witnesses signed with no more than a cross. Signing his own name, Pál Büki wrote "Paluo" instead of Paulo: one might suspect this was no more than a writing error, were it not for the fact that he wrote the village name as "Szent Ivanfalvacsi" instead of *Szent Ivánfalvensi*.[109] Both schoolmasters wrote in an ostentatiously beautiful manner, but their knowledge of Latin was less than perfect; with their signatures they unconsciously depicted the level of education of a whole class of society: only one in five schoolmasters in Vas County knew Latin as late as the 1770s.

In 1775 similar mistakes were made by the notary of Bükk in Vas County. One might think that his profession would presuppose strong writing skills.

Nevertheless, he not only wrote in a stiff and jerky manner but also seemed to have problems with writing his own name not in Latin but in Hungarian: instead of István (Stephen), he wrote "Istylyán". The reason he became village notary seems to be that he was the only literate person in the village at this time; all the other village inhabitants signed various documents with crosses. It is, therefore, not surprising that he also had difficulty with Latin phrases: he wrote *manó* (goblin, in Hungarian) instead of *manu* in the expression *manu propria*; thus the words "with his own hand" became "*with his own goblin*".[110] There were still some notaries in Vas County who copied the simplest of Latin phrases without knowing their meanings as late as the beginning of the nineteenth century. In 1806 the village notary of Köcsk made mistakes in his own signature and in the date: instead of Franciscum (Francis) he wrote "Trancisum", and instead of *Februarius* he wrote "Feburálius".[111]

Notaries and schoolmasters made attempts to appear to be educated men. At the end of the eighteenth century, the schoolmaster of Körmend drew up a list of his pupils writing, for the sake of refinement, in Latin. It appears that the writer of this document was a certain Márton Holtzapfel who, according to the church visitation of 1778, did not know Latin—a fact that should not be a surprise given that he became a teacher after obtaining his "qualifications" as an innkeeper in Vasvár. He wrote with curlicue letters, yet his knowledge of Latin did not even extend to the level of Christian names. It seems that he learned how to write these names in Latin from various lists and letters. This is proven by the odd assortment of grammatical forms he employed; he wrote some names in the nominative case, sometimes with priggish abbreviations, while other names appeared in the dative or even the vocative case, which was used only for addressing people: *Francisce*.[112]

In addition to trying to give the impression that they knew how to write Latin, some noblemen, notaries and schoolmasters liked to mix half-understood Latin words into their speech. In 1787 the noble writer and cavalry general József Gvadányi (1725–1801) defended the protagonist of his poem, the village notary, with the following words: it is true that "he mixed many Latin words into his verses, but in that I support him because everyone knows that village notaries are given to speak in this fashion so that they can make it public knowledge they had been to school".[113] People who had not gone to school did not want to be left behind. The 1827 edition of the Győr almanac included a short story that tactfully omitted the name of the locality concerned: "A noble village sheriff (who was otherwise a naturally sober-minded man yet had not learnt how to read or write) brought a legal suit against his debtor. Since the currency was not mentioned in the bill of debt, they argued over the amount due. The sheriff did not want to accept the judgment of the county court and exploded angrily with the following words: "I have a *gálya* (galleon) at home, and there is a *russzus* (Russian) in it with which to prove my claim; I am not afraid!" There was no warship full of Russian soldiers in this village—the sheriff had wanted to say *scala* (table) instead of "gálya", and instead of "russzus" he really meant *cursus* (rate of exchange). Yet, since he had not learned how to read, it is quite understandable that his knowledge of Latin was lacking. This little anecdote clearly demonstrates the conflicts that arose in Hungary in the sixteenth through nineteenth centuries as a result of the fact that the majority of the population did not understand the official language of the country.[114]

The mediocre knowledge of Latin displayed by lesser noblemen, who muddled the simplest of Latin words, stands diametrically opposed to the impression of Edward Brown, an English traveler, of the Hungarians' excellent Latin skills. In 1668 Brown wrote that many languages were spoken in Hungary, and this "makes them learn other languages and especially Latin, which very great numbers speak, especially gentry and soldiers. I have also met with coachmen, watermen and mean persons who could make themselves understood thereby. The Latin tongue is very serviceable in Hungaria and Transylvania", he concludes.[115] The travelogue of the Hungarian traveler, Márton Szepsi Csombor, confirms this from the other perspective: after a visit to London, Szepsi wrote, "I was astonished above all with the people's ignorance of Latin, since, proceeding among merchants, fur traders and tailors in three whole streets, I found no one who was able to speak a word of Latin to me." Nevertheless, it seems that Márton Szepsi Csombor must have been given directions in Latin on a number of occasions on the country roads of England; a few lines before, he drew attention to the different way in which Latin was spoken in England: "Latin-speakers do not use the word *milliare* [mile]; instead they use *passus* [foot] or *lapidibus* [milestone]. If someone asks how many miles, he is told the distance in so and so many *passus*, or *abest tot et tot lapidibus* [it is at a distance of so and so many milestones]." Thus it was only after his experience in the English countryside that Márton Csombor Szepsi expressed his surprise at the Londoners' "ignorance of Latin".[116]

In evaluating Edward Brown's admiration for the Latin skills displayed by Hungarians, one should take into account the fact that, in the Early Modern

Age, England stood out from the countries of the continent because far fewer of its inhabitants understood spoken Latin. At the beginning of the eighteenth century the English writer Daniel Defoe (who, however, had only second-hand knowledge of Poland) expressed his astonishment at how many people spoke Latin in that country. "A man who can speak Latin may travel from one end of Poland to another as familiarly as if he was born in the country", he wrote. "Bless us! What would a gentleman that was to travel through England and could speak nothing but Latin...I must lament his condition."[117] Miklós Bethlen (1642–1716), a Transylvanian aristocrat and future chancellor also noticed that Latin was a rarity even among the most educated classes of English society. Whereas the market town schoolmaster Márton Szepsi Csombor had tried to strike up a conversation in Latin with the artisans at the London market, Count Bethlen, a frequent visitor to the royal courts, attempted to speak with Oxford professors in Latin, but his efforts scarcely met with more success.[118]

Bethlen wrote in his autobiography that he studied English for five to six weeks before setting out for England from Holland in 1663, "so that I would at least know how to ask for food and drink, the study of which, despite being brief, was nonetheless much to my relief and affability in England, where one was forced to speak, however badly, in their language, for both priest and professor regard the speaking of Latin as real torture!" It is clear from Bethlen's words that he shared Márton Szepsi Csombor's impressions; both men found it strange that, in contrast to other European countries, in England there was no use of spoken Latin as the *lingua franca*. In Oxford the professors of the "great renowned academy" showed their respect for and entertained the traveler from Transylvania, "but they were reluctant to converse in Latin", and it is quite obvious that less learned men knew even less Latin. It could not have been easy for Szepsi Csombor to find speakers of the language on the English country roads.

At the end of the seventeenth century and at the beginning of the eighteenth century, other English travelers noticed how many people spoke Latin in Upper Hungary. In 1793 Robert Townson visited the Szepes County assembly in Lőcse and discovered to his surprise that the assembly was being held in Latin. Edward Clarke visited the country in 1802, and he wrote that Latin was used throughout Hungary; everywhere "we heard travelling Hungarian noblemen speaking Latin at the post houses". Richard Bright came to Hungary from the Congress of Vienna in 1814 and at the border met two men of commerce who spoke a number of languages, including Latin. In Bát, Hont County, the postmaster did not know German, and since Bright did not speak Hungarian, Romanian or Slovak, the two men chatted together in Latin. In Nagyszombat Bright was invited to a dinner at which the most distinguished guests were the mayor and a mustachioed and whiskered nobleman; these men engaged "in swift Latin discourse" and were joined from time to time by the whole company.

Conversation also was conducted in Latin at a Visegrád manor house where the English traveler William Hunter was a guest in 1799. In this case the noble lord and the local chaplain spoke Latin so that Hunter would understand them. The discourse was carried out in Latin, which the Hungarian nobles spoke "very fluently, many of them with classical elegance. This is truly the most important part of their upbringing, and knowledge of Latin is very necessary because even now, most legal proceedings are carried out in that language", he wrote in his travelogue.[119]

It was not only English travelers but also missionaries working in Hungary (most of whom came from Italy) who underscored how many people in Hungary understood Latin. In 1633 on a visit to the parts of Hungary under Turkish rule, the Albanian Archbishop Pietro Massarrecchi remarked with astonishment that schoolteachers in the Protestant villages surrounding Pécs did not allow children at school to speak in any language other than Latin, and therefore, "some very young children can speak Latin even though they cannot yet read well".

"In Hungary the peasants and the shepherds speak Latin more fluently than many priests do elsewhere", wrote a Flemish capuchin to Rome in 1633. Meanwhile, a year later the Italian Franciscan, Bonaventura da Genova, replied to the Holy Congregation for the Propagation of the Faith in a letter sent from Upper Hungary that "these people, down to the level of the smallest child, all speak Latin".[120]

Of course, these Italian friars emphasized the excellent knowledge of Latin displayed by people in Hungary in order to prove to the Holy Congregation for the Propagation of the Faith that they were able to convert the flock and, at the same time, to save face for the fact that they themselves had not learned Hungarian.

The Hungarian Franciscan, Kázmér Damokos, asserted in a 1657 report that the Bosnian missionaries in Transylvania spoke Latin very well. He wrote that, recognizing the reluctance of Hungarian friars to go to Transylvania, the Transylvanian Catholic lords had enlisted Bosnian Franciscans so that "they could at least hear their confessions in Latin". The Bosnian friars, Stefano a Salines and his companions who went to Transylvania, did indeed preach and hear confessions in Latin in the manor houses of the Transylvanian Catholic lords.[121] In Upper Hungary, the Italian Franciscans also heard confessions in Latin. In 1635 Bonaventura da Genova reported that he heard the confessions of some incorrigible heretics in Latin. In 1634 an Italian Franciscan, Francesco Leone da Modica, wrote to the Congregation about his missionary work in Szatmár where he "heard confessions and preached in Latin".[122]

Giovanni Battista Astori da Ferrara, a Franciscan missionary and the provincial of Hungary, defended the Italian missionaries when he wrote: "The Italians are more useful in these places than the ultramontanes because, although they do not speak the local languages and are thus of less use among the common people, they achieve more in the field of religious polemics, confessions and argumentation in Latin than those who in general know little and who live engrossed in lustfulness, drunkenness and other sins."[123]

The Bishop of Belgrade Luca Natale visited Upper Hungary in 1715. He preached in Latin, as his Croatian hardly would have been understood in Liptó or Turóc counties, but the bishop's oration was translated into German or Slovak by the local parish priest. Natale preached in Latin in Árva County as well. On this occasion he spoke to the noblemen and army officers in Latin while, over a period of two hours, his words were translated into Slovak for the people by the incumbent priest. Thus, the noblemen and the army officers did not need an interpreter, but it was only after the bishop's admonitions had been translated into Slovak for the local peasants that they declared with tearful eyes that they had never heard such a beautiful sermon in all their lives.[124]

The spoken Latin language was used in a multitude of ways by the inhabitants of Hungary in the seventeenth and eighteenth centuries. As noted earlier, knowledge of Latin greatly facilitated contact with foreigners. János Kemény (1607–62), an aristocrat and general who later became the prince of Transylvania, considered himself very honored to be able to speak with Emperor Ferdinand II without the aid of an interpreter: "He spoke very graciously with me for a long while in Latin, and I did so also to the best of my ability." When Kemény was travelling around Moravia, since he spoke neither Czech nor German, "he wanted to find the house of the priest or the school near the church so that he could ask in Latin" for directions, but the local villagers attacked him with clubs and axes. In the next market town, however, he was able to speak Latin with the Catholic priest.[125]

Even in the 1840s, Latin assisted the writer and future hero of the 1848 revolution, Mihály Táncsics (1799–1884), when he visited Paris. Táncsics earlier had written a Hungarian-French language book, but in Paris he conceded that it was "much easier to understand the language and to know the rules of the language than actually to speak it". Therefore he spoke with his acquaintances not in French but in Latin, although he wrote that "the peculiar pronunciation of Latin grated upon the ear" and that he found the way in which the French pronounced the Latin "*u*" especially odd.[126]

Soldiers formed a larger group of visitors to Hungary than did travelers in the seventeenth century. They also found it useful if they knew some Latin. General János Kemény looked for and found a Latin speaker among the imperial officers during the course of the campaign in Moravia, and in this way he was able to communicate with them.[127] As mentioned previously, Edward Brown also recognized the Latin skills displayed by the fortress troops. Furthermore, in 1670, at the time of the unraveling of the Wesselényi conspiracy (when imperial forces surrounded the Castle of Murány and a German officer went around the walls with a bugler to demand that the defenders of the castle surrender), the conditions for a free retreat were read in Latin, German, Hungarian and Slovak. In 1690, before the battle of Zernyest (which was to end in disaster for him), the Imperial General Donatus Heisler encouraged the Transylvanian troops by saying in Latin that the battle would be a ball because the Turks would all run away. He also gave instructions in Latin on how to coordinate the troop movements—instructions that the officers must have understood exactly.[128]

Latin served as a secret language that was used by the more learned to prevent others from understanding: the writer Táncsics mentioned earlier encountered this even in the early nineteenth century. Before learning Latin, he was with a teacher when the latter met "an acquaintance in town, with whom he always spoke in Latin; it was impossible not to notice that they were talking about me a lot and expressing great disdain for me". Later Táncsics's fellow students at the Buda teacher training college "spoke to one another in Latin and made me the subject of their mockery". After Táncsics learned Latin, however, he himself spoke the language to prevent others from understanding. Before his wedding he had an argument with the chaplain about the necessity of confession. He conducted the argument in Latin so that "those in close proximity would not understand".[129]

In 1766 a student of law who tutored in the homes of the inhabitants of Buda tried on a short fur-lined coat at the fair and declared that it was too tight. Once he had distracted the tailor, he bolted off with the coat. Here, the language they spoke was literally the thieves' Latin, for he and his fellow students outwitted the tailor "by speaking to one another backwards and forwards in Latin".[130]

For those who understood the language, Latin also could be used to prevent women from understanding discussions. Differences in male and female literacy rates were reflected in familiarity with Latin, too. Even noblewomen who could read and write were not taught Latin. In 1674 one of Transylvania's most distinguished lords, Dénes Bánffy, was sentenced to death and had to be summoned from his bedroom to receive his sentence. István Pataki, a theological professor in Kolozsvár, called out to him in Latin so that his wife would not understand. "Going quietly into the house, he wanted to wake the lord so that his wife, who was lying next to him, might not notice. But since she also awoke, he told him in Latin" that the death sentence had arrived.[131] A century later, in 1770, Emperor Joseph II had lunch in Sárospatak, and Ferenc Kazinczy (1759–1831), the future writer, participated in the meal, although he was still no more than a child. In his later memoirs Kazinczy recalls the "inquiries of the Emperor in Latin concerning where he could find horses on the way to Munkács". The Emperor did not speak Latin perfectly, and the Latin *vinum* became a masculine word as in the German word for wine, *Wein*: "Picking up the container and studying the color of the wine, he asked: '*Iste vinus Tokajinus?*'" At any rate, he conversed fluently with the county notables during the meal even if it was not at the level of classicism. Yet after dinner, Joseph II "turning to his ladies, flirted with them. But there was not one that understood the language". The noblewomen did not speak Latin.[132]

This is backed up by the will of Anna Tallián, the widow of a noble lord from Vas County and herself a member of a distinguished land-owning noble family. The noblewoman was able to write well, and yet she did not understand the Latin words that were intertwined in the Hungarian language at that time. She wrote in 1758 that "in my will, which is confirmed with the signature of my own hand, what is written in Latin has been explained to me in a satisfactory manner".[133]

In early modern Hungary, a living knowledge of Latin was quite commonplace among soldiers, because being a soldier was an international profession in this period; among the higher land-owning sections of the nobility; and of course among those in learned professions—professors, students, priests and lawyers. The English traveler and the Italian missionaries did not find this surprising but were stunned by the fact that even ordinary people could speak Latin. Indeed, the criminal law suits of the eighteenth century often bear evidence to the fact that ordinary people spoke Latin. This is especially clear in cases where the witness did not understand what had been said in Latin.

Disputes in Latin in Public Houses

In 1754 a peasant from Trencsén County stated that Ferenc Vitulay "came into the customs officer's room, where the flour merchant was sitting at a little table with the customs officer. The two men were chatting, but since Vitulay was speaking Latin to the merchant the witness did not understand" what the dispute was about. Subsequently, within a couple of minutes a considerable fight broke out. It is possible that they did not want the peasant to understand what was being said, but it is more probable that they wanted to bridge Slovak-Hungarian language difficulties with the help of Latin, though the fight rendered this attempt unsuccessful. It is a fact that they exchanged words in Latin in what was an absolutely commonplace situation with no trace of pomp or academia.[134]

It was also in a tavern and not in the halls of a college or Jesuit grammar school that the following conversation took place. Here, too, a substantial fight arose from the dispute. Both parties subsequently made petitions to the manor court and thus the sequence of events easily can be reconstructed. Travelling by cart from the Tisza River towards Pest, some fish merchants stopped at a roadside inn where they dined at separate tables because they were annoyed with one another. István Vidács alleged that János Rusa shouted at him from the other table, but he met the abuse with silence. Indeed, Vidács claimed that he himself remained seated quietly like "a stone idol". Rusa, on the other hand, recalled events differently. He testified that Vidács "met up with a German law student, and they spoke all kind of foulness about my dear wife in Latin"—obviously because the fish merchant did not know any German—and "another of them, who is a trader, understanding all of this because he knows Latin", obligingly interpreted the abuses directed against Rusa's wife. It may be concluded that Vidács, who became a fish merchant after working as a tailor, understood enough Latin to insult Rusa's wife in that language. The law student naturally understood this, as did the trader and voluntary interpreter. The Latin text, however, was "Greek" to the complainant fishmonger Rusa.[135]

The following discussion also took place in a tavern. In 1726 a peasant woman testified that many people were enjoying themselves in the tavern in Rozslonya in Gömör County. She saw "the lads going in and out, and they spoke in Latin and Hungarian", and then there was a fight during which an axe was brandished. Although the Slovak peasant woman stated that she had not understood a word of the half-drunk men's speech, it is not certain that the Rozslonya serfs in question really did speak in Latin; it is more probable that the witness was unable to understand their Hungarian. Yet the fact that the peasant woman supposed that they were speaking in Latin in a tavern shows that its use was not unimaginable in the mixed Slovak-Hungarian area.[136]

In 1778 in Perkupa in Torna County the local magistrate flogged the wife of a peasant. The village judge recounted that József Fekete, a nobleman, rushed to the scene (one can justifiably assume that he was the lover of the peasant woman), "inquiring from his honor the magistrate whether he was the cause of the beating. His honor the magistrate made a brief reply in Latin, which the witness did not understand, but at any rate his honor the magistrate continued beating her". The magistrate answered the other nobleman in Latin to prevent the peasants from understanding the transgressions of the lords. Nevertheless, another serf understood what the magistrate shouted at Fekete: "answering him in Latin, he told him that it was not because of him but for her other bad deeds" that he was beating her. Thus, this serf did understand Latin.[137]

These lawsuits show that, in areas where several languages were spoken, Latin was a language of communication, especially in Upper Hungary. "The town Eperjes is renowned for the fact that here four languages are fashionable: men of law, priests, tutors and students always speak Latin; the squires speak Hungarian as well; the burghers speak German; and Slovak is spoken by everybody." "I looked for Latin-speaking company in order that I might get rid of the long vowels learned in the college of Sárospatak, and fortunately I achieved this", the writer Ferenc Kazinczy recalled in the 1780s, when he was able to get rid of his college Latin accent, demonstrating that he really communicated in Latin in the town.[138] The Hungarian traveler quoted earlier, Márton Szepsi Csombor, who was so astonished by the inability of the merchants, fur traders and tailors of London to speak Latin, was a native of the market town of Szepsi in Upper Hungary. The area around Szepsi was the point at which three languages—Hungarian, German and Slovak—met. It was also a prosperous area of market towns and mining communities. Here, as the testimonies of the witnesses show, even peasants often understood Latin; in some cases they even spoke the language.

Knowledge of Latin was indicated in passports, since the holder was likely to use the language as a means of communication on the road. In 1737 Johann Michael Poliny, who was caught near Pozsony (Bratislava), erased the date in his passport and wrote a new one in its place. This swindler, a native of Graz who supposedly was collecting donations for the reconstruction of a burnt-down church, according to his passport, spoke German and

Latin.[139] When he was unsuccessful with German in the trilingual county of Pozsony, he tried to persuade potential donors by speaking Latin. In 1755 the search was launched for an inhabitant of Kassa in Upper Hungary who had left his wife. The official description of him stated that he spoke Hungarian, German, Slovak and Latin. In the same manner the authorities of Gömör County included "knowledge of Hungarian and Latin" in the passport of a nobleman from Tornaalja, with the impression that he would use both languages while travelling.[140]

Apart from those living on linguistic border areas, those who often traveled across multilingual Hungary in the course of their work used basic Latin as a kind of *lingua franca*, as they had to make themselves understood. Edward Brown did not make contact with the peasants and tillers, but he did speak Latin with noblemen and soldiers and also with coachmen and ferrymen, whose language skills were obviously similar to those of a twentieth-century taxi driver who converses with his passengers in German or English. The customs officer, the fish merchant and the trader in the lawsuits mentioned earlier all were required to make themselves understood at some basic level in distant provinces. The language of Cicero, which was still very much alive at this time, was of great use in such endeavors.

There were four living languages and four nationalities in western Hungary. One might suppose that there was a need for Latin to play a mediatory role, too. Yet German, Slovenian or Hungarian was the spoken mother language in separate districts that were divided sharply by linguistic boundaries, and the descendants of the Croatian refugees, who were quite dispersed, learned the language of their immediate environment, be it Hungarian or German. Most of the Hungarian lesser and middle noblemen lived in purely Hungarian areas where there was no need for Latin to play a mediatory role. Accordingly, there are no indications that basic Latin was a spoken language among the noblemen of western Hungary.[141]

In 1740 three noblemen made a friendly bargain in Nagykajd in the county of Vas. On the basis of the property divided among them, none seems to have been rich. Each was unable to write, they all drew crosses, and they had trouble with the Latin words that appeared in the Hungarian text. The county counselors who prepared the division of property read the agreement aloud, "and, where there were Latin terms, explained them word by word in Hungarian". These noblemen were not only incapable of conversing in Latin; they also did not understand even the most frequently used Latin expressions—just like those who muddled the Latin formal endings of letters and Christian names.[142]

Nevertheless, the Catholic majority of the population in Hungary heard Latin every week, even if they never entered a school. In the Early Modern Age, Latin terms, which were sometimes half-understood and more often not understood at all, buzzed in the air. These terms were interwoven with the contemporary official language, every official paper teemed with them, and the Catholic Church commonly used Latin as well. Until the second Vatican Council—the middle of the twentieth century—most Catholic services were held in Latin. During mass believers responded to the priest in Latin whether they understood the meaning of the words or not.

In 1613 a testimonial was written in Pécs, a town in Turkish-occupied territory, for a parish priest by the name of István who wanted to begin studying. The letter demonstrates that the priest really did need to study because, "apart from reading Latin—although he does not understand the text—he knows nothing".[143] In the savage conditions of the Turkish occupation, sometimes even priests did not understand what they read. During the sixteenth and seventeenth centuries, the period of the Turkish occupation, many Catholic *licentiatus* operated in this area; they were laymen who baptized, married and buried Catholics in villages where there were no priests. Some of the licentiati did not even know how to write. Clearly only a few of the literate ones could have understood Latin; they just read the Latin text out loud even though its meaning was obscure to them. Early in the eighteenth century, a nobleman wanted to have his patent of nobility read by "the *licentiatus* István Lengyel. But, Lengyel could not expound it", and therefore, the witnesses did not find out what the title of nobility concerned. The *licentiatus*, who did not understand any Latin, obviously only repeated the church services mechanically, and it is very probable that he distorted them as well. The common people understood these Latin texts even less well.[144]

On the other hand, at the turn of the eighteenth century, János Kis, a serf from Hollós, Vas County, was not just a "good literate person" for he also "knew how to speak some Latin". Thirty years earlier, in 1770, the schoolmaster in this village taught the basics of the Latin language; thus, János Kis acquired his knowledge locally in the village school.[145]

Just like literacy, Latin skills were an indication of social status. At the same time, it was largely determined by individual demand—a serf could learn some Latin from the village schoolmaster if he considered it to be important. In some other parts of the country, primarily in Upper Hungary where Germans, Hungarians and Slovaks lived together, some peasants understood Latin, while customs men and traders actively used the language, although hardly at the level of the classical orators. Nevertheless, the fact that at the end of the eighteenth century the case of János Kis is cited in a legal suit as a rare example worthy of attention is ample indication that a Latin-speaking serf was an unusual exception among the peasants of western Hungary. Most of the peasants not only did not speak Latin but also were illiterate and could not read.

A good part of the nobility in early modern Hungary heard Latin words daily even if many did not know Latin and could not read Latin texts because they had visited only elementary schools, if any. They heard these Latin expressions without seeing them, and they fixed them in their minds only in an oral manner without understanding their meaning. Yet this enhanced the prestige of Latin expressions. Distorted to the point of being funny, the many Latin words used by semi-illiterate lower noblemen were a reflection of the same effort as that of the illiterates when faking their signatures. Those who remained uneducated at least tried to feign knowledge of the language.

The gap between the culture of the landed gentry and the lower nobility, which was observed in their education, was also conspicuous in their knowledge of Latin. While many of the lower nobles could not so much as pronounce the words *corpus juris* correctly, a fair number of the landed gentry read Latin novels in the evenings.

CHAPTER 4

THE LOWER NOBILITY AND THE ORAL TRADITION

T HE lower ranks of the nobility in the sixteenth, seventeenth and eighteenth centuries were, for the most part, illiterate and lived in an oral culture. Therefore, they put little into writing, and little is known of their attitudes towards literacy up until the late seventeenth century. The ancestry cases studied when investigating the literacy of the gentry, however, serve as useful sources for examining the lower nobility's attitudes towards literacy in the seventeenth and eighteenth centuries.

Ancestry cases conducted in the eighteenth century aimed to separate genuine noblemen from fake ones. County committees checked the letters patent nobility presented, as well as the family's title to this document—that is, their genealogy handed down by word of mouth. If a nobleman lost his letter of nobility, he could bring in witnesses to testify that his letters patent had once existed, although he could not present it at that moment. In the course of these hearings, witnesses gave detailed descriptions of the history, lifestyle and daily routine of lower noble families, providing insight into the lives of the lower gentry, the so-called *taxalist* nobility, and shedding some light on their attitudes.

Ancestry Cases as a Historical Source

At the beginning of the eighteenth century, after the Turkish occupation ended, Hungarian society underwent major changes. There was no longer any need for the formerly populous warrior class that, with or without letters patent, was exempt from performing villeins' services in compensation for their sacrifices during the Turkish wars. In the seventeenth century Transdanubia and Upper Hungary were frontier areas beset by constant feuding and looting while the Turkish flag hung from the forts along the marches. After the defeat of the freedom fighters led by Prince Francis Rákóczi II in 1711, these regions became far removed from the frontiers of the Habsburg Empire. Landlords and the central government sought to redirect these warriors to productive labor by forcing freemen of dubious legal standing back into villenage as one of their priorities. One way to achieve this goal was to examine ancestries, and those who could not prove their nobility beyond a doubt were stripped of their privileges.[1]

Those subjected to these checks—*armalist* nobles, former servicemen from the border forts and freemen—comprised an ever-growing class between the nobility and the serfs in the seventeenth century. In addition, they were very much aware of the danger inherent in the investigation into their nobility. Former servicemen and their descendants reveled in nostalgia for the old times, when one's standing in society was determined by the sword and not by a piece of paper; when bravado and fighting skills against the Turks weighed more than legal cunning, sealed documents and—for a mostly illiterate class—unintelligible lawsuits conducted in Latin.

The testimonies genuine noblemen made during these hearings also revealed that, in an era when solid walls already separated the estates, the volatile conditions of the seventeenth century seemed to the gentry only a sidetrack in the otherwise distinct and uninterrupted history of the privileged nobility. One nobleman from Zala County, born in 1706 and thus raised in post-Turkish times, for example, said in an ancestry case that he "heard it said that, up until the nobility started to intermingle with the peasantry in times of war, the ancestors of the Szalai family of Tagyan too were privileged men living in the freedom of the nobility".[2] Though the year from which the landless but noble Szalai's letters patent was dated is unknown, there was some basis to presume that, contrary to the generosity of the oral tradition, they owed their nobility precisely to those "times of war", instead of having mingled as ancient nobles with the peasantry during the Turkish wars of the sixteenth and seventeenth centuries. In other words, it was due to the wave of ennoblement following the wars that they could have emerged from the peasantry.

The fact that counties initiated investigations asking for oral testimonies tracking lineage reveals much about the level of use of written records by the county administration. A plenitude of witnesses was questioned about when they had seen the lost document for the last time, which emperor had issued it and whose name they had seen written on it. County magistrates could have obtained more reliable information had they trusted the royal records kept in Vienna that contained, at least theoretically, copies of all letters patent ever issued instead of the memory of the elders.

Noblemen's chests yielded letters patent issued in the sixteenth and seventeenth centuries by Habsburg rulers, chiefly by Emperor Leopold I (1657–1705) in the late seventeenth century. Copies of all these letters-patent were available in Vienna, but the county administration apparently preferred the oral tradition of the local nobility—another proof that oral history continued to prevail among the Hungarian gentry. In a way, county officials were correct: even if they had procured attested copies of these documents from Vienna, the lineage of the male line would have had to be verified by oral histories—that is, the memory of local witnesses.

The eighteenth-century ancestry cases conducted in the Transdanubian counties of Vas, Győr, Sopron, Zala and Veszprém point to the existence of a layer of lower nobility in Transdanubia with a fairly uniform mentality: former servicemen from the border fortresses and lower nobles-turned-artisans migrating from county to county without their identity conforming to administrative boundaries. In order to see if these observations had any basis, the lawsuits related to ancestry cases in the two populous northern counties of Borsod and Abaúj and the smaller neighboring county of Torna were examined, only to find that these control groups were similar to those researched in Transdanubia.

The important factor was not whether these nobles lived in western or northeastern Hungary but rather that both regions were adjacent to the Turkish-occupied parts and, thus, suffered from constant raids and fighting during the seventeenth century. For this reason, in both regions a warrior class emerged and came to form an important segment of society in these counties. Part of this class conducted a bitter fight in the eighteenth century in order to be elevated into the ranks of the nobility. In Sopron County, near Vienna, which was less exposed to Turkish attacks, this warrior class, composed of members of the lesser nobility and freemen, was considerably smaller than in the counties of Vas, Zala or Veszprém. The lower nobles of Vas, as is apparent from their testimonies, were actually closer to the nobility of the remote Abaúj County than to neighboring Sopron in terms of lifestyle, mobility, mentality and attitudes towards literacy.

Illiterates and Fake Letters Patent

Unlike the documents written by village notaries, letters patent—ornate certificates issued at the royal chancery—were difficult to forge. These certificates were written on strips of high quality parchment, and self-appointed county nobles would have had a difficult time obtaining the raw materials alone. In addition, a forger would have had to inscribe the text in elaborate Latin, in gold and black ink, in calligraphic print; paint a coat of arms; forge a royal signature; and attach a seal. It is clear why, among the many thousands of lawsuits, not one case of complete forgery can be found—the difficulties involved deterred most of those aspiring to entitlement.

True, János Hornay of Abaúj County was indicted for forging a letter of nobility, but he did not fabricate a brand new certificate. He instead utilized a genuine document, issued by Emperor Ferdinand II in 1634 to the Tősér family, and altered it to suit his needs by scraping off the family name and inscribing his own. However, even this relatively simple method failed as the gold ink Hornay concocted was proven worthless when it soon turned green and gave him away.[3]

It was much easier, then, for a nobility-seeker to obtain a real letter and use it for his own family. Because of a general lack of birth registers in seventeenth-century Hungary, such letters were not tied to any contemporary family living in the eighteenth century, as the only link between the original recipients and their descendants was oral genealogy; that is, living persons and the written certificate were connected by memory only. Gifts, threats or promises, of course, easily manipulated oral tradition. This posed a great temptation for upwardly mobile freemen to obtain letters patent, make pacts with perjurers and bribe county authorities in order to be elevated to nobility in the post-Turkish society of the eighteenth century, when rising in social standing was much more difficult than in previous centuries. Freemen did not, therefore, lapse into villenage but went on to become privileged nobles instead.

A letters patent could also be purchased, and a real black market for such letters emerged in the early eighteenth century. Certificates that were sold came from three principal sources: they were either letters lost during the Turkish wars, certificates of a family that had died out or letters pawned and never redeemed. Many letters patent "went astray" during times of war, and those who stole them tried to sell them at as high a price as they possibly could.

There were also those who requested money to return the letters to their rightful owners. Serbian soldiers stole the letters patent of the Klinger family in Rum, Vas County, when they raided the village in 1705 and "emptied all the pit-stores". The looters asked for a ransom of thirty forints to return the document, which, according to a damage list drawn up in the same year, cost its owner the same amount of money as if two of his oxen had been driven away.[4]

In most cases, however, thieves did not offer the documents for resale to their original owners but sold them on the black market. Potential buyers whose names somehow could be connected to the family inscribed in the letters patent—either because it was a common name or because the orthography of the time, still quite malleable, left enough room for interpretation—stood a better chance of making use of it. For example, the Vörösmarty family petitioned the county to revoke the letter of a László Vörös, by force if need be, who could not verify his kinship with the Vörösmartys and was taking advantage of a superficial resemblance in their names, made possible by the fact that family names had not been fixed yet in oral tradition.[5]

János Tislér, on his part, wanted to become a member of the Varjas family by presenting a letters patent in the name of Varjasy. In 1746 Ferenc Varjas, Junior recounted that two years earlier "János Tislér, upon hearing that [his] family name was Varjas, accosted him thus: 'Brother, I am also of the Varjas family; if we wanted, we could show our nobility because I have in my possession the letters patent of nobility of the Varjas family. I wish Ferenc Varjas, Senior would come here…so that I could learn more about our kinship ties.'" The gist of this barely concealed offer was that the letter of nobility possessed by Tislér in the name of Varjasy should be united with the oral genealogy of the Varjas family during the ancestry case; the Varjas family should accept Tislér as their kin so that, by virtue of the combined power of oral tradition and a written document, all of them could become members of the nobility.

The original letters patent of the Varjas family was lost during the wars, which might help to explain their interest in the resurfaced document. Ferenc Varjas, Senior's son-in-law lived in the market town of Simontornya, where Tislér and the older Varjas first read the old tattered letter with the royal seal attached. Their host, a nobleman-turned-blacksmith, testified that he had not read the document because he could not read. This man, who worked as a blacksmith despite his nobility, was only twenty-nine years of age, leading to the conclusion that it was his education rather than his eyesight that was less than perfect. However, Tislér tried in vain to state his case to those present in the house of this illiterate lower nobleman by claiming that the letter belonged to the Varjas family, and he could not convince his alleged kin that it would be worth their while to jointly petition for recognition of their nobility. Tislér, "having failed to satisfy himself with obtaining nobility through the possession of a letter in the name of Varjasy [not Varjas!], put his letter back into his chest", much to the disappointment of his newly found kin. János Tislér, however, did not give up easily and continued trying to rise to the ranks of the privileged classes. He wasted no time attempting to pass himself off in other villages under different names, such as János Eörsy and János Lajos, then obtained two letters patent in the names of Halasy and Drághy and set out prior to his arrest to find his "kin" under either of these false names.[6]

In western Veszprém County, the case of the Márton family is especially characteristic of attitudes among the lesser nobility, even though they held genuine nobility. In 1682 Pál Márton fought the Turks bravely—even his horse was shot from beneath him. His commander, a lieutenant from Győr, brought a reward for his bravery in the form of a letters patent issued by the king and duly announced it in Győr County. The letter, however, was taken to another region by a relative who served as a bootmaker's apprentice there. Despite their nobility, the lack of a land base forced the Mártons to continue living by their trade. Their only option was to buy a new—and needless to say, fake—letter of nobility. They soon found someone willing to sell his certificate. Ferenc Márton of Keszthely, having failed to become a nobleman by presenting his letters patent in Zala County, had sold his certificate to somebody in Győr. The Márton family bought this document for seventy-five forints and found someone "present at the bargain of the letters patent of nobility" to attest to the originality of the document. This certificate, however, could not have been the rightful possession of the seller, who had the common name of Márton but was not a noble at all. He soon sent a warning that the rightful owners "were after the document...therefore they should somehow strike a deal and claim kinship with them"—to unite again the written document and oral genealogy. The rightful owners, in pursuit of the original certificate, then went to claim their valuable document. The Mártons, however, refused to return it, although all they could read in the text was their own family name, for which reason they had it read by the local notary public. This case clearly shows that as the lower nobility still lived in an oral culture, the Márton family thought it better to give up on the tedious pursuit of the original certificate and the equally tiresome and time-consuming process of demonstrating their genuine nobility, and instead started looking for a certificate in the same name.[7]

As outlined earlier, the lesser nobility were for the most part illiterate and could not read their letters patent of nobility. It is no wonder, then, that buyers could not always tell if they could use their expensive documents at all. In 1760 witnesses in Rádó, Zala County, testified that some twenty years earlier a stranger brought such a letters patent to one Gergely Sidi. The next morning, as one witness related, Sidi "showed him the letters patent of nobility, saying that he had given away a pair of oxen for it and would be willing to give more, even his remaining two oxen, just to keep the document. Upon hearing this, the witness said: 'How could you possibly give more for it when you can't even tell if it concerns you at all?'"—implying that Gergely Sidi could not read the letter. However, Sidi did keep the certificate, "paying sixty forints on top of the two oxen". Local nobles found special pleasure in later discovering that the letter proved worthless for Sidi, as it was in the name of another family. What the deceived peasant may have done with the letters patent afterwards is not contained in the witness's testimony, but it safely can be assumed that he went on to sell it in order to recover his investment, and the letter probably ended up on the black market.[8]

Sidi was not the only illiterate man to make a bad bargain for a letter issued to a different family. "I remember it as if it happened today", the widow of a Tállya noble began her testimony in 1764, "that in the good old days the late János Czimbalmos was suffering mightily from many an illness, and during the last bout of the disease he implored his honor, the late Pál Király, to take mercy on his son". As it turned out, Czimbalmos, strapped for money, had pawned his letters patent for six forints and asked Király to redeem it, promising to return the favor should he ever recuperate. In response to his plea, Király did redeem the letter and presented it to Czimbalmos "before the very own eyes of the present witness, whereupon Czimbalmos thanked him for his brotherly kindness and died soon afterwards". Some time later, the younger Czimbalmos came to the village and gave Király two oxen and four bushels of wheat for his expenses and loyalty. However, the younger Czimbalmos, an illiterate simpleton, was cheated—Király had given him a letter in the name of another family. It was only after his death that his sons realized that this friend had given their grandfather the wrong certificate.[9]

A similar event must have transpired in the case of István Horváth of Lak, who bought the letters patent of a family whose male line had died out, either without first reading the document or having it read by someone else. Horváth bought the certificate for only an apron, but county officials conducting the ancestry case refused to accept it because it was in somebody else's name. Evidently Horváth was unable to read even the family name in the letters patent. Horváth returned the now useless letter and bought a new one from a widow for twelve forints, this time in the correct name, even though the document was not his.

There were many lower noblemen who could not decipher their certificates and had to have them read by someone else. In Garadna, Abaúj County, witnesses related how a man took out a letter with a big seal from his haversack but had to ask the local priest and schoolmaster to read it, as he himself could not. A nobleman from Miskolc held a letters patent of nobility jointly with the Barta family that, as he told the judges, he had seen but not read; had he known how to read, he certainly would have read the document. Nor did the swineherd of Rudabánya know what his document contained until his former comrade-at-arms read it to him. However, this swineherd did not seek his nobility even after realizing the value of the document he had in his possession, saying that he "would not give even a loaf of bread or a good axe for it"—a statement that did not seem as much out of place at the beginning of the eighteenth century as in 1776, when a reputedly one-hundred-six-year-old witness recalled the case.

The letters patent of nobility also must have puzzled another nobleman who appeared before the census takers of Borsod County in 1697 and, "pulling out his own letters patent from the sleeve of his shepherd's coat, handed it over to the clerk". Upon reading the document, the clerk told him to take better care of the letter and store it in a special case, "for it deserved to be kept in a box now that thou art a true noble man".[10]

Nor could the Bodons of Radnót, Gömör County, read the precious document to which they could thank their ennoblement. Their case is especially interesting, as it was not the letters patent of nobility itself they purchased, but the entitlement to it—the oral genealogy. Their namesakes, living at the other end of the village, recognized the Bodons as their kin for the price of a pair of oxen, "as if they had held privileges jointly". The Bodons even received a letters patent from the county, which their illiterate offspring took to a Radnót nobleman to have read. The letter revealed, however, that the Bodons had redeemed their freedom and villein's share of land from their lord only sixty years earlier, while their letters patent dated back eighty years—twenty years prior to their release from villenage. "Any literate and honest man looking at this document will see what truth Your Honor's nobility holds", and the deceit would soon be exposed, said the noble reading out the certificate. He advised the Bodons to abandon suing and not to dwell too much on the subject, "for they would suffer mighty damages and only regret it all later".[11]

Widespread illiteracy was also the cause of a misunderstanding in connection with a letters patent issued by Emperor Maximilian II (1564–1576) and announced in Vas County. The innkeeper of Révfalu remembered clearly how an acquaintance had arrived to his inn one day in 1754, looking tired, and produced a large certificate from his haversack, saying: "'Look here, my friend, I went to much trouble and expense to lay my hands on this—our letter of nobility!' But since he could read neither Latin, nor Hungarian", the innkeeper went on, "he did not look at it as thoroughly and diligently as would enable him to testify about it. He could not even remember if it had a seal or if it was written in gold letters or on parchment. The only thing he knew for certain was that it was a large document." The only lasting impression the illiterate innkeeper had of the certificate was, then, its size. A serf from the next village, who happened to be drinking in the inn at the time, although he could not read either, observed the letter and the coat of arms more thoroughly. The document was indeed a letter of nobility, but neither this man nor his brother-in-law could make any use of it because they were only linked to the Beke family, in whose name the certificate was issued, through their wives—a kinship not recognized in Hungarian law as permitting transmission of a nobleman's title. This family only spent money on the letter because "they deemed it to be a title deed"— a title not only to nobility but to a noble's estate as well. In this they were bitterly disappointed.[12]

Illiterate lower nobles could not read the information contained in these documents and not even the family name, inscribed in large golden letters, held anything of informational value to them. What these analphabets saw in such a document was an expensive, valuable object to possess rather than a certificate that was meant to be read.

Writing as an Object

When chief magistrates investigating ancestry cases tracked down lost or perished letters patent, most witnesses—due to widespread illiteracy—could only resort to their visual memory. In other words, they could remember only how the letter looked and were unable to say anything about its content.

Even for someone living in the twentieth century, the first feature that catches the eye when looking at a letters patent in a museum are the words (the king's title and the recipient's name) inscribed in gold letters; the large, round seal appended on a silk cord; and the painting depicting the coat of arms in the upper left corner of the document. These were also the attributes illiterate witnesses in the eighteenth century tended to remember: "Though the witness himself cannot read", a serf from Gyarmat testified in 1756, "he could clearly see that the letter was written on a large strip of parchment in golden letters with a large seal appended on a silk cord". A nobleman from Körmend remembered in 1744 that the names on the certificate were all written in gold. When the "letter was laid out on the table", a weaver from Pákod testified, "he saw that there were golden letters in two or three places". "Though she herself cannot read", a woman of Vitány acknowledged in 1756, "she can nevertheless clearly remember that there was a large wax seal with an impression on the letter and, furthermore, that it was written in golden letters". Nor could a petty noble from Meszlén say anything about the contents of a letters patent in 1733, although he could testify in good conscience that he had seen the letter in question "countless times with his own eyes—it was written in large, golden letters, and it had a large seal appended on a silk cord". In 1792, a nobleman from Miskolc remembered a letters patent as having had a "seal as large as a plate dangling from it".[13]

Some witnesses were most impressed by the tin case in which these letters were kept; they too were interested only in the visual attributes of the document. When questioned, an eighty-seven-year-old serf from Kovácsi said that a noble "did show the witness the letter attesting to his nobility, which he kept in a tin case, and he also saw the large bulge of the seal".[14] All an eighty year-old freeman from Zala County could remember in 1724 was that the letter, which its owners were trying to save from the Turks, was "in some tin case that was opened with a small key".[15] A serf from Somod, though "his lack of literacy did not permit him to know" if the letter presented to him by a nobleman was indeed a certificate of nobility, testified in good conscience that "on a number of occasions when German officers were billeted in his house", the nobleman in question "took a letter written in large golden letters that also had a silk cord and a large seal attached to it from a tin case and showed it to his German guests, who took off their hats upon reading it". This was because it was forbidden to billet soldiers in noble houses, and it seems that—at least on the above occasion—this regulation actually was observed. While the German officers, before taking off their hats, read the document conferring on its bearer a certain status in society as well as exempting him from the nuisance of billeting, the testifying serf, being illiterate, only saw the certificate and was, therefore, most impressed by its tin case.[16] The document, then, commanded respect among illiterates not as a *writing* but as an *object*. There were even some whose interest was aroused by the tin case rather than the royal letter itself.

The royal seal attached to the certificate was proof of authenticity. This was all the more valuable to illiterates, who could not do much with the text of the letter—it was the size of the seal rather than its text that made a lasting impression on them. To them, the seal was not of any informational value; if it had a certain authority, it was on account of its being large rather than belonging to a certain king. There were few witnesses for whom the seal represented a means of authentication. A herdsman from Gérce, although he hardly could have been a learned man, did recognize the figure on the seal of his master's letters patent: "Seeing a large seal on the letters patent of nobility, the witness had inspected it and recognized the coat-of-arms with the two-headed eagle, as he was able to recall even now", the witness, who claimed to be ninety-eight years of age, concluded his testimony. A lower noble from the same county also recognized the imperial seal on the certificate, but these testimonies are the exception; predominantly it was the size of the seal that was captured by the memories of witnesses.[17]

Appended to the letter "was a wax seal attached to a silk cord and shaped like a bowl in which coins are kept", testified an eighty-eight-year-old witness from Gönc about a seal he had seen almost seventy years earlier. For him, the fact that the seal was large was proof enough that the cryptic writing was indeed a letter of nobility. A serf recalled having seen a document salvaged from a fire. "This witness judges it to have been a letters patent from the red seal in yellow wax attached to it in the shape of a small bowl." A letters patent was recognized by the large seal, a nobleman from Kisberzseny concluded: "the letter had a seal as large as the center part of a plate, so it must have been a letters patent of nobility". A ninety-two-year-old witness from Lengyel put it in an even more straightforward manner: he saw a letter with a large seal appended, but since the villagers could not find anyone to translate it (reading it alone must have posed considerable difficulties), he did not know what sort of document it was. "He does surmise, however, that it was some kind of a royal deed, for it had a seal attached to it on a cord."[18]

During the wars of independence, the Szabó family from the Őrség district hid their letters patent under a fallen tree where it rotted away. Due to the lack of professional care, the document became illegible and was destroyed as a piece of writing, but as an object it still retained a certain value, and the Szabós continued to display the large seal and what was left of the parchment as proof of their nobility. Witnesses remembered this damaged certificate even forty-seven years after the war. In view of widespread illiteracy in the Őrség district, witnesses hardly could have recounted more, even if the document itself had not become illegible.[19] Similarly, the members of a lower noble family of Nemesnép buried their letters patent during Rákóczi's war for freedom to protect it from Serbian marauders, but the document rotted away in the damp soil. Although the letter itself was destroyed, the family did keep the seal with Emperor Leopold's coat of arms impressed on it and presented it in 1728 to county officials as important proof of their nobility. Even less was left of the certificate of the Balás family from Győr County: when the Serbs pried open their chests, they also took their letters patent, and all that there was left for this family to show was the case of the original document.[20]

Lesser nobles who buried their letters in the ground or hid them at the approach of insurgents or the Serbs, although aware of the value represented by these writings, had too little experience with books and papers to know that they needed different care than that required by the family gold and silver. Many nobles hid their certificates in hollow trees where they rotted, were nibbled by rodents or were stolen by shepherds. The members of the Borbély family from Jánosháza put their documents of nobility in a chest that they lowered into a lake—the letter, of course, perished. The members of the Borsos family of Zala County buried their certificate in a copper pot during the war, which led to its decay.[21]

Apart from golden letters, tin cases and large seals, the coats of arms painted on the certificates were also vivid in witnesses' memories. A nobleman from Peremarton recalled concerning another noble's letters patent that "in the middle of the coat of arms there was a pelican depicted. The witness recalled it as if he were looking at it now, at this very moment". While this letter was adorned by a pelican, nobles living in the marches received warriors' coats of arms. "As far as he can recall, the coat of arms depicted a sword, and on the sword, there was the severed head of a Turk", a witness testified of the crest of the Répási family of Veszprém County. Nobles testifying in Borsod County remembered a white dove, a lion with eagle's wings and a lion holding a star as coats of arms on letters patent long lost, but it was not unusual for a Turkish head on a lance or sword or a warrior on horseback leading a Tartar prisoner to emblazon letters patent as reminders of a life spent in the border forts.[22]

Coats of arms played an important role in ancestry cases. The letters patent presented to county officials by those seeking to establish their nobility were linked to families through an orally transmitted lineage. Witnesses, therefore, needed to *recognize* the letter and testify that it was indeed the one they had seen in the hands of an ancestor many years earlier—that is, that it was not a stolen document or one purchased on the black market. However, since most witnesses could not read, they could only resort to their visual memory.

In 1746 a nobleman from Simontornya testified that although "he could not read, having inspected the letter brought before him by the honorable tribunal, and it not being as tattered and torn and old" as the one he had seen in the possession of the family in question, it could not have been the letter for which they were looking. The illiterate witness could not say anything about the content of the certificate, but his visual memory that had preserved the document as an object revealed the fraud.[23]

The memory of a perished certificate of nobility was sufficient proof of a family's status, even if witnesses only could remember it as an object they had seen once and not as a document they had read and understood. This prompted nobles to show their letters to as many people, including illiterates, as possible.

A letters patent was the pride of a nobleman, especially if it was the only possession that set him apart from his neighbors who, although peasants, were not necessarily worse off than he was. Lower nobles, therefore, flaunted their letters patent at every opportunity. Showing off such certificates lent them a degree of respectability vis-à-vis family members and neighbors. A bootmaker from Szepsi asserted his nobility when fighting with his wife: "what do I have to fear from you, or your father, when I'm as much of a nobleman as he is"; then "in his great agitation he jumped on top of the workbench, produced a letter from a case and shouted to his wife: 'your father treats me as though I came out of his behind, but behold this certificate—it proves that I'm just as noble as your father is.'"[24]

However, it was not only out of pride or resentment that nobles flaunted their letters patent to people. It was much rather a conscious way of imparting information; they were thus transmitting the memory of their certificates orally—not as understood texts but as visible objects.[25]

Noblemen were well aware that the more people who saw their letters patent of nobility, the more secure their titles. People who lived through the raids of the Turks and Serbs and had seen several fires were concerned with the possibility of their documents being destroyed. Therefore, they showed the letters to as many people as they could, even if most could not read them, since they later could be called on to testify their existence. A nobleman from Zemplén County, witnesses recalled, often declared that "he had a nice letters patent and that he would become no one's serf, and he proceeded, although the witness was illiterate", to show him the certificate. Gergely Horváth from Dőr was "no man of letters", remembered another nobleman, but when the latter was visiting Horváth's house, "his host brought his letters patent of nobility to the table to display the document". While the witness, having said nothing of the text of the letter, was probably illiterate, and it is certain that Horváth could do no more than show it around, the latter nevertheless seized the opportunity to lay the writing on the table, as even an illiterate man could make a good witness later. In 1762 János Fekete, a seventy-year-old nobleman from Miskolc, recalled during an ancestry investigation that a fellow nobleman often had shown him his letters patent before it was lost. However, since neither of them could read, they could not say which king had granted the title. The two nobles, both analphabets, only showed their documents to each other as objects of value, not as fully understood texts. The widow of a Miskolc nobleman also could not read, but János Barta (who also was nicknamed "Cobbler" after his trade) often showed his certificate to her. Decades later this widow did indeed testify at the age of seventy-eight that the certificate, by that time lost, did exist once, although she could not say anything about its content.[26]

A nobleman from Vas County often took his letters patent from his chest and showed it to his servants, although they could not read. Vince Miklós served as a shepherd despite his nobility, and his master would often show him his certificate on holidays when they were drinking together, saying, "you can see here, lad, the letters patent of nobility proving the nobility of my family". The master, a lower noble himself, did not want his noble servant to think himself better than he, although it did not occur to either that the shepherd actually should read the document. Nor did the serfs of Megyehida, read the letters patent of György Pálffi, but they saw it often when Pálffi, "in his better moods", would show it to peasants from the neighborhood. Pálffi did well to flaunt his letter, because serfs were able to recall the lost document easily forty years later.[27]

In 1775 an eighty-eight-year-old nobleman testified about events that took place in Veszprém County at the beginning of the century. He struck up a friendship with János Vörös during the freedom fights, and Vörös showed him his letter of nobility, saying, "take good note of this certificate, my pal, and should my sons be separated from me, tell them about you having seen my letters patent of nobility and enlighten them as to their nobility". Vörös only showed his army friend the document in question; reading it never occurred to them, most probably because neither of these valiant freedom fighters would have been able to do so. The witness never-theless could remember this letter seventy years after the war of independ-ence. From Vörös's words it is clear that winning respect from his contem-poraries was not among his motives for showing off his certificate; rather he was considering his sons' future and ensuring the transmission of this in-formation.[28]

A bailiff from Muraszombat also sought to ensure the survival of this in-formation when displaying his letter as an object. A serf was taking him to town in a cart when the nobleman "opened his chest and pulled out a letter attached to a long cord" and, waving it, he said to the serf, who could hardly have been capable of examining the text of the certificate: "Remember, my friend, that I am a nobleman so that you can tell others about it".[29] The same behavior led a lower nobleman from Szergény to lay out his letters patent for a neighbor, saying that "as he had offspring and inheritors, he would like others to be able to testify later about the letters patent of nobil-ity he is entitled to have," which is why he showed it to him. The nobleman was not disappointed: the witness testified in 1753, at the age of seventy, about the letter he had seen in his youth.[30]

There are many more examples of noblemen displaying their letters pat-ent as objects in order to preserve their memory. There were also some—though far fewer—who aimed to ensure the survival of their certificates as texts that had been read and understood. These noblemen showed their letters patent of nobility primarily to schoolchildren. As a child beaten at the village border was able to remember border signs in his older years, so did school-children preserve the information entrusted to them for a long time.

"The letters patent of nobility in question was in his hands countless times when he was a student under this schoolmaster", a serf testified in Hosszúfalu, Vas County, "and he also read it many times". The letter be-longed to the schoolmaster, who often used it as a reading exercise. He was not disappointed either; although the certificate disappeared without trace during the freedom fights, its memory and the schoolmaster's chance to reclaim his title to nobility survived thanks to his former pupils.[31]

It was a good idea to show these certificates to schoolchildren even if they were not asked to read them. In a society that continued to transmit infor-mation by word of mouth, children were able to preserve the memory of a certificate for a long time. The public notary of Kásmárk, who was also a schoolmaster, read his letters patent in front of his students and said: "Bear in mind that I, too, have a coat of arms and a letter of nobility." His efforts were not in vain—fifty-four years later, one of the boys could recall even that the then-lost certificate was granted by Ferdinand III. A freeman from Nagyvázsony was a twelve-year-old schoolboy when a relative gave him a letters patent to read: "here, little cousin, look at my certificate of nobility". The boy must have had a good look, for he was able to give a detailed description of it thirty-eight years later. A nobleman from Nagyalásony was also twelve when he was shown the letters patent of another noble. Although he did not read the letter, it was read to him, and he and a childhood friend could evoke the memory of the lost certificate sixty-three years later.[32]

Orally Transmitted Genealogy

The lineage of lower noble families was transmitted by word of mouth and preserved only in the memory of witnesses. True, in the second half of the eighteenth century village birth registers became more common, and at the request of the county officials, priests and pastors in remote villages often copied data from their registers. However, it was more common for them not to be able to provide the information requested because the old books were lost or the request pertained to a period when a village register did not exist. However, individual data, scattered as it was, could only be linked by oral history even when written entries were found. Village registers might have recorded the deaths and births of some relatives, but family descent could only be traced through witnesses' testimonies.

Nobles providing testimony in response to questions from county officials presented their elaborate family trees in great detail—information that was transmitted from generation to generation by word of mouth. A seventy-year-old illiterate noble provided a detailed list of both the close and distant relatives of a nobleman from Bajánháza, which he was more than ready to relate as "he had heard from the elders in Őrség district as the commonest news".[33] Other old noblemen testifying in the lawsuit also had heard from two older villagers, ninety and ninety-five years old respectively, as the family tree passed from generation to generation. Similarly, a ninety-year-old serf from Sidahegy had heard it said by numerous other elders "whence the ancestor of the family seeking their nobility had come to the village".[34]

The genealogy of the lower nobility was, for the most part, preserved only in memory. In eighteenth-century Vas County, only two exceptions were discovered, both related to Protestant noblemen living in the northern, more developed part of the county. In 1757 a seventy-seven-year-old nobleman from Felsőőr who like the rest of the village was probably Calvinist, outlined his family tree based not on the narrative of his grandparents but on the village register (that is, a written document). In his words, he had "seen and read the family lineage from the baptizing book".[35] Lutheran noblemen from Nemescsó testified in a case not involving the verification of nobility but the discovery of an illegitimate child's father. This fellow nobleman from Nemescsó was indicted for "deflowering" a girl who was, to make matters worse, his own goddaughter—an act that was, according to the morals of the time, as incestuous as if he had sinned with his own daughter. In this case, which continued to make ever greater waves, the only item that is of relevance to the history of literacy is the fact that the Lutheran nobles of Nemescsó, instead of remembering the feast that followed the ceremony or questioning the elders of the village, testified that the nobleman was indeed the godfather of the pregnant girl, a fact they had "read in the baptismal book".[36]

These two incidents are, however, exceptions to the rule. The lower nobility continued to live overwhelmingly in an oral culture at the end of the eighteenth century. Elders had good reason to tell narratives as a deliberate means of passing on information about family trees. In 1728, during an investigation conducted into the ancestry of the Horváth family, a fifty-eight-year-old witness recounted the sophisticated genealogy of his noble family, which he learned in his childhood when his mother "conversed with the witness, her son, for him to remember in times to come".[37]

Lesser nobles, among whom the oral tradition still prevailed, were well aware of the importance of information stored in the memory of the elders; they knew that with every generation gone, important and irreplaceable knowledge was lost. Dying men, on their part, were aware that they might take important information with them to the grave, causing whole branches of families to fall from common memory and, consequently, the privileged classes.

Noblemen about to die did not want to take the memory of their relatives with them "together with their soul" and thus strove to transmit information on their lineage before their deaths. The eighty-year-old father of a nobleman from Vat "ordered his son not to deny the orphans of an uncle their family rights and title to nobility". A nobleman living in the town of Pápa said on his deathbed: "my sons, the sons of Mihály Horváth are true noblemen like ourselves and, should they seek their nobility in the future, you are not to deny our relation to them".[38]

However much dying elders would have liked to ensure the survival of these family trees, not even oral tradition could transcend the limits of human memory. In peasant oral tradition, memories generally went back as far as three generations (two generations prior to theirs). The same was true for lower nobles; they knew members of their family personally from their grandfathers' generation, but they knew those who had come before them only from hearsay. An older witness, of course, might have known younger generations and have listed them in his testimony; this, however, did not affect the reach of his memory back in time. In 1743 a nobleman in Zala County claimed to be ninety-five years old. In his testimony, he claimed to know three living noblemen from the family in question, their respective fathers, their common grandfather as well as their great-grandfather and his brothers, whose deathbeds he attended. However, he only knew from others that the great-great-grandfather of the three noblemen in question was once a soldier in a border fort and was named Márton.[39]

The witness who pushed the bounds of memory the farthest was the one attesting to the nobility of the Králóczy family. At a 1767 hearing in Pápa, a supposedly ninety-six-year-old witness claimed to have known the tailor János Králóczy, the great-great-grandfather of the family seeking to establish its nobility, who lived to be almost a hundred. The grandson of the tailor—that is, the grandfather of the petitioners—had been a standard bearer at the siege of the Kanizsa castle in 1690, seventy-seven years earlier. Assuming that the witness, who claimed to be ninety-six, lived to be at least ninety, he could well have remembered the standard bearer and could have childhood memories of his grandfather, the tailor. In any case, another witness, a nobleman from Keszthely who was "merely" sixty-five years old, said he only remembered the standard bearer's father "as if from a dream", although he seemed to recall a childhood memory of having attended the latter's funeral. When the supposedly ninety-six-year-old János Hatvani later died, the long-dead grandfather of the late standard bearer fell from common memory, and all that was left was a "dream image" for the following generation. With each death among the oldest members of the community, another segment of human history plunged into darkness.[40]

Oral genealogy could not transcend the limits of human memory. A nobleman from Zala County could not trace the family tree of the Dienes family when he was called upon to do so. He could remember that the Dieneses received their nobility from Emperor Maximilian II (1564–76) but "to say what relation they bore from generation to generation to the Dieneses in question was beyond human memory, and he could offer no testimony to that effect". Other witnesses also could not provide information on this subject. The sixteenth-century document, the certificate granted by

Emperor Maximilian, had not and could not be linked to the eighteenth-century world of the witness by oral tradition. The witness, therefore, was right in noting that this case had surpassed human memory.[41]

It is evident from the case involving the lost and found letters patent of the Symon family of Vas County that witnesses zealously asserting the authenticity of the Symons strove to bridge the time gap with knowledge passed from generation to generation.

In 1743, an eighty-two-year-old lower nobleman from Andrásfa referred to his father's narrative: "he heard it from his late father who, when he was around ninety, often told him that the forebears of the Symons had been true noblemen, living in the freedom befitting nobles", although they had no letter of nobility. "The late father of the said witness claimed to have seen the letters patent and the robes of the Symons in the castle of Egervár before they were lost" when the Turks looted the place. Egervár was burned down by the Ottoman Grand Vizier Ahmed Köprülü in 1664, seventy-nine years before the deposition. If the witness was really eighty-two years old at the time of his deposition, as he claimed to be, he was a small child at the time of the incident, and his father could well have seen the Symons trying to save their documents. Witnesses testifying in the same case fifty years later were, however, in a more difficult position. The lower nobleman questioned in the case at that point could not refer to the memory of his father when testifying about a document that had disappeared one hundred twenty years earlier and, suspiciously enough, resurfaced ninety years later. He testified that his grandfather, another lower nobleman, who "lived to be one hundred eight and served in the Turkish wars told him countless times when he was a boy of fifteen that the ancestors of the family in question had taken their letters patent to the castle of Egervár along with others and proceeded to fight the Turks at Kanizsa, but the Ottoman army, defeated in the battle, looted the fort of Egervár and took all the letters and other tools with them". According to the witness, who claimed to be seventy-three, he heard the story in 1735 at the age of fifteen. His reported age was based on careful calculation as the witness thought that if he had claimed to be younger than fifteen at the time of the story, county officials might have found his testimony unreliable for being too young at the time to understand what the story was about. On the other hand, were he to claim to have been much older than fifteen, his grandfather would have had to be well over the age of one hundred to have given a credible description of an event that had taken place one hundred twenty-nine years earlier, a fact that might have diminished the authenticity of his testimony.[42]

Among the many thousands of suits involving ancestry, only one case was discovered in which the memory of family descent seemed to have been successfully maintained beyond the third generation. The title to this family's claim was based also on a certificate issued by Emperor Maximilian II. The letters patent dated from 1571, and the chapter of Vasvár made a copy of it in 1725 "as far as it was legible on account of its age". In 1740 this letter came to form the basis of a major lawsuit. A serf from Tormaföld, allegedly ninety-three years of age, claimed to know the father of Márton Hermann from the time of the Turkish wars "where he was a fellow soldier of the witness in the military camp". He also knew his grandson of the same name and his cousins, the three István Hermanns, and although he did not remember the forebears of the Hermanns, he knew the father and grandfather of the other three Hermanns well. Although he had not known the three great-grandfathers personally, he told the judges, he had heard of them. He also had heard "from the elders of old" that their common great-great-grandfather was named Pál; his father, Mihály; and Mihály's father, István, whose name already figured in the sixteenth-century document in question, which had been issued to István's father. The elaborate family tree, going back as many as eight generations, was again recited by another seventy-four-year-old witness when testifying afterwards about the genealogy he had heard a number of times from the elders. Miklós, the frontier soldier, also was remembered by this witness; he had heard that his father, István, was shot dead during the Tartar raid of 1664. However, from the generation of the great-grandfather he remembered slightly different names than witnesses before him, and he said that he had heard countless times from the elders that "the father of the three brethren was Pál; Pál's father, Mihály; and Mihály's father, the István who figures in the deed", as well as the fact that "Balázs Hermán, the father of István, having won his nobility as a reward for his bravery in battle, had his son's name inscribed in it, too".

This beautiful family tree is a real triumph of human memory—even if not of knowledge handed down from generation to generation, but of route-learning prior to the testimony. Other testimonies revealed that the Hermanns, flaunting the letters patent that they obtained from the chapter, always had been working serfs. Witnesses whose motives hardly could have been selfless tried in vain to bridge the vast gap of some one hundred seventy years between the issuing of the letter by Emperor Maximilian and their own time with references to the memory of the elders. Two witnesses, allegedly ninety-three and seventy-four years old, had heard from the elders that the great-grandfather of the great-great-grandfather obtained the letters patent of nobility in the sixteenth century, but society did not give much credence to their memories. The county tribunal ended up rejecting the Hermanns' claim, since they could not trace their nobility to the ancestor who was granted the letter.[43]

Credibility of the Memory of the Elders

The most important channels for sharing information in societies with a predominantly oral culture were the memories of the elders. It is difficult to ascertain at what age one was considered old, but the age limit was definitely earlier than in the twentieth century. One witness in Páty stated in 1779 that "although, being so old he rarely went among people", he nevertheless still knew something about the case in question. This "old" man was actually only sixty-seven years of age. Average life expectancies were low, and people aged rapidly. Anyone who lived to the age of seventy could consider him- or herself as well "over the hill" indeed.[44]

Many court witnesses claimed to be between one hundred and one hundred ten years old. The schoolmaster of Ság in Vas County, who was able to sing in church without spectacles, "was an extremely old man, and as he himself professed, was one hundred ten years old", a witness stated in 1747. When asked his age, a Kisgyőr serf said he was one hundred six in 1737, and, consistent with his original statement, claimed to be one hundred ten in 1740. Many other examples can be cited from testimonials of practically every county. Claims to being one hundred years old were uncontested by eighteenth-century jurors during court cases. In the course of a 1779 ancestry case in Hernádkak in Zemplén County, for example, a witness claimed to be one hundred, and subsequently the counsel for the defense argued that, as he was born in 1679, he was an excellent witness of the family tree of a family of lower noble origin. Ultimately the county court recognized the nobility of the litigating family.

Witnesses apart, there were others who claimed to be older than one hundred in the seventeenth and eighteenth centuries. Missionaries working in Hungary kept records of the age of people when they were converted to the Catholic faith. An older age in this context indicated the efficiency of missionary activity; it meant that the new believers had turned away from Protestantism after a century of "erring". Missionaries were fond of stressing in their reports that their brethren had become Catholics at the end of their long lives: at one hundred twenty and one hundred ten year of age two

Lutherans of Besztercebánya (Banská Bystrica) became Catholics, as did several who were one hundred twelve and one hundred fifteen years old in Lőcse and Liptó counties. This implies that a great many people in Hungary at the time professed to be over one hundred and, more importantly, their peers believed them.[45]

Even in the eighteenth century most people were unaware of exactly how old they were, reflecting the fact that oral tradition held strong in their society. In societies where literacy prevails, dates of birth are registered and birth certificates issued when necessary—and they often are. Time is expressed in numbers, recorded and divided into equal periods, and does not rely on mortal witnesses' vague memories.

In oral societies, however, many people professed to be older than one hundred. A petty nobleman of Terestyénfa claimed to be one hundred four years old in 1764 when recalling sixty-year-old battles.[46] In 1718 Mihály Salamon, a nobleman, first maintained that he was one hundred ten but changed his mind and reduced his age to one hundred eight in order to make his confession seem more accurate and credible. Age rendered authority, and old village men who thought themselves to be one hundred keenly would go around telling people their age. "As he himself often told me, he was one hundred ten years old", a witness in Bogács confessed in 1778, speaking of István Kozma, an old nobleman. Another eighty-five-year-old witness also believed from what he had heard that Kozma was more than one hundred. The third witness, who was ninety-three at the time, explained that "he has lived to a fine old age", but never had he seen a man as old as István Kozma, who not only claimed to be older than one hundred, but even the elders at the time generally thought him to be older than themselves.[47] Another ancestry case featured some even taller tales: an Alsópáhok peasant declared he was just eighty, but—presumably in order to make a dubious confession credible—claimed that his father (who had once told him that the family seeking out its noble roots did have a letters patent) was one hundred thirty.[48]

The memory of the elders in the peasantry and the lower nobility enjoyed great authority. Miklós Osvált, a shepherd, testified twice in a border dispute between two villages. Judging by the age he dictated to the scribe in each case, he aged thirty years in just twenty-one, between 1724 and 1745.[49] Shepherds were not alone in such rapid aging but shared this propensity with members of the lower nobility, as they all lived in an oral society. Even in the eighteenth century most people knew their actual age only more or less, and the witness's age in confessions more often than not was preceded by "circiter"—that is, "approximately". The older one was, the fewer contemporaries one had to verify one's memory. A nobleman, Pál Gombossy, in Vas County professed to be seventy-six in 1726. In 1732 he made two depositions: during the first he claimed to be eighty-three, and in the second, eighty-nine. In another deposition in 1737 he said that he was ninety-eight at the time. A fellow witness, a nobleman himself, aged eleven years in just four; he was only seventy-two in 1733, but eighty-three by 1737.[50]

A lease-holding serf of the Esterházy family in Csesztreg was called as a witness in an ancestry case. According to his testimony, the weekend of the trial took ten years off his age: on Friday, 7 January 1741 he claimed to be eighty, but by Monday, 10 January he was only seventy. The latter was most likely his real age, because in another testimony at Christmas the same year he restated that he was seventy. The record holder in this respect is probably Gergely Vörös, a Veszprém nobleman, who aged just a year but did so in an hour or two. On Saturday, 24 February 1742, the jurors of Veszprém County questioned witnesses in the cases of two, formally neighboring, families. Vörös told them twice what he knew about the same royal deed of gift; he first professed to be sixty-four, and later, sixty-five.[51] A Miskolc noble aged eight years in a day. He was called as a witness in an ancestry case in 1767 and stated that he was eighty-six years old. On the following day he announced that he upheld his testimony in every respect but one: he was ninety-four instead of eighty-six. Presumably he had deliberated overnight and decided that eighty-six years of age did not give him enough authority.[52]

The fact that witnesses provided different ages each time they were asked is no mere accident. They would profess to be older if they were called to confirm a fact in the past. The above Csesztreg serf, who became ten years younger in three days, spoke of the present legal status of the family claiming to be seventy years old. However, when it came to recalling events that happened before his own lifetime, he was left to draw on oral tradition, and hence stated that he was eighty. He told the judges that when he was a young lad and a shepherd, he heard partly from his father, who lived to a fine old age, and partly from "a cottar who lived with them, a very old man indeed" how the members of a noble family had once forbidden the use of a mill ages ago. László Kupai of Abaúj County claimed to be seventy-eight in 1745; three years earlier in another ancestry case, however, he said he was eighty-eight. This was not accidental: in the first instance, he was called to speak about a much older event involving the long-dead grandfather of a nobleman.[53]

Witnesses, then, would adjust their ages to suit the event, the recollection of which was still their duty in an oral society. In 1741 an Abaúj County lower noble claimed to be forty-six in an ancestry case, but nine years later he professed to be twenty-one years older. In 1750 he asserted that, "the witness hath seen his letters patent also, as a stripling of twelve years of age". The scribe initially wrote fifty-seven years as the age of the witness—which is what the witness must have dictated to him in the first place—and given that witnesses rarely, if ever, knew their exact ages, it could not have been very far from the truth. However, the next witness, a sixty-eight-year-old nobleman from Aszaló, also had seen the letters patent as a child of fourteen. So the first witness adjusted his own age to this nobleman's testimony and changed fifty-seven to sixty-seven. Now, practically the same age, they both were able to remember fifty-four to fifty-five years back and the deed that had disappeared in the meantime.[54]

In the oral tradition of the peasantry and the lower nobility, however, events of the past were never tied to actual dates, and so witnesses could never know how old to claim to be in order to provide credible testimony about the event in question. Asserting an old age served to overinsure: anyone over one hundred must certainly remember the event in question. In 1737 a nobleman of Boldva, who had his age changed from one hundred to one hundred ten, remembered how "in olden days, being roughly ten years of age, when the Poles attacked and massacred many in the church of Beregszász (Beregovo) town", the noble in question was killed. This Polish attack occurred at the time of the military campaign of George Rákóczi II (the prince of Transylvania) against Poland in June 1657; that is, exactly eighty years before the testimony. So, provided the witness was at least ninety at the time of his testimony, he might have remembered that terrible day. What he did not know, however, was exactly in which year the tragedy had occurred. He figured it must have been at least a hundred years ago, so to be sure he was a lad of ten on the day of the massacre, he had to be one hundred ten.[55]

In 1638 witnesses were called to testify that King Mathias Corvinus (1458–90) had freed their village, Mályinka in Borsod County, as a reward for being wined and dined there. This legendary visit happened almost two centuries before and thus there was only one major event to which the witnesses could relate the king's visit: the loss of Dédes castle, which previously controlled the area, to the Turks. This happened merely seventy-one years earlier on 2 April 1567—seventy-seven years after the death of King Mathias, a date that the witnesses could not specify. Consequently, they reckoned that in order to be able to remember an event that happened "ages and ages ago", they would have to be at least a century old. So when the peasants alive at the time of the fall of Dédes were called in as witnesses, "bidding" began. The first man claimed to be one hundred; the second, one hundred two; and the third, one hundred eight. Jakab Válint of Vadna thought he was about seventy-seven, and he reckoned there was no way he could remember an event that ancient: "I was not yet born when the Turks besieged the castle of Dédes", but he was told about it by his aunt, he said. However, if his age was given correctly, he was already six when the castle was captured.[56]

The Borsod lower noblemen and peasants, who in the mid-eighteenth century tried to recall the previous century (the Turkish era), thought they needed to be at least one hundred. A one-hundred-year-old Alacska witness recalled the decapitated head of the pasha of Arad, while a serf, purportedly one hundred seven, could remember the Eger pasha's decapitated head; both were spoils of war. Very few fighters from that period were left by the mid-eighteenth century who might have told these peasants that the Hungarian soldiers most probably would not have killed pashas, but lower-rank Turkish officers, and there was never a pasha in Arad.

The examples above illustrate how witnesses underwent "accelerated" aging—as they grew older they professed to be more so than they actually were. However, some examples of the opposite also have survived the years. In the 1752 ancestry case of the Pázmándi family a witness declared that he was exactly one hundred fourteen years old. Presumably he assumed that he thus might have fought alongside a Pázmándi upon whom one of the emperors Ferdinand had conferred a patent of nobility. As Ferdinand III died in 1657, this must have been no later than the mid-seventeenth century. Five years later, in 1757, however, when the same witness was called to repeat his testimony about the same warrior, he claimed to be just one hundred fifteen—he had aged just one year in five years. Presumably he decided that by initially saying he was one hundred fourteen he already had stretched the age limit far enough, being even older would have sounded unbelievable.[57]

The lower nobles and peasants of the seventeenth and eighteenth centuries could not link military events or plagues to specific dates, and so witnesses often would "remember" events that—even according to the age they claimed to be—they could not have seen in reality. In other words, sometimes a witness would fail to adjust his age to his testimony. In 1794 a nobleman was called as a witness in the ancestry case of the Czélia family. He told the court that "when Péró [the peasant revolt leader] attacked, he remembers well Mátyás Czélia complaining to his father of his fear that he might have to fight in the noblemen's militia", and so he concealed his nobility. The noble, who claimed to be sixty-three, was only four at the time of the Péró rebellion (1735), so it is unlikely he could have remembered the dialogue. Either he was in fact older than he claimed or more likely he remembered an event he had been told.[58]

The record holder in claiming to be of an extremely old age was not a lower noble, but a roaming beggar discharged from the army. In 1776 János Jávortsik of Szentpéter was questioned about the notorious highwayman Jánosik, the whereabouts of whose hidden treasures he boasted to know. He went on to say that although he had not known the highwayman personally, he had "seen him hanged and dangling". The famous robber had been hung sixty-three years before, in 1713 in Liptó County. All Jávortsik knew was that it happened a long time ago. So in order to give his words credibility, when he was asked his age, he announced without hesitation: "I shall be one hundred thirty next St John's Day." The witness was a shepherd before he joined the army, and of course he did not know his exact age. He certainly could never have made note of it, since, as he himself admitted, he could neither write nor read, and so he had someone else read the letter about the hanged highwayman's treasure hidden in the mountains.[59]

In 1754 Pál Kelemen, a nobleman, professed to be sixty-nine years old in his testimony. Thinking his ancestry case would be judged favorably, he fiercely claimed to have fought the Turks at Nagyvázsony on his grandfather's side. The scribe realized that the zealous soldier would have been only a three-year-old child at the time of these fights, and even at the time of the Carlowitz peace treaty (1699) at the end of this war, he would have been no more that fourteen. Without batting an eye, Pál Kelemen altered his age from sixty-nine to ninety-six. The three-decade jump indicates that beyond a certain limit, roughly over seventy years, any given number was merely a synonym of "very old".[60]

A draft copy of the testimony of a petty Hollós nobleman contains no less than four versions of his age. The scribe first wrote seventy, but later modified it to seventy-four, then seventy-five, and finally the witness claimed he was a full eighty years of age. Even if he had owned a certificate of baptism he could not have verified his age, since, as he put it, he "could not read".[61]

Exaggerating one's age was encouraged by the fact that in this society, where even among the nobles oral traditions prevailed, the older one was, the greater authority one had. Consequently, people preferred to appear older than younger—in sharp contrast to twentieth-century customs. The only exceptions were women. A noblewoman of Kásmárk, for example, could not decide whether to say she was thirty-six or forty-six, nor could a "noble virgin" in Liszka make up her mind very easily. The scribe barely could cope with making all of the changes: first thirty-one, then thirty-three and ultimately forty-four. In a testimony given on 16 March 1763, a noble-woman of Abony thought she was about fifty-three years old, but when she was called as a witness five weeks later, she decided that admitting she was forty-six would be sufficient.[62]

Male witnesses, however, sought to give their testimony the greatest credibility possible, and so, if they are to be believed, they lived to biblical ages. However, in the latter half of the eighteenth century the credibility of oral tradition began to crumble concurrent with the spread of literacy and the use of written records. The illiterate mentality, as opposed to the literate, does not relate age to specific dates. Consequently, after sixty or seventy years one's age and placing past events in time become dubious matters. One example of the transition from one mentality to the other is a noble of Szil in Sopron County (a developed, literate region) who claimed to be ninety-nine in 1763. He kept a record of his age and was proud of doing so. The letters patent, with which the inquiry was concerned, "he had oft held it in hand...it was a gift of Emperor Leopold (1657–1705), and it is but two years older than the witness", he established with barely concealed pride. The given age of the witness was merely synonymous with "very old" (unspecified old age), but the literate old man had compared the age he was thought to be in the oral tradition with the exact date in the written document.[63]

By the mid-eighteenth century the credibility of the testimonies of very old people sometimes was called into question. In the 1748 ancestry case of the Rácz family a serf who claimed to be one hundred was called as a witness. The county court refused to accept his testimony on the grounds that, due to "his old age and many years, and because of the weakness of his memory, he keeps changing his testimony". Similarly, seeing the disbelief of the jurors concerning his deposition on age-old events, an Emőd serf admitted in 1793 that he could not remember the family tree of the noble family in question because "his memories are so vague that the family could not have appeared in his mind". In a border dispute in 1765 six middle-aged peasants between thirty-one and fifty-five years old unanimously declared that a Vas County peasant, "past his prime of life and being old, knew not from one hour to the next what he spoke. He was losing his mind, and if he was asked to say anything, like a little child, he could be persuaded." However, these were just a few cases; the credibility of the testimonies of elder witnesses was still generally accepted in eighteenth-century villages.[64]

In the second half of the eighteenth century, particularly in the last two decades, the jurors conducting a case increasingly sought to verify the witnesses' ages. The jurors asked the witnesses how old they were at the time of the 1697 Hegyalja uprising, the 1686 recapture of Buda from the Turks, the Tartar invasion of 1717 and the great plague of 1741 respectively and proceeded to calculate the witnesses' real ages from this information.

By the 1780s, as a result of the spread of literacy and the use of written records, jurors would consult birth registers to determine how old the witnesses were. In 1785 a district magistrate did not content himself with believing what the witnesses told him about their ages but looked up the information in the local birth register in Nagymihály in Borsod County and gave the exact ages of the witnesses on the basis of the parish register.

In 1792 an inquiry was launched in Lovas (in the Upper Balaton region) into the noble relatives of the Szakál family. The court did not content itself with unconditionally accepting the extraordinarily high ages of the witnesses, and so—in an attempt to find out how far back the witnesses could accurately remember—the county jurors, all noblemen, also asked how each of them knew his or her age. The first witness said, "I know I am fifty-eight because I was twenty-five when I got married, and I have been married for thirty-three years now." The next witness, a peasant woman, knew that the previous witness, when he served at their house, was said to be three years older than she, so she concluded that she must be fifty-five. A widowed woman also measured her age in relation to her marriage. She told the court she knew she was sixty-eight because her husband had died thirty years ago, they were married for twenty years, and she had married at eighteen. Another witness claimed to be fifty-seven. "I know my years for I have always kept count of them", he proudly announced. Mrs. Mihály Szakál, a noble woman who had died long ago, the witness declared, "must have been at least one hundred years old, not least because she herself said so and because she could scarcely walk anymore". The lady was extremely old, so there was no question about her being past one hundred. "She herself professed to be one hundred two; yes, dear, I am past a hundred, a hundred two even", she kept saying. The witnesses who were able to determine their own ages numerically on the basis of the maiden-wife-widow periods of their lives relied, however, on the oral tradition when it came to establishing the age of a long deceased lady. Old people's testimonies and the authority of oral traditions were not unquestioned among the nobility at the end of the eighteenth century.[65]

An inquest in Abaúj County in 1784 set out to establish the genealogy of a noble family. A decade or two previously the county noble delegates would not have batted an eye on hearing the Litke serfs' unanimous testimony regarding the family tree. Towards the end of the eighteenth century, however, it occurred to the nobles interviewing the serfs to question the witnesses' knowledge of the long-deceased nobleman and his sons. The records note that because no birth register existed at the time, the age of both witnesses could not be established for certain. The case records make it clear that only registered dates of birth were considered authentic by the noblemen conducting cases at the end of the eighteenth century.[66]

In these oral societies a great deal of information was preserved only in older people's memories, and it is hardly surprising that as the years went by few of them could recall events precisely, let alone the ancestry of individual noble families. The noblemen under investigation surely often welcomed spontaneous memory flaws. Undoubtedly, many testimonies in ancestry inquiries were false, and certainly both the questioning and the testifying nobles acted as best suited their interests. The decisions they made determined the fate not only of individuals but also of entire families; either they granted an individual and his descendants entry into the privileged class or denied him the opportunity to climb the social ladder for good.

The historian's position, in one respect, is more favorable than that of individuals who lived in the seventeenth or eighteenth century. The historian is not concerned with whether the given family deserved the patent of nobility or not, but rather with the literacy level and mentality of those who testified. Consequently, even false testimony can provide genuine facts. It has to be said on behalf of the false witnesses that they were seeking to make their testimonies sound as plausible as possible, and even if they were a little on the inadequate side, they were nevertheless characteristic of the mentality of the witnesses' social strata.

Testimonies of ancestry and noble descent did not appear spontaneously, and winning the goodwill of a witness had a price. Painstaking negotiations preceded the summoning of a witness before the court. These secret pacts only came to light if the parties involved came into conflict with each other later. In 1747 a noble of Zala County told the court that a certain György Tik had complained about Márton and Ferenc Tik because they "enticed me into dwelling here at Szentandrás" and promised to "support me decently in my old age" as long as he testified that they were his relatives and, therefore, also nobles. This was, of course, not the case.

Obviously the Tiks were neither the witness's relatives nor noblemen. They were originally called Kövér (fat), and Tik was a nickname they had acquired for being notorious hen thieves ("tik" is the Hungarian word for hen). The family later was able to capitalize greatly on this sobriquet, because they discovered the genuine noble György Tik, who gave them written evidence of his nobility and taught them the orally transmitted ancestry of the Tik family. However, György Tik later regretted his perjury, because these new namesakes of his were atrocious to him: "they have joined me in the nobility and not only do they not behave accordingly, but they starve me". They made the old man run errands on the farm. The price of obtaining nobility was a settlement ensuring support for life; however, the new noblemen did not keep their word, and yet on account of the false testimony, the deluded witness complained, "his soul was also lost, because as a liar he would be punished by God".[67]

Perjury—making changes to orally transmitted noble lineage—was not unheard of in Abaúj County either. In 1742 the Idránys tried in vain to persuade two serfs claiming to be eighty-five and eighty-eight to confirm the family's false genealogy with the authority of their long memories. "Heard nothing about the relatives from his father who is said to be one hundred ten", one of the two serfs said, and Idrányi was wasting his time trying to persuade the other serf to accept a "pail of barley to testify in his favor", because, "not wanting to challenge his faith, he did not accept" the price for perjury—at least that is what he kept telling the district magistrate.[68]

Not all were daunted by lying in court, however. Two lower noblemen of Nagymizdó in Vas County frequently testified in ancestry cases, and one of their neighbors "frequently heard them talk about their good luck because the Devil did not bear them off for false witnessing".[69]

Candidates for the upper classes had to pay substantially for supporting testimonies. In turn, however, the new nobles were entitled to sell their own testimonies. Some made money from their new and expensive patents of nobility. József Mészáros of Zala County was "for his diverse obsequiousness dear to the county sub-prefect", which was how he was able to enter the privileged class. Mészáros (butcher) was not an uncommon name in Hungary, and some thought he had stolen his letters patent from a wanderer he once had boarded. Having fraudulently acquired nobility with the help of this letters patent, József Mészáros helped others into the peer club—at a price. For example, he claimed that the Peremarton vicar was a relative of his in exchange for two hundred forints and a cart of wheat. A shepherd, also by the name of Mészáros, promised to support him until the end of his life if he could become a noble by József Mészáros claiming he was a relative. Later, however, they quarreled, and as with the previously mentioned case of György Tik, the perjury-for-eternal-livelihood deal turned out to be a great disappointment for József Mészáros. The new noble, the shepherd Mészáros, owed him approximately one hundred forints, although he admitted to having received the other presents he had been promised.[70]

Primarily illiterate, the lower nobility traced its ancestry orally. The conferee's name on a written patent could be scratched off and a different name written in. But forging memories or spoken testimonies in a society living in a predominantly oral culture was an even easier matter.

Memories of Heroic Deeds in the Oral Tradition

The lower nobility orally preserved not only its genealogy, its ancestors' names and relationships but also the heroic deeds of its forebears. The legal grounds for a noble title was armed service, a principle often quoted by the nobles or at least the literate ones, who could read the lawbooks of the time.[71] This rather abstract concept of privilege gained through heroic military service assumed concrete meaning in the stories of eighteenth-century lower nobles' accounts of the wars against the Turks. The theory of a title earned by arms in practice meant a detailed record of the heroic deeds of one's forefathers. The less a lower noble's way of life, clothing, house and (lack of) estate revealed his blue blood, the more important it was to differentiate himself from the peasants. Such differences, however, were mostly illusive; in Hungarian villages the lower nobility lived together with the peasants whose fathers and grandfathers had themselves participated in the Turkish wars as free peasant-soldiers or border castle defenders back in the seventeenth century.

Looking back one hundred years, memories of heroic pasts held certain people to be noble who, in fact, never were. In 1783, one hundred years after the siege of Vienna, which triggered the war of liberation from the Turks, two *agilis*es (seventy and seventy-five years old) claimed that the members of the Boda family were nobles. The agilises themselves were sons of noblewomen but not noblemen and were, therefore, on the periphery of the noble class and not legally real gentry. The evidence they provided was that "when they were in camp, being true noblemen, their fathers and grandfathers had to fight and to be attentive to the extent that, on twice hearing the report of the old cannon of the castle, they were to go directly to the castle, mounted and armed". Perhaps the Boda family was noble, but in the seventeenth century, the military duties outlined in the above testimony were, in fact, the duties of the liberated soldier-peasants—the Haiducks—living in the villages around the castle.

Orally transmitted memories of the past were similarly distorted in Borsod County. An eighty-year-old freeman, who was called as a witness in an ancestry case in Miskolc in 1747, claimed he was sixteen in 1683 when the Turks besieged Vienna. He remembered the lower noble in question being a soldier at Ónod castle and could even recall him once bringing home the decapitated head of a Turk from the siege of Eger. He reasoned that if he had fought the Turks so valiantly, and—as the villagers remembered—also had taken part in the battle of Vienna, he must have "valorously fought the pagan Turks out of fidelity to our royal majesty". However, the county jurors knew history better and remembered the elaborate turns of seventeenth-century Hungarian politics. As a result, they cross-examined him to the point that the witness conceded that the nobleman in question really had been there at the siege of Vienna—on the other side, fighting alongside the Turks under the Hungarian insurrectionist Prince Imre Thököly, an ally of the sultan. It is unlikely that sixty-four years later the witness was trying to prove a long-dead warrior's loyalty to the emperor. In the mid-eighteenth century memories of the chaotic front lines must have mingled in the oral tradition to the extent that brave soldiers always were considered to be on the right side.[72]

In the lowest—essentially illiterate—stratum of the nobility, the heroic past and the memories of the Turkish wars were handed down orally. András Chutor did not even have a house, and he lived as a poor cottar in a freeman's house, yet he fondly recalled his forebears as "great peers and arms bearers". The crestfallen old nobleman could not read himself the letters patent he had inherited from his ancestors, so the village pastor read it to him. The preacher praised the letters patent for being "a good letter indeed, by which András Chutor could ennoble himself". The patent of nobility also recounted how the conferee, an ancestor named János Chutor, had encountered "the Turks under a castle, and being a captain, he and his few men overcame the Turks and took an officer prisoner. He heard this news from many a man", an eighty-four-year-old freeman told the court in 1735. The old heroic deed, the story of the captain taking prisoners, must have been the talk of the small Zala County village, as András Chutor told numerous people what the preacher had read in the Latin letters patent. He did so in an attempt to prevent loss of prestige, which went hand in hand with social degradation and poverty. In this way, a *written* story was handed down *orally* among the illiterate.[73]

Witnesses to the Turkish wars were still alive at the beginning of the eighteenth century. In 1733 a seventy-five-year-old Peremarton noble was called to testify in the ancestry case of a nobleman because he was an adult when his uncle was killed in the battle of Fejérvár. He "even saw his head impaled on the wall of the Turkish border castle, displayed to the public".[74]

A decade later, in 1746, an eighty-eight-year-old Vat freeman was able to recall how sixty years before he had met the grandfather of a Csorna noble-man in the camp of the army besieging Buda, the capital of Hungary. He was with a noble from the next village who claimed to be eighty years old. At the time of the recapture of Buda in 1686, he said he was "roughly a youngster of eighteen", which, adding up the years, must have been true.[75]

Time passed, and the battles of the Turkish era became distant memories. The number of people who purported to be able to recall these memories did not dwindle, but the credibility of their tales did. Two decades later there were far fewer Turkish war veterans alive. In 1765 an ancestry inquiry was held in Vas County regarding the nobility of the Mazali family. A seventy-one-year-old noble learned from the elders that the grandfather of the two Mazali boys, who were trying to prove their nobility, had been "killed under the Turkish castle of Kanizsa in the Turkish war". Claiming to be eighty-nine, György Németh of Körmend knew about this from his own experience, or at least that is what he tried to tell the county court. He stated that he had known the old István Mazali well, as they had fought together at the siege of Kanizsa. However, Kanizsa was recaptured by the Christian armies seventy-five years before, in 1690, so there was no way an even near ninety-year-old György Németh could have fought to liberate this strategically important castle.[76]

Only the latest battles of the seventeenth-century Turkish wars were preserved in the consciousness of the eighteenth-century lower nobility. Witnesses could recall the campaigns against the Turks, including the recapture of the castles of Buda, Fehérvár, and Kanizsa from 1686 to 1690. Some even spoke of the Turkish campaign of 1663–64: the abortive attempt to take Kanizsa, the famous battle of Szentgotthard, the general Montecuccoli and the "Tartar invasion", the plundering Crimean Tartars who swept across the country with the Sultan's armies. The horrors of these events were crucial experiences in the lives of an entire generation. Nothing from the war-laden history of the Turkish era, which began in 1526, could be remembered from before 1664: the oral tradition failed when it came to recalling events more than seventy to one hundred years before. Anything that happened before then belonged to the world of legend.[77]

The further away from the heroic deeds of the Turkish wars, the hazier the stories became. In 1727 an old soldier, who claimed to be one hundred seven and a defender of Ónod castle, remembered a fellow soldier chopping off the head of the pasha of Eger and said the head was hung on the castle gate. If he was not the pasha himself, as he remembered, then he was at least a Turkish soldier. This old man personally fought with the decapitator. However, forty years later, the witness knew from the stories of his father and mother only that at the siege of Vienna (1683)—that is, eighty-five years before—the lower noble in question had been a soldier "who presented the emperor with three Turks' heads in exchange for which the emperor conferred upon him a patent of nobility". The story—a century after the siege of Vienna—is somewhat like a folk legend: Emperor Leopold personally received this heroic lower noble with the decapitated Turks' heads and instantly issued him a letters patent in reward. The treasured but not understood written document—the letters patent—was *material* evidence of the heroic deed, and as such, it confirmed the orally handed-down tradition of a glorified past in the eyes of the lower nobles.[78]

In 1742 Veszprém County initiated an inquiry into the nobility of the Kalocza family. A nobleman of the town of Veszprém, Gergely Vörös, told the court that forty-six years earlier, after he married a girl from the Kalocza family, he traveled to the village of Szabadi (the name means "free village" in Hungarian) in Somogy County with his new wife. There he read the royal charter giving liberty to this village, which included the family name Kalocza (presumably the deed had been used by the girl's family to prove her nobility to her future husband). During the same visit, the village elders told him the story about "one of these Kaloczas: when King Louis fought the Turks on Mohács plain, the pin of the coach's wheel came out, so he plugged his finger into the end of the axle, and carried the king for some time in that fashion". His wife recalled the family tradition similarly: "She heard as a child from the elders that the Kalocza family members themselves were facing the pagan enemy as true noblemen should; one of them, when the pin from the wheel of King Louis's coach fell out, put his finger into the end of the axle. He died in that battle."

The source of this legend can be traced with the help of another nobleman's testimony. The noble told the court that Szabadi's royal deed of gift was granted by "the deceased King Louis". The deed already had been lost by the time of the deposition, but it seems probable—from intelligence gathered from other, similar deeds—that the free village's royal deed was given not by King Louis II of the Jagellon dynasty, who was killed in the battle of Mohács in 1526, but by the fourteenth-century Louis I the Great of the Anjou dynasty (1342–82) who issued numerous similar charters to free villages. When in 1696 Gergely Vörös proposed and the lower nobles of his wife's village read the name "Ludovicus" heading the Latin deed, both King Louises had been dead for long enough—one for three hundred fourteen years, the other for one hundred seventy years—to fall outside the span of memory. However, the battle of Mohács and the death of Louis II, being the beginning of the misery of sixteenth- and seventeenth-century Turkish-dominated Hungary, were "living memories" in common knowledge. This explains why the village nobles connected Ludovicus, the Latin name read in the written document, with the memory of Louis II.

That the legend cannot be rooted in reality hardly needs to be explained. The noble finger stuck into the end of the wheel was unlikely to have substituted successfully for the lost pin. Genuine accounts of participants in this famous battle tell us that from the beginning of the battle of Mohács until his death, Louis II fought on horseback. The legend, however, compared the historical figure to the contemporary ruler; the Szabadi elders, subjects of Emperor Leopold I (1657–1705), who never would approach a battlefield, only could imagine a king at war with the Turks arriving at the scene in a coach.[79]

Patents of Nobility Destroyed by Illiterates

Regardless of whether or not they could read, individuals during this period were aware of the significance of a written patent of nobility. When a family lost everything—whether they were robbed or their house burned down—it was always the loss of the letters patent they bewailed most. The loss of letters patent appears in the court records in dozens of ancestry cases. When the house of a Nemesnép nobleman burned down, "if only the cupboard in which the letters were kept could have been rescued from the flames", his wife complained, "for he feared the loss of those more than all his wealth". "More than any of my damages I am most sorry about my letters", a noble of Lengyel in Zala County exclaimed. When another Zala County nobleman's house was devoured by flames, "with tears in his eyes he complained...he would easily forget all his charred possessions, if only his letters patent had not burned". In 1682 Turks plundered the village Pereszteg, recalled a noble, and one of the noblemen "did not bewail any of his stolen goods more than the Turks having carried off his letters patent".[80]

Even illegible remains of a written document entailed the right to nobility. In an ancestry case in Vas County witnesses told the court that when a lower noble's house was struck by lightning, all of his furniture was destroyed. They tried to rescue the letter—his most important property—from the flames, "but merely tiny and just half-inch pieces of the letter" could be salvaged. The nobleman, "unable to rescue his letters, fell to the ground with grief and anguish." Or at least that is what the original testimony said; later, however, he felt it necessary to add that "a fraction of parchment…that shriveled up due to the fire" and became illegible was in fact saved. The charred and illegible piece of writing made a strong case later in the inquiry.[81]

This nobleman was not the only one who, among all his possessions, was most devastated by the loss of the letter warranting him class and prestige. The Horváth family's letters patent was lost during the Kuruc wars. They were forced to flee with their valuables when they were attacked by marauding Serbian soldiers in a forest. "Breaking open the trunk on the carriage…the said privileges were taken out and away…their mother implored the robbers at least to return those privileges to secure the future of her children". Apparently the attackers were unmoved and rode away with the document. Evidently they, too, were aware of the value of the patent, knowing they would be able to extract a decent ransom for it or sell it to another family. Whether the attackers were killed in the turmoil of the war or, exploiting the commonness of the family name Horváth, sold the letters patent issued by King Ferdinand III is unknown, it was never found again.[82]

"Indeed, the throats of my children have just been slit", a noblewoman of Abaúj County wailed after she learned that German soldiers had carried off her patent of nobility.[83] The exception that proves the rule in this respect was the wife of a noble of Gönc. During the war of independence led by Francis Rákóczi, German soldiers turned his cellar upside down, and from that time on he would remind himself over and over again how he was devastated by nothing except the letters patent that his forebears had "earned with bloodshed". His wife would then start bickering, "unable to comprehend what a treasure it might be". The sarcastic remark came from a woman who was illiterate herself and therefore only mourned her lost dresses and jewelry.[84]

Cases of someone destroying their own patent of nobility, although infrequent, nevertheless were known to have happened. A widow of Katafa in Vas County did not want to make money from the letters patent of her late husband—she was more inclined to take revenge. In 1744 a nobleman told a court that, "following the death of the husband, his wife took it [the letters patent] into the garden, and since her marriage had been childless, she burned the letters patent. When the servant asked the woman why she burned the letter, she replied, 'so it is of no use to others.'"[85] This illustrates that this widow was fully aware of the value of the patent. However, unlike ladies worried about the future of their families, her sole concern apparently was to do harm to her husband's presumably hated family by destroying the treasured writing.

The case of the Csajtai family was quite different. They underwent legal proceedings for the recognition of their nobility in Sopron County; however, they were unable to present conclusive evidence—that is, their patent of nobility. A noble told the court that he had known the old János Csajtai, a bootmaker, as a young man. "He remembered how the previously mentioned János Csajtai had made his letters patent into a pattern-design for boots." The witness inquired of the widow "if it was true that her husband had cut up the letters patent to make it into a pattern-design for boots, to which the said widow not only replied it was true", but "also presented to the witness the pattern-design for boots made from the letters patent. Holding it in hand, the witness observed that the letters of the parchment were lengthways down the bootleg, seeing which the witness rebuked the widow for having allowed her husband to do so. The widow claimed not to have been at home at the time, and when she scolded her husband afterwards, her husband said—with the pride of a real nobleman—that he was a noble even though he did cut up his patent." However, Csajtai was desperately wrong. In 1725 the county court refused to recognize his nobility on the grounds that he was unable to present his (cut-up) documents. His son proceeded to take the case to court twice, a quarter- and a half-century later, but his petition was refused for the same reason. For generations the Csajtai family was cursed for having destroyed the precious document, and ultimately the grandsons of this ignorant nobleman became serfs.[86]

This example is in such sharp contrast with all the other testimonies, which speak of the letters patent being treasured and kept safely hidden, that one would think it an isolated case. A Torna County lower noble, however, ruined his letters patent in a similar fashion. At the end of the eighteenth century, Mihály Herke, a Miskolc flask maker, took his ancestry case to court in Torna County, from which all the Herke family had come. However, by then the Herkes of Torna County had all died. The district magistrates only were able to question the eighty-three-year-old daughter of their former maid. She had seen and had often dried the letters patent in question, but never read it. She remembered to have "heard it said that the letters patent had been conferred upon him by his royal majesty Leopold". The letters patent was later found mutilated, without the royal seal. Another nobleman, who was called to witness in the case, recounted what had happened to the seal. He told the court that his mother-in-law, a Herke girl, had lived in his house for eighteen years, and among her letters was one said to be the Herke letters patent. He himself "little understood reading and writing, having had a simple upbringing in hard times", and so, together with his brother-in-law, they "removed the large wax seal hanging from the letters patent, broke it in half, shared it and used it to make waxed thread for sewing boots. They also cut off the cord made of twisted blue, yellow and red silk and, being smokers, they wound it onto pipe stems." Luckily for the flask maker, his relatives never thought of a better way to use the parchment, and so at least the mutilated and discredited letter survived. The forty-nine-year-old nobleman failed to recognize, then, the significance of the document, and together with his brother-in-law only saw the elaborate letter as a source of raw material otherwise hard to come by. A noblewoman called Zsuzsanna Visolyi similarly was oblivious to the significance of the deeds. She removed a letters patent that was airing on a rod by the hearth, and "because the seal was hung on a thick cord, the witness told her mother that it would do well as a headdress tie, and suggested cutting it off since it was good strong stuff", but her mother—fortunately for the relatives later seeking to prove their nobility—would not allow her to mutilate the letters patent, arguing that it was worth nothing without the seal and cord.[87]

A third effacer of letters patent, a Szepsi noble, was also a bootmaker. His grandson took his ancestry case to court, but his letters patent lacked the royal seal. An eighty-year-old Szepsi told the court that he had served two months in the Balogh household, and he knew that "the royal letters patent that belonged to him was kept in the cabinet for a while, and he also knew that János Balogh himself cut His Majesty's wax seal off the silk cord appended to the letters patent and melted it in with other wax to spread on thread". This bootmaker, too, refrained from cutting up the parchment, so we know the letters patent was issued to the Balogh family by Emperor Leopold I (1675–1705). This eighty-year-old witness must have served with the Baloghs fifty to sixty years previously, around 1690–1700, so it was not an old inheritance that the ignorant bootmaker mutilated, but a freshly issued document from the ruling king.[88]

In 1745 the Kőszeghy family of Szántód also declared that their letters patent had been destroyed. The letter always had been truncated, they said, because the tutor of the orphan János Kőszeghy, "has thrown the letters patent, together with many other letters, onto the dunghill, which was where it was then found with a dung fork". The witnesses claimed that the tutor confessed, "I did it to dispossess the Kőszeghys of their inheritance". The tattered document later was found in the trunk of Kőszeghy's brother-in-law György Toronyai, a tax-paying serf. "Knowing little about writing and reading" he had his son read it to him. His son, recently returned from the famous Calvinist school, Debrecen College, read the name Kőszeghy, but Mrs. Toronyai (née Erzsébet Kőszeghy) gave the letters patent "to her children to play with, and the little that could be read was torn up".[89]

The story certainly raises doubts: the destroyed letter was seen only by Erzsébet Kőszeghy and her stepchildren, and no one knew about it in Szántód. Due to the fact that noblemen would make a show of their letters patent precisely in order to prove their existence, it seems probable that the two Toronyais, father and son, wanted to help the Kőszeghy family into the noble class. It is fairly suspicious that the tutor did not burn it but dumped it on a dunghill, and even more so that Mrs. Toronyai, after her Debrecen graduate son read the letters patent—illiterate as she was, she must have grasped the fact that the letter truthfully belonged to her brother—have it to her children to play with. One is inclined to believe that the family was not nearly as indifferent as they sought to convince the court and that the letters patent, said to have been tossed about quite a deal, never had seen a dunghill or been shredded by children's hands, because it never actually existed.

The Torna and the Szepsi bootmakers removed the authenticating seal from the letters because they were illiterate and ignorant of the significance of the document. As one witness stated, they "understood little about reading and writing" and defaced the documents out of sheer ignorance. The third bootmaker's foolish act attests to quite a different mentality. János Csajtai, the Vas County nobleman who cut out a pattern-design for boots from his patent, was not altogether ignorant, although he did sign his name with an "X" on the contract selling his house. However, a seventy-year-old noble could remember going to school with him. Even though this bootmaker could not write his name, he presumably could read, though his reading skills did not enable him to cope with a letters patent written in Latin. As opposed to the case of the Torna County noble, this seemingly similar moronic act attests not to ignorance of and indifference to writing, but rather is an extreme manifestation of the self-assurance of a nobleman living in an oral society.

In 1744 a Keszthely freeman recalled that a seventeenth-century castle defender, when asked about his patent of nobility, "placed his hand on his sword and said: 'In these times, this is my letters patent!'" Similarly, a Komárom soldier announced that he had "no need of any privilege, since he had his sword, and that was [his] privilege".[90] When, also in the seventeenth century, one member of the Lázár family visited his relatives serving in a border castle to persuade them to inquire about their lost letters patent, they "rattled their arms hanging on the rack and said 'we have our letters patent here.'" In other words, they thought it superfluous and humiliating to have to give written evidence of their nobility, which they took for granted.[91] The previously mentioned bootmaker, János Csajtai, was of the same opinion. He figured that whether or not he cut up his letters patent, he would still be a noble. Yet by then, he had a history of destroying papers; previously, the county sub-prefect had him flogged for having torn up an official county document—a petition submitted against him.[92] Such gestures were spectacular outbursts against the written law abounding in strange Latin lingo, seedy shysters' ruses and writing in general. They were manifestations of a mentality of an oral society that disbelieved writing but credited words uttered by an honest person. By the mid-eighteenth century, however, with the spread of literacy in Sopron County, neither the hazy memories of the honor of the sword nor oral testimonies were worth much against writing. Thus, the Csajtai family remained excluded from the nobility.

Illiterate College Student: A Swindler's Lesson

A Vas County court case sheds light on the problems of oral traditions, literacy and illiteracy. In 1733 János Körmendi, the eldest son of a lower noble family of Kolta in Vas County, set out on a long journey; the Calvinist boy had decided to attend a higher school in Miskolc. Although his mother had a premonition that she never would see her son again and grieved greatly, his father was adamant that he go. He dressed János, supplied him with books, sewed travel money into his coat and set him on his journey. The eighteen- or nineteen-year-old young man was a lean, tanned lad with a round face, black hair, thick eyebrows, black eyes and "a little black down on his chin". A year later he wrote his mother from Miskolc and then disappeared forever. Whether he died of disease or failed to return for other reasons was never discovered.[93]

Thirty years later, however, a young lawyer appeared in Kolta and told the villagers he was the barrister of the Nagyvárad (Oradea) Chapter, was named János Körmendi and claimed he was none other than the son of the student who had disappeared. He paid a visit to his "grandmother" and asked her to recognize him as her grandson. According to witnesses, the noblewoman told the youth she never had seen before, "My dear sir, I might call you my son judging by your years, but that you should be the son of my son János, I cannot believe". In other words, he was too old to be her grandson. The mentality of the age is well characterized by the fact that this was not all that persuaded the lady to distrust the man. Not only did his features not resemble those of the vanished student, but also "her son and all her family had been Calvinists, but this one was a Papist". Her distant grandson tried to put her doubts to rest by saying his father had become a Papist, when he married, and "he won many goods and chattels, and I myself have serfs and have no desire to live in this land". That is, the Kolta nobles did not need to worry—he had no intention of sharing the estate or claiming his inheritance.

What was the lawyer up to, then, when he visited his so-called relatives? The answer became clear: nobility. Sándor Körmendi, the Kolta nobleman, was the guardian of the family's letters and deeds. The Nagyvárad lawyer was put up in his house and asked to see the family documents, especially the letters patent. The suspicious Sándor Körmendi, however, denied he had the letters patent. Well-educated in matters of law, the young man then went to the chapter of the next town, which was where such matters were dealt with in the county, and demanded a copy of the document.

Hundreds of miles away in Nagyvárad, János Körmendi told quite a different story about his journey to Vas County. He said he had visited his sister, who was the wife of the Vas County magistrate, and went to Kolta because his grandmother had "expressed a desire to invite her grandson to live there". This circumstance set even a not particularly suspicious nobleman thinking: "How come", he asked the lawyer, "she recognized you as her grandson so soon, never having seen you before?" Körmendi had the answer ready: "My grandmother was as hospitable as if she had seen me all my life." Because János Körmendi wanted to prove his nobility to the county court, his relatives—so the lawyer said—offered to issue him a certificate. This, however, he refused, saying "I have enough letters recently issued by the chapter and will use these for evidence more easily than such a certificate".

János Körmendi, as one would rightly assume, was no nobleman. He did use his real name, though, and his father (his namesake) really had gone to

Nagyvárad from Vas County. But these constitute just about the only true elements of his story. János Körmendi's real father belonged to another socially mobile layer of society—he was an itinerant craftsman. That the witty lawyer nearly successfully forged his ancestry and entered the noble class, and that in the end his swindling was denounced, is largely due to the level of illiteracy in eighteenth-century Hungary.

The older János Körmendi, the lawyer's father, arrived in Nagyvárad from Vas County and registered with the local guild as a tailor roughly at the same time that his noble namesake, a student, set off to Miskolc and disappeared. His fellow guild members remembered the older János Körmendi to be different in every respect from the lean, tanned student with a little black down on his chin: "he was short and stout, had a round face, blonde hair and moustache, with ruddy complexion". What caused his would-be-noble son's failure, and what set the tailor apart from the college student, were not only exterior features, but also that the tailor could not read or write—a fact everyone knew.

"János Körmendi was an uneducated man", remembered the tailor quoted above, "to the extent that he couldn't even write down his own name. That he might have been a college student is unimaginable." Eight other Nagyvárad witnesses unanimously asserted that the one-time tailor's being a "college student is unthinkable, since he knew not how to write". "He was illiterate", stated a noble lawyer with whom János Körmendi had lived eighteen years before. "He couldn't even write his name, and it is impossible that he should ever have been a college student, for he knew no Latin. He did mention, however, that he used to be a swineherd, and used to make his own moccasins from bark."

The illiteracy of the tailor was revealed in his environment several times. His colleagues noticed he never wrote a letter to his distant relatives, and when he was elected guildmaster, "he had his sums written by another tailor named Sartoris". A Nagyvárad citizen's curiosity was roused by the fact that the elder Körmendi "could not spell out his name, and this he knows because when on one occasion he borrowed money, he had the contract formulated by another, and even had his name signed by this other, in the presence of witnesses".

Two decades beforehand, János Körmendi spoke about his being a swineherd in Vas County, yet when he became an acclaimed craftsman and head of the tailors' guild, he recalled his bygone youth in quite a different way. He kept flaunting his nobility, and the distant relatives in Vas County grew more and more distinguished. In the months preceding his death he went so far as to claim his sister was the wife of the Vas County magistrate. His behavior must have been occasioned by the fact that his sons were apparently even more socially upwardly mobile than their father, who had risen from being a swineherd to become a guildmaster. One son went to grammar school and eventually entered the clergy. The other, János, who sought to prove his nobility in Vas County, was also well educated and became a lawyer. This social rise cannot have escaped the attention of the family's environment. One member of the Nagyvárad tailors' guild, who was a noble himself, remembered how he used to joke with his colleague János Körmendi: "Now that his son János attended school"—the old witness used to tell the old János Körmendi often—"You have a school-goer son, old man, and before you know it, he will be a better man that yourself, for he learns Latin", referring to the fact that his father could not even write his name.

János Körmendi, when he was a young tailor in the town, told his host that his former name was Ivánczi and that he had learned the trade in Körmend. He was unwilling to recall his modest start later, but an itinerant tailor exposed him. These itinerant craftsmen served as a form of eighteenth-century communication. A Nagyvárad tailor, Körmendi's fellow guild member, had heard "from a relative that he is only called Körmendi because he learnt his trade in Körmend. He might well call himself a nobleman, yet he is no more than a peasant named Ivánczi."

There is just one circumstance the vast amount of case records fail to clarify: where the son of the tailor, the younger János Körmendi, learned about the existence and disappearance of his namesake. They cannot have been schoolmates, because the young Kolta nobleman was a Calvinist; the tailor, a Catholic. Maybe he heard about the death of a man with his name or came across a grave bearing his name. As aggressive a social climber as he was, the young lawyer realized the opportunities that ubiquitous illiteracy and scanty communication links between the remote regions of the country had to offer. So he set himself to the task of shifting class. He applied to the Vas County administration for the recognition of his nobility and brought up his grandfather's "recently found" will.

The will actually had been formulated by János Körmendi. However, he underestimated his prospective family members, who were far above average with regard to literacy among Vas County lower nobles. Both of his "uncles", Simon and Sándor Körmendi, were literate and Latin-speaking people—a point that they proudly stressed in their testimonies—and both kept the family letters in good order and "read them on countless occasions". The will, they announced, was a fake. Although their father had been a lieutenant in the rebel army, their uncle, contrary to what the will stated, was never a soldier, and "no memories of their armor or arms mentioned in the will have in truth been preserved in the family". The will suggested that János Körmendi was Prince Francis Rákóczi II's captain, but he had not been born in 1711 when the Rákóczi war ended, nor were his parents even married then. In addition, the goods and chattels mentioned in the will were not among the family's possession, and no Ádám was known by the family, the other uncle said. Anyone around when István Körmendi died could testify that he never could have dictated the will, because he died five years before the will was written. The witnesses of the will were fictitious, and "the witness never had heard of such people".

The counterfeit will was written by a clever shyster—János Körmendi was aware he could not leave anything to himself, or he would have the family up in arms against him. Consequently, he only sought to prove his descent. For the sake of greater credibility, his "father" János apart, he created a son called Ádám, likewise given up as lost.

The court case dug up the shyster's real family roots. Old Nádalja serfs unanimously maintained that they could remember a serf who fit the description: he had been a short, round-faced, blond-haired man with a red moustache who went to Körmend to learn the tailor's trade and later sent a message to his relatives from Nagyvárad.

The lessons of the story of the hapless shyster seeking to prove his nobility are many. The role of the witnesses is important; whether they signed their name with an "X" or properly, they were considered suitable to be called upon and could give verbal testimony concerning the authenticity of a written document. Consequently, the will containing unknown witnesses immediately gave it away as a forgery. The noble family kept account of its family tree and its relatives, for only then could they guarantee the order of succession and guard themselves against problems caused by sham relatives turning up and demanding their share. In a society that was more or less immobile and whose members rarely embarked on long journeys, geographically mobile persons such as students, soldiers and itinerant craftsmen assumed an important role in conveying information.[94]

In addition, people were aware of who could write and who could not, and even decades later they could remember that the guildmaster had his name signed by someone else. There were no identity cards back in the eighteenth century, nor had photography been invented yet; and therefore, when it came to describing people, literacy was considered to be one of an individual's distinguishing features.

Illiterate Lower Nobles in a Contemporary Comedy

The fundamental methodological problem with the history of mentality is that this type of research cannot reveal what percentage of a given group is characterized by the diagrammed state of mind. One of the most popular eighteenth-century plays—or to be more precise, an interlude in a school drama—entitled "The Marriage of Mihály Kocsonya" clearly shows that the image and system of beliefs of the illiterate and orally minded lower nobles drawn from ancestry cases is not unlike the way their contemporaries saw them.

The interlude, probably written by the Pauline monks Márton Billisics and Mihály Szabadhelyi, was first performed in 1756 at the Sátoraljaújhely grammar school. In the play, Péter Berbencze, an indigent Hungarian nobleman, tries to marry his rather old daughter to an even poorer nobleman, Mihály Kocsonya, who when asked about his estate does not reply but scratches his head instead.

The play opens with the father dressed in tattered clothes poking about in a trunk filled with old letters. Enter the suitor, Mihály Kocsonya, and Berbencze hands him his letters patent. Kocsonya exclaims, "Ho, ho, Mister Berbencze, sir! I see you are a nobleman." To which Berbencze replies, "Certainly, I have always considered myself one. I am about to present my letters patent as evidence. I am surprised that the honorable county should dare to call me into question", and he continues to enumerate the heroic deeds of his forebears, going back to the times of King Béla the Blind in the twelfth century. "If you believe me not", he goes on, "read this charter or take a look at the royal seal. You are, perhaps, a more literate man than I am." However, neither the suitor nor the father is able to read the royal deed. The future son-in-law then draws his own letters patent from his bootleg and sticks it under the father's nose, saying "If you do not believe, here, read this." The would-be father-in-law then stops being skeptical (as he could not read it) and says, "I believe you, my dear sir", and so both give up trying to decipher the letters patent.[95]

Mihály Kocsonya is a caricature of the eighteenth-century estateless poor noble. Messing up Latin legal terms—saying "porcus juris" (law's pig) instead of *corpus juris* (body of law, i.e. lawbook)—and flaunting their only treasures—the letters patent—due to their illiteracy, in light of the ancestry cases the two lower nobles were not grossly exaggerated figures.

CHAPTER 5

AN OUTLOOK IN TIME: NATIONALITIES AND THE SPREAD OF LITERACY AFTER THE AUSTRO-HUNGARIAN COMPROMISE

A researcher on the literacy of peasants and nobles in the sixteenth through the eighteenth centuries has no choice but (1) to collect the crosses and signatures on available documents of the period from archives and (2) to read through testimonies that reveal whether someone could read or simply had a thorough look at letters but, being illiterate, did not comprehend their contents.

A literacy researcher is better off when he or she examines the period after 1870. From that date, censuses were held every ten years that gathered information on literacy and illiteracy and even noted the number of people who only could read. The first such census, which surveyed the entire population, presented a frightening picture. In 1870 three-fifths (58.16 percent) of the population of historic Hungary (which consisted of Hungary, Transylvania, Croatia and Slavonia, Fiume and the marches) above the age of six could neither read nor write. In Hungary alone this figure was 51.01 percent; in Transylvania, 78.67 percent; and in Croatia and Slavonia, over four-fifths of the population (84.1 percent).[1]

The data gathered in the censuses also depict the dynamic spread of literacy as a result of the school reforms initiated by the minister of education, Baron József Eötvös. In 1868 elementary schooling became obligatory. Despite these efforts, however, the world of written culture remained foreign to significant groups of the population even in the early twentieth century. Additionally, the statistics on literacy in the counties highlights the vast differences among the diverse geographical and economic regions that constituted historic Hungary (see Maps 5.1 and 5.2). The censuses indicate

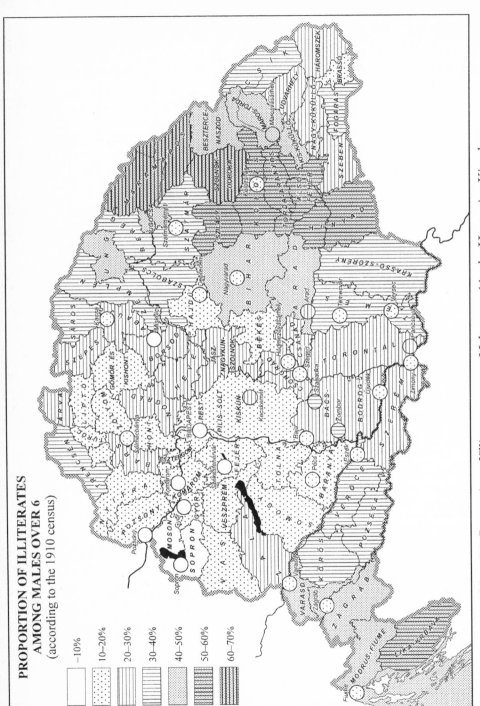

Map. 5.1. Proportion of Illiterates among Males over 6 in the Hungarian Kingdom

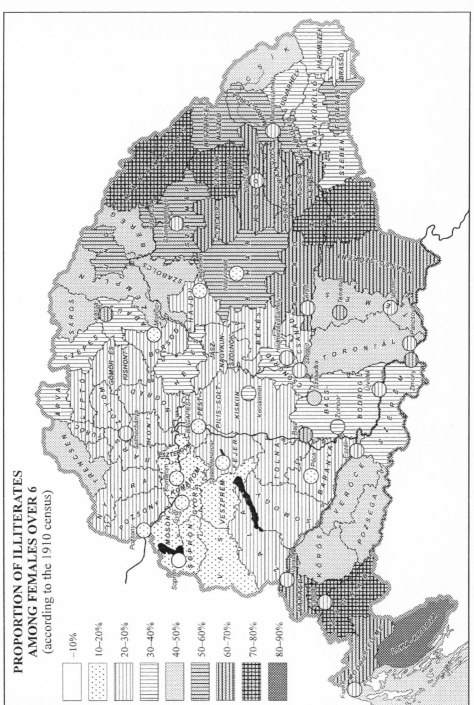

PROPORTION OF ILLITERATES AMONG FEMALES OVER 6
(according to the 1910 census)

- –10%
- 10–20%
- 20–30%
- 30–40%
- 40–50%
- 50–60%
- 60–70%
- 70–80%
- 80–90%

Map. 5.2. Proportion of Illiterates among Females over 6 in the Hungarian Kingdom

that of all of Hungary's geographical regions, literacy was most widespread in Transdanubia (the region most exhaustively covered in this book for the period comprising the sixteenth through eighteenth centuries), while the strongholds of illiteracy were Croatia, Slavonia and some Transylvanian counties. More important than regional differences, however, were the discrepancies in the spread of literacy among individual nationalities.

The 1870 census—the first to investigate literacy—did not devote enough attention to the different levels of literacy among the various nationalities. However, from the 1880 census on, the highly diverse literacy indices of individual nationalities were recorded. In 1890 almost two-thirds of the German population and over half of the Hungarians could write, but the proportion of literates among Ruthenians was less than ten percent (see table 5.1).

Table 5.1

Proportion of Literates in Hungary by Nationality in 1890
(Including Children under Six)

Native Language	Men (%)	Women (%)	Total (%)
Hungarian	59.1	48.2	53.6
German	68.1	58.2	63.0
Slovak	50.6	36.7	43.2
Croatian	50.2	34.7	42.4
Serbian	39.4	22.2	30.9
Romanian	10.9	8.2	14.1
Ruthenian	12.6	6.8	9.7

The high literacy figures in Transdanubia can be explained by the fact that the two most educated nationalities, Germans and Hungarians, constituted the majority of the population in this area.

Data on Vas County, the focus of this research project, are quite abundant, since the village summaries of the 1870 census, which were destroyed in other counties, have survived. These provide detailed information on how many women and men were literate, illiterate or could only read.

In Vas County 46.3 percent of the population could neither read nor write in 1870. There were huge differences, however, within this figure; the literacy rates of individual districts reveal a strong division between a preponderantly literate northern section and an illiterate southern region (see table 5.2).

Table 5.2

Percentage of Illiterates in Vas County in 1870 (of the Entire Population)

District	Illiterates (%)	District	Illiterates (%)
Szombathely	40.9	Felsőlendva	53.8
Rohonc	21.9	Sárvár	39.4
Felsőkemenes	37.1	Répcemellék	32.1
Németújvár	47.3	Kőszeg	26.1
Körmend	48.0	Vép	39.7
Füzes	42.0	Pornó	40.7
Pinkafő	25.7	Felsőőr	36.6
Őrség	53.2	Kiscell	33.8
Alsókemenes	46.5	Jánosháza	46.2
Csákány	45.4	Petánc	74.9
Hegyhát	57.6	Muraszombat	75.8
Szentelek	52.7	Szentgotthárd	57.2
	Vas County Total: 46.3		

In the district with the lowest rate of illiteracy, Rohonc, only 21.9 percent of the population was classified as illiterate, while the district with the highest rate, Muraszombat, had a 75.8 percent rate of illiteracy. Vas was a county of sharp contradictions when it came to the spread of literacy; there were far fewer differences in most other Transdanubian counties. In Veszprém, another large county, the best results came from the town of Veszprém (37.5 percent illiterate) and the worst from the Csesznek district (47.7 percent), but the difference between the two is merely 10 percent. Even in the large Zala County illiteracy ranged from 43.2 percent to 77.4 percent. In Sopron County the district of Sopron headed the list with an illiteracy rate of 32.8 percent, but even the least-developed Rábaköz district only had 9 percent more illiterates. The great difference between the Rohonc and the Muraszombat districts in Vas County clearly indicates that the area was comprised of two differently developed regions; that is, the divide between a more literate northern Transdanubia and an underdeveloped southern Transdanubia ran through the county. True, in 1870, Vas County had the highest number of districts (twenty-four) in all of historic Hungary. However, in adjacent districts the rate of illiteracy was roughly identical, indicating natural divides.

Vas County's rate of illiteracy fell in the middle of those of the Transdanubian counties (see table 5.3), and the northern counties of Transdanubia overall were more advanced. In 1870 in Moson County only 29.6 percent of the population (including children younger than six) were unable to read and write, and in Sopron County, only 35.0 percent. Vas County's southern neighbor, Zala County, however, had an illiteracy rate of 64.1 percent.

Table 5.3

Percentage of Illiterates in Transdanubia in 1870
(of the Entire Population, Excluding Royal Towns)

County	%
Moson	29.6
Sopron	35.0
Veszprém	40.9
Győr	42.0
Komárom	43.9
Tolna	44.4
Vas	46.3
Fejér	46.3
Esztergom	47.7
Baranya	50.9
Somogy	52.9
Zala	64.1

The differences in Transdanubia, however, were inconsequential compared to the contrasts among the individual regions of historic Hungary. While in the northwest Transdanubian counties of Sopron and Moson, not far from Vienna, one-third of the population was illiterate, in parts of Transylvania and Partium (the Kővár region, Doboka, Hunyad and Zaránd counties) over nine tenth of the population was unable to read or write in 1870. In Zaránd County, 96.5 percent of the population (including children under six) could neither read nor write, and only two percent of all women could write.

The two largest regions of Hungary, Transdanubia in the west and Transylvania in the east, also bear comparison. The twelve Transdanubian counties had a population of 2.469 million, 47.44 percent of whom (1.166 million) were illiterate. Transylvania had a population of 2.101 million in 1870, 1.726 million of whom could neither read nor write (78.67 percent). Despite significant regional differences and high illiteracy rates in its three southern counties, Transdanubia was, as a whole, one of the country's most developed regions.

In calculating the proportion of crosses and signatures Transdanubian data from the 1870 census can be compared to the results of the 1769 socage survey that provide information about the literacy of the village and market town élite (village mayors, jurors). This comparison reveals the same, at first glance surprising, conclusion that has been established often in Western Europe—namely, that the regional distribution of literacy fundamentally characterizes a society and therefore proportionally changes very slowly.[2]

Both in 1769 and a century later, in 1870, Transdanubia's two most developed northwestern counties, Moson and Sopron, stand out. In 1769 forty to fifty percent of the village and town principals (village mayors, jurors) could write their names, and by 1870 only 29.6 to 35 percent of the population was illiterate. The other pole of the region remained similarly unchanged: in both 1769 and 1870 southern Transdanubia (Zala, Somogy and Baranya counties) was the least developed. Less than five percent of village mayors could write in 1769 in these counties, and in 1870, 50.9 to 64.1 percent of the population could neither read nor write. Between the northwestern positive and the southern negative poles was the Transdanubian center, consisting of Vas, Fejér, Győr, Veszprém and Tolna counties. Slight changes did occur in this area within the one hundred-year span between the two surveys. In 1769 Fejér County was ahead of Veszprém in the spread of literacy; a century later the situation had reversed. However, this did not affect the overall picture significantly, and the literacy map of Transdanubia essentially remained unchanged during the period under discussion.

The 1870 census, therefore, confirms what the Hungarian historian Kálmán Benda (1913–94) concluded from the answers given to the questions in the 1769 survey: the spread of literacy in villages largely depended on whether or not the villagers were willing to move out of their narrow world to trade in distant towns where they might gather new and different experiences, thereby triggering a desire to be able to read. Northern Vas County opened such trade links—Vienna, Graz and Sopron must have been enticing—but the areas south of the Rába River were left out.[3]

Whether considering the results of the 1910, 1870 censuses or of the 1769 investigation, the borders between the three Transdanubian groups—

(1) the widely literate northwest, (2) the underdeveloped southern areas and (3) the in-between areas—did not change with regard to the spread of literacy. In 1910 Moson County topped the literacy list in Transdanubia, and Zala came last, just as they had forty years before. The change is nevertheless immense: while in 1870 the two counties were separated by a rate of 37 percent (60 percent literacy in Moson, and a mere 23 percent in Zala), the difference was only 13 percent by 1910. With the introduction of compulsory schooling in 1868, the differences leveled out, and the less literate areas developed at a faster pace than the more advanced. While in Zala County the proportion of literates increased from 23.1 percent to 75 percent between 1870 and 1910, Moson County only experienced an increase from 60 to 80 percent, even though it was more advanced in the first place. Evidently compulsory schooling accounts for this development, a point that is confirmed by the distribution of writing ability among the different age groups. The older the individual was, the lower the probability that he or she could write. In 1880, 42.6 percent of the population in Hungary from age fifteen to nineteen was illiterate; this proportion among the age group over sixty was 58 percent.

Not only the individual Transdanubian counties but also Vas County's smaller regions underwent a leveling process at the end of the nineteenth century (the county, divided into twenty-four districts in 1870, was later reorganized, the district borders were altered, and the same county was divided into ten new districts). By 1900 the regional differences had diminished in comparison to three decades earlier. Southwestern Tótság, inhabited by Slovenes, was still the least developed region. Even in 1900 this area had an illiteracy rate of fifty-four percent, while thirty years prior only one-quarter of its population could write. A new division then emerged in Vas County. The villages southeast of the Rába River approached the northern districts in literacy rates, and so the western regions on the Austrian-Styrian border—the Tótság, Szentgotthárd and Némettújvár districts—comprised Vas County's least developed sections. All other parts had a literacy rate of sixty-five to seventy percent. This leveling process continued; a decade later, in 1910, the larger, developed part of the county had a literacy rate of sixty-nine to seventy-three percent, and the Szentgotthárd and Nemetújvár districts followed suit with sixty-three to sixty-four percent. The most backward area developed at the greatest pace in this case; between 1900 and 1910 the literacy rate increased from fifty-four to sixty-three percent in the Tótság region.

In response to the realities of the time, census writers created a separate category for people who could read but not write. This kind of partial literacy, which was very difficult to measure in earlier centuries, was primarily characteristic of women (see table 5.4). Writing was a man's task in a peasant society, and it was generally considered enough if women could read prayer-books. Girls, therefore, were taken out of school earlier, and most of them would have learned only to read by then, not write. As they did not have the opportunity to practice, women forgot writing skills more easily than men did.

Table 5.4

Percentage of Readers-Only in Hungary in 1870 (over the age of six)

	Men (%)	Women (%)
Hungary (in the narrow sense)	8.16	17.46
Transylvania	3.85	6.08
Croatia–Slavonia	0.65	1.01
Fiume (Rijeka)	0.11	0.08
Marches	6.11	4.77
Hungary (in the whole kingdom)	7.14	13.88

The number of women who could only read was uniformly higher than that of men. Before compulsory schooling was introduced, this strange type of literacy followed the distribution pattern of the population that could write. That is, those who could only read were in abundance in areas where there were numerous writers as well. The reverse was equally true: where there were few writers, there were fewer people who only could read. However, with the introduction of compulsory schooling, the reading-but-not-writing form of literacy gradually disappeared, and everyone who went to school learned to do both. In 1880, 6.5 percent of the population could read but not write; in 1900, the same figure was only 2.9 percent.

The lines of development in the spread of literacy are fairly clear on county or district maps. However, upon closer examination of the districts, a relatively clear picture transforms into a multicolored patchwork.

For example, Berkifalu and Harasztifalu in Vas County are separated by three kilometers. Both used to be inhabited by Croatian Catholic peasants, and both belonged to the same estate. In 1870, 58.9 percent of males over the age of seven could write in Harasztifalu, but the same figure was only 39.6 percent in Berkifalu. Also in Vas County, in the Szentgotthárd District there were four German Catholic villages on the Rába River: Nagyfalu, Badafalva, Raks and Gyanafalva, each two to four kilometers apart. Geographical vicinity notwithstanding, the rate of literate men varied immensely: in Badafalva it was 38.2 percent; in Raks, 42.7 percent; in Gyanafalva, 62.8 percent; and in Nagyfalu, 80.1 percent.[4]

A number of historical sources on these villages have survived, yet there seems to be no explanation of the variations in literary rates. For example, in two neighboring German villages, Kertes and Németsároslak, the literacy rate varied greatly in 1870. Eight hundred people lived in Németsároslak at this time, and five hundred eighty in Kertes—all German and all Catholic. However, in Kertes only 21.8 percent of all men could write, while in Németsároslak three times as many were able to do so (64 percent). Kondorfa and Farkasfa are adjacent Hungarian Catholic villages on the Szentgotthárd estate. Four hundred thirty-seven people lived in Farkasfa in 1870, and seven hundred forty-three in Kondorfa. In Kondorfa 29.7 percent of the men could write, but in Farkasfa only a handful (4.4 percent) were able to do so.

Similar examples can be found in the northeastern regions of Vas County. Kissitke and Nagystike (Small and Big Sitke), Alsószeleste and Felsőszeleste (Lower and Upper Szeleste), Szentivánfa and Uraiújfalu are neighboring villages with purely Hungarian inhabitants, yet the literacy level differed greatly among them. In Kissitke 46.9 percent of the men could read; this figure was 78.6 percent in Nagysitke. True, while Kissitke had a majority of Catholics, only one-third of the population was Catholic in Nagysitke. However, both Alsószeleste and Felsőszeleste were Catholic villages and had roughly the same population (325 and 367, respectively). Nevertheless, in Alsószeleste 73.7 percent of the men were literate, but only 46.6 percent were in the slightly larger Felsőszeleste. Szentivánfa and Uraiújfalu were also neighboring villages, and both were half-Catholic and half-Lutheran. The literacy rate was worse in the more populous Uraiújfalu, where 31.3 percent of the men could read and write, while 68.4 percent could in the smaller Szentivánfa.

Studying literacy in seventeenth-century England (from a richer assortment of source materials than in Hungary), the English historian David Cressy observed that while the differences between the greater regions could be pinpointed safely, researchers are at a loss to account for the discrepancies in literacy between villages that were otherwise identical.[5] Individuals cannot be lumped under narrow headings, and neither can villages. A closer inspection of the literacy rates among individual peasants and nobles revealed that within the broad limits set by the given class, literacy largely depended on personal mentality. The spread of literacy is a multidimensional phenomenon, and it cannot be explained by a single factor. The above examples call attention to just that: the level of literacy will vary in neighboring villages otherwise identical in religion, nationality, geographical location and economic and social status. An assertive teacher, a priest who paid greater attention to his congregation than other clerics, may have fostered a desire to learn to read and write. Perhaps the example of a bright, educated peasant returning from town might have encouraged others. Scholars probably will never know why it happened. It is certain, however, that the historical magnifying glass should be focused on the districts, and then the whirling colored patches reveal a clear picture: the dividing lines of literacy.

An Outlook in Space: The European Context

The differences between the literacy rates of Early Modern Hungary and those of the most developed countries of Europe (such as England or France) are striking. England and the Netherlands were the most literate countries in the world during this period. In the mid-seventeenth century, during the stormy years of the Civil War, Englishmen had to sign oaths of allegiance several times; consequently there is ample data concerning the state of literacy in various parts of the country in the form of thousands of signatures and signs. On examining these, David Cressy found that in England in the 1640s some seventy percent of men and ninety percent of women were illiterate. With the sixteenth-century situation, however, only estimates can be made. Cressy avers that in the middle of the sixteenth century, eighty percent of men and ninety-five percent of women could neither read nor write. The percentages around 1500 may have been ninety and ninety-nine respectively, although this is a mere conjecture as even in England no statistical data about literacy can be identified for this period.

The situation in eighteenth-century Britain is better known. According to David Cressy's estimates based on available sources, at the beginning of the century fifty-five percent of men and seventy-five percent of women could write their own names. In 1754, it was stipulated by law in Britain that the marriage register had to be signed by both bridegrooms and brides.

From that time on, therefore, the development of literacy can be traced on the basis of precise data. By the middle of the eighteenth century, the majority of men knew how to write, with only forty percent being unable to do so, while the rate among women was sixty percent. In the second half of the eighteenth century, however, this dynamic progress came to a sudden halt until the early nineteenth century. This most probably was due to the social transformation that was took place as a consequence of the Industrial Revolution—internal emigration and early child labor were not conducive to literacy. In the second half of the nineteenth century, though, illiteracy in Britain all but disappeared. Between 1850 and 1911, the proportion of illiterate men decreased from thirty to one percent and that of women also fell from forty-five to one percent.[6]

The most researched of all countries with regard to literacy during this period is France. From the age of Louis XIV, it was compulsory for brides, bridegrooms and witnesses to place their signatures in the register when marrying, thus leaving material for literacy researchers. In the eighteenth century the number of literate persons almost doubled in France, even though at the time of the outbreak of the French Revolution they were in the minority. From 1686 to 1690, the proportion of literate persons in France grew from twenty-one percent to thirty-seven percent from 1786 to 1790. French women also lagged behind men; literacy among them grew from fourteen to twenty-seven percent within a hundred years, while among men the rate increased from twenty-nine to forty-seven percent.

Averages that apply to entire countries, however, happen to hide what is really relevant—the huge regional differences that were so characteristic of France. The seventeenth-century imaginary dividing line connecting Geneva and Saint Malo, which separated the literate northern and eastern parts of France from the more backward western and southern parts was still clearly visible a century later and, in the case of women's literacy, as late as 1866. This indicates that the regional divisions of the spread of literacy, as an important index of development, take a long time to equalize.

At the time of the French Revolution, there were huge regional differences in the literacy of men. In Normandy and in the counties north and east of Paris, ninety percent of all bridegrooms signed the register. In Brittany and on the Atlantic coast, less than ten percent did so. In central France, in the secluded regions of the Massif Central, sixteen percent of men signed the marriage register while only four percent of women did. In Alsace-Lorraine the numbers were eighty-three percent and forty-four percent respectively. These differences did not decrease until the second half of the century. In this respect there was some similarity between Hungary and France, even though the literacy rate in France was much higher than in Hungary.

By the end of the nineteenth century, illiteracy effectively was eradicated in France. While in 1854 thirteen percent of bridegrooms were unable to sign the marriage register, the number decreased to a mere five percent by 1900. The proportion of illiterate brides decreased from forty-six to six percent within the same period. Compulsory schooling put an end to the differences between male and female literacy, which had been a significant feature in earlier centuries.[7]

Due to a lack of relevant research, there is no statistical data on literacy available from the Austrian provinces of the Habsburg Empire from the sixteenth to eighteenth centuries, although this information would have been highly useful in exploring the Hungarian scenario. After modern censuses were introduced, the data testified to huge discrepancies among the provinces, in comparison to which the differences among the various French or British regions are dwarfed. In 1900 in the most developed provinces of the Habsburg Empire, in Upper and Lower Austria and in Bohemia and Moravia, the rate of illiteracy among members of the population aged ten and above was a mere three to four percent. At the same time, in Galicia, fifty-six percent of the population of those ten years of age and older was illiterate; in Bukovina, sixty-six percent; and in Dalmatia, seventy-three percent.[8]

There are ample sources in Italy on the spread of education and culture and on schools in the Early Modern Age; however, no statistics are available on literacy before the introduction of censuses in the second half of the nineteenth century. In the vicinity of Turin in 1710, excluding the town itself, ninety-four percent of the brides and eight-one percent of the bridegrooms were illiterate. By 1790 the percentages decreased to seventy and thirty-five respectively. In the Campania province of the Neapolitan Kingdom in the mid-eighteenth century, 76.3 percent of those submitting tax returns could put only a cross on the document, although only well-off men were expected to prepare them at all. The marked difference between the northern and southern provinces is evident even from this single piece of information. Censuses reveal that in the whole of Italy in the late nineteenth century, illiteracy—which earlier had reached astonishingly high proportions (indices of illiteracy were higher in Italy than in Hungary)—was rapidly diminishing. On the other hand the gap between northern and southern Italy was enormous and did not disappear by the early twentieth century—in the northern region of Piedmont in 1901 eighteen percent of the population above six years old was illiterate, and in Sicily the figure was seventy-one percent.[9]

It is especially useful to compare the spread of literacy in Hungary and Poland. In the voivodeship of Cracow at the end of the sixteenth century, the landed nobility was largely literate: 96.7 percent of the nobles who bore the title *generosus* and usually owned several villages could sign their names, and this figure remained unchanged for the next two centuries. The literacy of women, however, progressed rapidly: while in the late sixteenth century, fifty-one percent were analphabets, by the seventeenth century only twenty-two percent remained so. Women continued to catch up with men in the eighteenth century, when a mere fifteen percent put crosses on documents instead of signing their names. In the lower ranks of the landed gentry (*nobilis*), who owned one or at most two villages, the proportion of illiterates was twenty-four percent in the sixteenth century and sixteen percent in the following century.

In another study, the literacy of Polish noblemen was examined on the basis of tax returns submitted in and around Cracow. In 1564 forty-three percent of all noblemen were illiterate. There were vast differences between various strata of nobles: among those who had no serfs, ninety-one percent could not write their names, and the higher the position they occupied in the hierarchy, the higher the literacy rate. Only twenty-two percent of those paying over ten zloty in tax were analphabets.

Literacy was much more common among the nobility near Cracow than in western Hungary. This is no surprise, as it was the most developed region in Poland, and Cracow—the capital until 1569—was a large city, a trading center with a university and schools; the intellectual fervor of the town must have spread around its vicinity.

The vast Polish kingdom, however, comprised regions with very different levels of development, as did historic Hungary and France. In the voivodeship of Sandomierz in the seventeenth century the circumstances were very similar to those of the voivodeship of Cracow. Ninety-nine percent of the noblemen bearing the title of *generosus* and seventy-five percent of the *nobili* could write. On the other hand, the voivodeship of Lublin lagged behind: while the *generosi* were almost entirely literate, only sixty-five percent of the women, rather than four-fifths, could write. Of the *nobili*, compared to the eighty-four percent in and around Cracow, only seventy percent signed documents, while only one out of ten women could write their names in this social layer.

Even this appeared highly developed in comparison to Eastern Galicia, where eight percent of the magnates (*magnifici*), eleven percent of the *generosi* and seventy-two percent of *nobili* put crosses on documents instead of their names as late as the early eighteenth century. In 1764 two-thirds of the participants of the diet (*sejm*) could not authenticate documents with their signatures.[10] The rate of literacy of the nobility in western Hungary was behind that in the Cracow Voivodeship but significantly more developed than in eastern Galicia.

There was a large gap between Hungary and the developed, northwestern part of Europe with regard to schooling and the literacy rate. However, across the Hungarian border to the east and south, the vast differences between Hungary and Russia and the Balkan countries were conspicuous: with regard to literacy, Hungary was much more developed.

No reliable data is available on illiteracy in Russia for the sixteenth through eighteenth centuries, but Jeffrey Brooks, a historian of Russian literacy, gave his work on the period between 1861 and 1917 a telling title: *When Russia Learned to Read*. According to the 1897 census, only twenty-one percent (twenty-nine percent of men and thirteen percent of women) of Russians could read. Literacy attained the highest proportions in the Polish provinces of the empire, even though this was relative: twenty-nine percent of men and twenty-three percent of women could at least read. In the European part of Russia, twenty-eight percent of men and ten percent of women could read, while the relevant percentages in Siberia were only sixteen and three respectively. Rapid development, however, took place in the fifty years preceding World War I: while in 1880, four-fifths of new conscripts did not know how to write, in 1913 only thirty-two percent of these young men, just past school age, were illiterate.[11]

The Danube River and the Carpathian Mountains, which separated Hungary from the Balkan Peninsula, demarcated the line between two worlds of literacy. Catholic missionaries, accustomed to Latin and Italian, noticed in seventeenth-century Moldavia and Wallachia not only that they could understand the Romanian tongue of the people living there better than of those in neighboring countries, but also that hardly anyone knew how to read or write, and even some of the Greek Orthodox bishops could read only with difficulty. "Of the nobles and tradesmen, few know the Ruthenian or the Slavic script", and even the majority of priests were illiterate, so the Jesuits found, although they may not have been impartial. In addition, in the seventeenth century youths aged sixteen to eighteen were sent from the Dalmatian, Bosnian and Albanian provinces to the Pontifical Illyrian College, which was set up in Fermo, Italy, to train missionaries, where they were expected to study theology and philosophy. These boys were mostly illiterate or at best semiliterate—they could read but not write.[12]

The population in Serbia was largely illiterate as late as the early nineteenth century. Hardly any of the leaders of the Serbian uprising could read or write; the ruling Prince Miloš was probably the only illiterate head of state in Europe at the time. According to his contemporaries, when Serbia became independent, neither the priests nor the monks could read or write. There was little improvement in subsequent decades: the 1866 census revealed that ninety-six percent of the population was illiterate; by the turn of the century, the figure was eighty-three percent. The Balkan peninsula remained very much a region of illiteracy even at the turn of the twentieth century: around 1900, of the population above six years of age, seventy-two percent in Bulgaria, sixty percent in Greece, seventy-eight percent in Romania and eighty-seven percent in Bosnia were illiterate.[13]

When compared to northwestern Europe, Central Europe's literacy rates were depressing, however, the gap that divided the Russian Empire and the Balkan countries from this region was not any smaller—compared to these areas, Central Europe appeared very developed indeed.

CONCLUSION

Whether contemporaries rejoiced or feared it, the spread of literacy was vastly overestimated in early modern Europe, especially literacy of the peasantry. In 1533 Thomas Moore wrote that three-fifths of England's population read the Bible fluently; twentieth-century English historians, however, inferred a much lower level of literacy from archival documents.[1]

In Hungary the engineer Ferenc Kováts suggested in the review *Mindenes Gyűjtemény* (Miscellaneous Collection) published in 1789 that a special newspaper should be produced for field workers, packed with useful tips about agriculture.[2] Kováts overestimated the circle of village readers, as did the Palatine and Archduke Alexander Leopold of the Habsburg dynasty in 1795 when, in his memorandum written for his brother, Emperor Francis, he expressed concern over the propaganda of the French Revolution having reached Hungarian villages and the Hungarian peasants reading anarchistic papers. The palatine thought he could thwart the excessive literacy of the peasantry by quietly closing down small village schools. "Regarding village schools, I am frankly at a loss to account for the need for them, and I fear they might pass knowledge to peasants that they have no need of whatsoever...Teaching reading and writing to village folks is, in my opinion, unnecessary here [in Hungary]...Experience has shown that once a peasant has learned to read and write...he will abandon the kind of field work that suits him best to waste time reading papers, books and pamphlets." The palatine echoed a recurrent fear of the eighteenth century: if too many peasants learn to read and write, who will harvest the crops?[3]

Mátyás Bél, the early eighteenth-century Hungarian polymath, also overrated the literacy of the peasantry. In his description of the Hungarian Kingdom, he focused on the peasants of Vas County and wrote, "Letters, too, are here in high esteem. In consequence, in order to be able to read books and write as village life demands, both sexes are willing to learn." True, he added, they learned only what they deemed necessary. In the first half of the eighteenth century, as noted earlier, very few Vas County peasants could write their names, and very few peasant children ever went to school. Where the great scholar obtained his perspective on the education of Vas County peasants is unknown, but the image he presented of peasant boys (and girls) flocking to school and of serfs reading books and writing is certainly not the picture that available resources support.[4]

Miklós Misztótfalusi Kis (1650–1702), the typographer, was more acutely aware of the sluggish spread of literacy in Hungary. After returning from developed Holland, he was shocked to see the contrast between Hungary's backwardness in the field of literacy compared to the level of Europe's most developed zone. In Holland, he wrote in the preface to his psalm book in 1686, "one would be at a loss trying to find one who could not read, among either the men or women". In Hungary, however, the spread of literacy was a goal that the printer argued for with anger and enthusiasm. "Understanding writing…is indeed a treasure, a noble thing, a whole world and happiness…to a nation and any private person; as opposed to illiteracy, which is filth, commonness, gloom, fear and plague." A knowledge of reading already had spread among "other good Christian nations…among whom we hide clandestinely, and seeing their immense pleasure in reading and writing, we cannot but laud their condition and be ashamed of our own".[5]

Ubiquitous illiteracy in Hungary not only caught the attention of Miklós Misztótfalusi Kis but also of foreign Catholic priests. A Franciscan monk in 1659 reported from Lippa to Rome that he operated a school as when he arrived there, "I was able to find but three people in the entire mission [meaning eight to nine hundred Catholics in Lippa and three villages] who could write or read".[6] The general circumstances under Turkish occupation here probably impeded the spread of education more than in the other Hungarian regions. Nicolaus Gotthal, vicar of the Bishop of Zagreb, however, reported to Rome in 1712 on the Zagreb area, which never had been occupied by the Turks: to dispense plenary indulgence was a problem there, because hardly anyone could recite the Salve Regina prayer "of those who could not read. Indeed there are many more, not only among the peasants but also the town-dwellers, who cannot read than who can read. I think the situation is similar in other places where there are fewer parish schools than in Italy." Based on his own experience, the vicar then decided that most citizens and peasants in Croatia and Hungary could not read in the early eighteenth century.[7]

There was, however, an Italian traveler who at the end of the eighteenth century was astonished by the high level of literacy in Hungary. The young Giuseppe Melograni arrived in Selmecbánya (Banská Štiavnica) from the Kingdom of Naples to study mining. In his letters, published by a Neapolitan paper, he presented Hungary to the people of southern Italy as an example to be followed: "nowhere to be found is such a miserable and forlorn person who could not write and read well…we are pleased to see that while their ladies speak of love elsewhere, their maids in the rooms, books in hand, argue about the laws of nature and all that concerns the rights of mankind".[8]

This spirited Italian student wrote these words during the intoxicating initial months of the French Revolution in May 1790. We have to consider that in his homeland in southern Italy, eighty to ninety percent of women were illiterate, even according to nineteenth-century censuses. One might have doubts about every maid in late eighteenth-century Selmecbánya discussing human rights with a book in hand; however, the civilized college town certainly must have appeared to be a highly developed place in the eyes of the excitable traveler who had come from a backward region in Italy. However, Selmecbánya, like many other small but civilized towns, was but a tiny spot of light on the primarily dark Central European literacy map. In this region the task of eradicating the "filth, gloom and plague" of illiteracy was left for the twentieth century.

APPENDIX

Table A1

Literacy in the Counties of Hungary (1870)
(proportion of those who could neither read nor write in the population above six years of age, including towns in the territory of the given county)

County	Men and Women	Only Women
Moson	16.88	19.16
Sopron	22.16	25.34
Gömör	22.56	23.30
Torna	28.78	29.49
Veszprém	29.25	33.40
Győr	29.95	34.35
Liptó	30.30	32.89
Pozsony	32.87	37.71
Komárom	33.06	37.92
Hont	33.10	35.67
Tolna	33.56	39.46
Zólyom	33.61	35.69
Fejér	34.30	39.06
Békés	34.69	37.71
Vas	34.96	38.63
Pest	36.50	42.21
Hajdú	36.71	39.71
Esztergom	36.97	40.99
Borsod	40.11	43.06

Table A1 cont'd

County	Men and Women	Only Women
Nógrád	40.14	39.70
Turóc	41.00	42.79
Baranya	41.24	44.34
Nyitra	42.21	46.14
Bars	42.30	43.68
Somogy	43.12	46.20
Jász–Kun	43.27	46.52
Abaúj	43.49	47.49
Árva	44.13	46.38
Szepes	44.53	45.83
Segesvár	44.73	47.86
Beszterce	46.25	47.81
Kőhalom	48.72	51.61
Brassó	49.88	57.40
Nagy-Sink	50.23	55.11
Medgyes	50.95	54.93
Heves	52.89	54.70
Csongrád	55.77	61.71
Csanád	55.88	61.36
Zala	56.69	60.42
Szabolcs	56.69	62.72
Bács	58.01	64.66
Szeben	59.21	65.03
Udvarhely	59.81	67.23
Bihar	59.94	62.20
Trencsén	60.71	64.00
Zemplén	61.10	64.94
Sáros	63.61	65.35
Torontál	64.50	70.10
Szatmár	66.59	72.38
Újegyház	68.70	76.27
Háromszék	69.93	76.77
Temes	70.82	76.69
Maros	72.62	81.60
Bereg	73.53	79.08
Aranyos	75.60	84.60
Ung	77.06	80.10
Kraszna	79.31	81.81

County	Men and Women	Only Women
Csík	79.34	84.16
Arad	79.40	83.16
Szászsebes	79.90	85.28
Kolozs	80.90	83.86
Szerdahely	81.00	86.30
Naszód	81.65	90.11
Ugocsa	81.69	86.08
Küküllő	82.19	85.03
Közép-Szolnok	82.66	86.48
Szászváros	83.66	88.18
Felső-Fehér	83.68	87.50
Krassó	85.15	91.74
Torda	86.99	90.37
Máramaros	87.58	91.43
Fogaras	87.67	93.69
Alsó-Fehér	89.61	92.62
Belső-Szolnok	89.66	93.03
Kővár	92.77	96.00
Doboka	93.20	95.19
Hunyad	94.50	96.78
Zaránd	95.70	98.07

Table A2

Proportion of Those Able to Write in the Counties and Towns of Hungary
(above six years of age)

	1880	1890	1900	1910
Hungary (without Croatia)	43.5	53.2	61.4	68.7
1. Right Side of the Danube River				
Baranya County	51.5	64.2	70.1	77.6
Pécs Town	71.6	74.5	81.2	84.9
Fejér County	62.5	71.3	76.9	80.7
Székesfehérvár Town	72.3	79.9	87.9	90.2
Győr County	63.0	73.0	79.1	83.4
Győr Town	73.0	78.5	87.8	89.7

Table A2 cont'd

	1880	1890	1900	1910
Komárom County	65.8	75.2	80.0	83.2
Komárom Town	68.6	76.6	85.9	89.9
Moson County	76.6	83.1	85.9	88.9
Somogy County	50.1	63.7	72.9	80.1
Sopron County	70.6	80.5	85.4	88.2
Sopron Town	82.1	85.2	92.1	95.0
Tolna County	61.4	72.2	77.2	81.7
Vas County	61.7	71.4	79.1	83.6
Veszprém County	63.5	72.5	79.5	83.9
Zala County	39.9	54.2	65.8	75.1
Total	58.4	69.1	76.4	81.8
2. Left Side of the Danube River				
Árva County	34.0	47.9	56.4	67.9
Bars County	51.3	60.1	67.4	75.9
Esztergom County	58.3	71.2	77.4	83.9
Hont County	54.3	67.2	74.1	81.4
Selmecbánya Town	62.3	67.5	73.5	81.4
Liptó County	54.1	66.6	73.1	78.7
Nógrád County	44.5	58.1	66.7	76.1
Nyitra County	47.3	59.8	68.5	75.9
Pozsony County	55.8	68.2	75.2	80.8
Pozsony Town	77.1	82.2	87.7	90.5
Trencsén County	29.8	42.3	52.4	62.1
Turóc County	50.3	61.3	67.8	76.7
Zólyom County	51.9	63.1	71.9	79.1
Total	48.1	60.1	68.2	76.0
3. Between the Danube River and the Tisza River				
Bács–Bodrog County	44.9	57.8	67.0	73.7
Baja Town	54.0	62.9	71.4	76.7
Szabadka Town	26.1	36.4	49.5	61.1
Újvidék Town	55.6	66.7	73.6	78.2
Zombor Town	37.6	44.9	55.1	64.7
Csongrád County	43.6	52.0	63.1	71.7
Hódmezővásárhely Town	61.8	71.5	78.6	82.3
Szeged Town	53.5	61.8	72.3	79.3
Heves County	39.1	52.4	64.8	73.0

	1880	1890	1900	1910
Jász–Nagykun–Szolnok County	75.8	54.1	63.4	70.3
Pest–Pilis–Solt County	55.9	66.2	73.8	79.8
Budapest (Capital)	76.3	81.7	87.6	92.5
Kecskemét Town	51.3	58.5	64.8	72.7
Total	53.6	64.1	73.2	80.0
4. Right Side of the Tisza River				
Abaúj–Torna County	44.2	56.3	65.4	73.4
Kassa Town	64.3	70.6	78.8	84.8
Bereg County	28.7	37.5	46.4	57.2
Borsod County	50.7	61.8	69.6	76.3
Gömör and Kishont County	64.9	72.6	76.7	80.7
Sáros County	22.7	33.9	46.2	58.6
Szepes County	46.0	56.1	62.5	69.8
Ung County	23.7	32.3	41.3	53.0
Zemplén County	32.9	41.1	51.6	61.6
Total	40.0	49.6	58.5	67.2
5. Left Side of the Tisza River				
Békés County	64.2	73.0	78.3	81.8
Bihar County	37.5	42.3	46.8	51.5
Nagyvárad Town	65.2	71.4	77.5	84.8
Hajdú County	64.1	72.1	75.9	79.4
Debrecen Town	72.6	75.8	81.4	84.1
Máramaros County	12.3	17.6	21.3	26.8
Szabolcs County	38.0	47.5	56.0	64.3
Szatmár County	31.7	40.1	47.4	55.0
Szatmárnémeti Town	65.6	71.5	76.3	81.0
Szilágy County	19.1	26.2	32.8	41.5
Ugocsa County	20.5	28.4	37.5	47.8
Total	38.1	45.1	50.9	56.9
6. Between the Tisza River and the Maros River				
Arad County	20.0	29.8	37.7	47.0
Arad Town	54.9	62.8	72.4	78.6
Csanád County	46.4	56.0	65.7	74.5
Krassó–Szörény County	24.1	32.4	42.9	50.7
Temes County	35.3	46.0	55.0	62.1

Table A2 cont'd

	1880	1890	1900	1910
Temesvár Town	63.3	71.6	77.2	80.9
Versec Town	56.9	65.6	73.7	76.8
Torontál County	38.1	48.0	57.2	64.7
Pancsova Town	51.8	65.8	72.8	74.8
Total	33.4	43.2	52.5	60.2
7. Transylvania				
Alsó-Fehér County	14.6	20.1	31.2	40.8
Beszterce–Naszód County	28.1	38.5	46.5	52.3
Brassó County	56.2	67.4	75.1	82.3
Csík County	23.2	34.8	45.4	58.9
Fogaras County	22.3	35.5	47.6	58.2
Háromszék County	36.0	48.0	57.6	66.9
Hunyad County	15.0	15.8	24.9	33.9
Kis-Küküllő County	22.4	29.2	38.4	49.8
Kolozs County	12.1	19.7	25.8	35.6
Kolozsvár Town	58.9	65.4	71.6	78.4
Maros–Torda County	25.6	33.3	41.8	51.1
Marosvásárhely Town	55.4	64.8	72.6	79.8
Nagy-Küküllő County	44.9	53.6	61.5	69.1
Szeben County	40.9	51.6	62.3	70.2
Szolnok–Doboka County	10.7	15.7	21.0	28.6
Torda–Aranyos County	15.0	21.6	27.1	37.1
Udvarhely County	35.0	49.1	60.4	69.1
Total	25.2	32.9	41.5	50.5
8. Fiume	49.6	66.3	74.9	83.2
9. Croatia (with Slavonia)				
Belovár-Körös County	28.8	38.2	52.2	59.4
Lika-Krbava County	11.8	13.8	21.3	25.1
Modrus–Fiume County	18.0	24.0	34.8	43.2
Pozsega County	28.6	38.1	52.8	59.7
Szerém County	33.8	43.0	58.1	66.6
Zimony Town	65.1	69.6	76.4	83.5
Varasd County	22.2	29.6	41.5	47.7
Varasd Town	66.2	70.1	75.9	79.4

	1880	1890	1900	1910
Verőce County	24.6	34.4	46.4	57.8
Eszék Town	66.5	68.6	76.7	81.7
Zágráb County	17.5	22.4	31.2	39.8
Zágráb Town	70.0	73.8	79.8	83.9
Total	24.9	32.3	44.4	52.6
Hungarian Kingdom Total	41.3	50.6	59.3	66.7

Sources: The censuses of 1870, 1880, 1890, 1900, 1910.

NOTES

Chapter 1

1 The Lutheran church visitations of the region: Stromp, *Magyar Protestáns Egyház-történeti Adattár*, 11–193; Payr, *Egyháztörténeti emlékek*, 102–128. The Catholic church visitations in the same region: Visitatio canonica Stephani Kazó, 1697–1698, Diocesan Archives, Szombathely (film copy: HNA Film 52; partial edition of its text: Házi, *Die kanonische Visitation*, 2); Visitatio canonica Batthyanyana (1754–1758) Diocesan Archives, Szombathely (film copy: HNA Film 5197–5201); Visitatio canonica Szilyana (1778–1781), Diocesan Archives, Szombathely (film copy: HNA Film 23720–23724).

2 HNA Film 23721, Fol. 77, Fol. 43, 50.

3 Mészáros, "Népoktatás Nyugat-Magyarországon", 315.

4 HNA C 39, Acta fundationalia, Lad. E. Fasc. 12, I, Vas County, Tótság 1770; Melton, *Absolutism*, 13–14; La Vopa, *Prussian Schoolteachers*, 11–24.

5 HNA C 39, Acta fundationalia, Lad. E. Fasc. 12, I, Vas County 1770; HNA Film 5198, Fol. 1128; Juhász, *A licenciátusi intézmény Magyarországon*; for comparison, see Tóth, "Deákok (licenciátusok)", 139–148; and Tóth, *Relationes missionariorum*, 8–28.

6 HNA Film 23724, Fol. 196.

7 HNA Film 52, Fol. 798.

8 Payr, *A dunántúli evangélikus egyházkerület története*, 273, 218; HNA Film 52, Fol. 700; *"E numero Lutheranorum unus erat praedicans crebris adhortationibus nostrorum permotus, publice damnata haeresi et orthodoxae fidei professione facta, nunc de ordinarii facultate in licenciatum ordinatus ferventem catholicae veritatis agit propugnatorem"*, APF, SC Ungheria Transilvania, Vol. 2, Fol. 252, 1687; Vas County Archives, Inquisitio nobilium, IV/5, Fasc. 2, No. 23, 1758.

9 Vovelle, "Y-at-il eu une révolution culturelle", 89–141.

10 Payr, *A dunántúli evangélikus egyházkerület története*, 891.
11 HNA Film 23720, Fol. 38, Fol. 73; 23721, Fol. 164, Fol. 199, Fol. 277, 354; 23721, Fol. 97; 23723, Fol. 73; 23721, Fol. 75; 23722, Fol. 320, Fol. 176, Fol. 15; 23724, Fol. 54; 23723, Fol. 282; 23722, Fol. 8, Fol. 74; 23721, Fol. 14; 23721, Fol. 66.
12 HNA Film 23721, Fol. 188; 23722, Fol. 12; 23722, Fol. 165; Rába Múzeum, Körmend, 13/81, 62; HNA Batthyány Family Archives, P 1313, Majoratus, Lad. 8/a, No. 11; HNA C 39, Acta fundationalia, Lad. E. Fasc. 12, III, No. 1, 1770; HNA P 1322, Batthyány Family Archives, Acta scholarum, 1, No. 4:2; Vas County Archives, VK 36/MV 6, Fasc. 4, No. 100, 17; HNA C 39, Dept. Schol. Nat., 306, 1804/4, No. 125; Tóth, "Iskola és reformáció Körmenden", 10–21.
13 HNA Film 23721, Fol. 242; Pferschy, *Atlas zur Geschichte des steirischen*; Weiss, *Geschichte der österreichischen Volksschule*; Helfert, *Die Gründung der österreichischen Volksschule*; Engelbrecht, *Geschichte des österreichischen Bildungswesens*; Klingenstein, "Akademikerüberschuss als soziales Problem", 165–203; Heiss, "Konfession, Politik und Erziehung", 13–63; HNA Film 23721, Fol. 87, 148, 43; 23722, Fol. 109.
14 HNA Film 5198, Fol. 1180; 5200, Fol. 116, 318; HNA C 39, Acta fundationalia, Lad. E. Fasc. 12, I, Vas County.
15 HNA C 39, Acta fundationalia, Lad. E. Fasc. 12, I, Vas County.
16 HNA Film 23724, Fol. 57; 23723, Fol. 165; 23721, Fol. 108; 23722, Fol. 51.
17 Mészáros, *Ratio Educationis*, 69, 91; Fináczy, *Magyarországi közoktatás*, 233–36, 240–41; Kosáry, *Művelődés*, 403–450; Benda, "Felvilágosodás és a paraszti műveltség", 292–296; HNA C 39, Acta fundationalia, Lad. E. Fasc. 12, I, Vas County.
18 HNA Film 5197, Fol. 755; HNA C 39, Acta fundationalia, Lad. E. I. Fasc. 12, Vas County; HNA Film 23721, Fol. 75; 23730, Fol. 31, Fol. 122; HNA P 1322, Batthyány Family Archives, Sedis dominalis, 191, p. 522; Vas County Archives, Divisionales, IV/1/v, Fasc. 9, No. 25; HNA Film 23721, Fol. 124, Fol. 75; Film 23721, Fol. 73; Film 23720, Fol. 218; Film 23721, Fol. 128.
19 HNA Film 23724, Fol. 112–113; HNA Film 23720, Fol. 13, 75, 128, 122, 174, 218; 23722, Fol. 8, 49, 165; 23723, Fol. 129.
20 HNA C 39, Acta fundationalia, Lad. E. Fasc. 12, I, Vas County; HNA Batthyány Family Archives, P 1322, 191; Sedis dominalis, 522; Vas County Archives, IV/1/v. Divisionales, Fasc. 9, No. 25.
21 We can check the credibility of schoolmasters' careers as described in the church visitations by the deposition of a schoolmaster as a witness in a criminal case. The schoolmaster of Keresztúr told exactly the same facts in 1775 at the landlord's court about his age, the schools in which he taught and the times he changed villages as he did in 1779 during the church visitation. HNA Film 23721, Fol. 90; HNA B 1322, Batthyány Family Archives, 192, Sedis dominalis, 1775.
22 HNA P 1313, Batthyány Family Archives, 25, Majoratus, Lad. 7, No. 43/4, Sároslak 1754.
23 HNA Film 23720, Fol. 95; 23722, Fol. 70; 23723, Fol. 73–74; 23723, Fol. 112, Fol. 237, Fol. 235, Fol. 248; 23724, Fol. 172; 23724, Fol. 68, Fol. 86, Fol. 130; HNA C 39, Acta fundationalia, Lad. E. Fasc. 12, I, Vas County; HNA Film 5197, Fol. 999–1031.
24 HNA C 39, Acta fundationalia, Lad. E. Fasc. 12, I, Vas County.

25 Ibid.

26 Vas County Archives, IV/1/f, Orphanalia, Fasc. 4, No. 49.

27 HNA C 39, Acta fundationalia, Lad. E. Fasc. 12, I, Vas County. Even in Prussia the local schoolmaster had less prestige than the ox herder of the village because of his poverty. See Melton, *Absolutism*, 18.

28 ŠOBA Bratislava, Pozsony County, Processus criminales, A XII, No. 99, 1774.

29 Vas County Archives, XI/604, D Vol. VII, Fol. 107/v, 135/v, 141, 200, 202; and Vas County Archives, IV/1/Fol. Orphanalia, Fasc. 4, No. 49. For comparison, see Morineau, "Budgets populaires en France", 204–212; Chartier, Julia, Compère, *L'éducation en France*, 42.

30 Brooks, *When Russia Learned to Read*, 3; Marker, *Publishing, Printing and Origins*, 70–83.

31 Mészáros, *Középszintű iskoláink kronológiája*.

32 Fináczy, *Magyarországi közoktatás*, 303.

33 This method was used in Hungary by Domokos Kosáry and in France by Dominique Julia. See Kosáry, *Művelődés*, 450–457; Chartier, Julia, Compère, *L'éducation en France*, 42–44; Thirring, *Magyarország népessége*, 66–68; HNA C 39, Acta fundationalia, Lad. E. Fasc. 12, I, Vas County; HNA Film 23720–23724; HNA Film 23720, Fol. 164–165, 195–196; 23721, Fol. 55, 77; 23722, Fol. 80, 137. On schoolbuildings: HNA C 39, Acta fundationalia, Lad. E. Fasc. 12, I, Vas County, HNA Film B. 1368, Veszprém County Archives, Acta nobilitaria, Fasc. H./III, No. 24, Fol. 1, Hericz 1754; Vas County Archives, IV/5, Inquisitio nobilitatis, Fasc. 2, No. 73, (1766). Schoolmasters taught in the fields due to the lack of school buildings, even in Brittany in France. See Meyer, "Alphabétisation", 335–336. For comparison, see Quéniart, "Les apprentissages scolaires élémentaires", 3–27; Marchesini, "Copier à l'école en Italie", 29–33.

34 HNA C 39, Acta fundationalia, Lad. E. Fasc. 12, I, Vas County.

35 Ibid., Vas, Pozsony, Sopron counties.

36 Ibid., Zala and Vas counties. Generally in Europe, children attended schools only in winter when they were not needed in the fields. However, in Tyrol it was precisely in winter that children did not come to school because of the high snow in the mountains. See Helfert, *Die Gründung der österreichischen Volksschule*, 59–60.

37 HNA C 39, Acta fundationalia, Lad. E. Fasc. 12, I, Sopron County.

38 Mészáros, *Ratio Educationis*, 67. Regarding the calculation capacities of rich and poor peasants, see for comparison Norden, "Die Alphabetisierung", 141–143.

39 Mészáros, "Az iskolaügy", 394.

40 Stromp, *Magyar Protestáns Egyháztörténeti Adattár*, 152–155.

41 Mészáros, "Népoktatás Nyugat-Magyarországon", 314.

42 Mészáros, "Az iskolaügy", 282.

43 HNA C 39, Acta fundationalia, Lad. E. Fasc. 12, I. Moson County Lajthafalu (Potzneusiedl); Ibid., Pozsony County Engerau.

44 HNA Film B 1368; Veszprém County Archives, Acta nobilium, Fasc. H/III, No. 24, 1754.

45 "Kis János Emlékezései", 815, 821.

46 ŠOBA Bratislava, Pozsony County, Criminalia, A XII, Processus criminales, No. 99, 1774.

47 For learning to read and write outside schools in early modern Europe, see Spufford, "First steps in literacy", 407–436; Vigo, "Quando il popolo cominciò a leggere", 812–814, 824–827; for comparison, see Schutte, "Teaching adults to read", 3–16; Hébrard, "Comment Valentin Jamerey-Duval apprit-il à lire?"; Schenda, *Volk ohne Buch*, 50; Ducreux, "Lire à en mourir", 279; Johansson, "History of literacy in Sweden", 151–182.

48 ŠOBA Banská Bystrica, Gömör County Processus magistrales, 656, Fasc. VI, No. 307, 1753.

49 Táncsics, *Életpályám*, 66, 130.

50 Csongrád County Archives, Szentes, Károlyi Family Archives, Sedis dominalis, IV, A. 53, a. 24, 1746; ŠOBA Prešov, Sáros, Criminalia, No. 287, 1726.

51 ŠOBA Bratislava, Pozsony County, Trestné spisy, Processus criminales, A XII, No. 68; ŠOBA Prešov, Sáros County, Criminalia, 515, 1755. Schram, *Magyarországi boszorkányperek*, 349.

52 Vas County Archives, Processus nobilium, IV/1/d. Fasc. 1, No. 23, No. 24.

53 Mikes, *Összes Művei*, 107; Borsod County Archives, Acta nobilium 1770, Nagy.

54 Vas County Archives, Archivum Capituli Castriferrei, Testamenta, Fasc. 2, No. 18, 1753; HNA P 623, Széchényi Family Archives, Vol. 379, Fol. 36; Vas County Archives, IV/1, Fol. Orphanalia, Fasc. 3, No. 41, 1778.

55 Tóth, *Vas vármegye*, Vol. II, 153.

56 Mészáros, "Az iskolaügy", 292–307, 362–363; Andritsch, *Studenten und Lehrer*, passim.

57 HNA P 701, Vidos Family Archives, 2, No. 4, 1696–98; Vas County Archives, IV/1/Fol. Orphanalia, 4, Chernel; Vas County Archives, Chernel Family Archives, Vol. 5–10, 16, passim. For comparison, see Benda, "Magyar köznemesség", 87–92.

58 "Kis János Emlékezései", 827–829; Mészáros, *Tankönyvkiadás története Magyarországon*, 48–66.

59 Kosáry, *Művelődés*, 151–152.

60 Mészáros, "Népoktatás Nyugat-Magyarországon", 306–328.

61 Benda, "Iskolázás és az írástudás", 123–132.

62 For the edition of the text of this church visitation, see Varga, "Győri székesegyházi főesperesség", 177–221.

63 Benda, "Iskolázás és az írástudás", 123–132; Vitéz, *Minden munkája*, I, 557–558.

64 Pferschy, *Atlas zur Geschichte*, 59/I–IV; Pietsch, *Die theresianische Schulreform*, 47.

65 Engelbrecht, *Geschichte des österreichischen Bildungswesens*, 408–409; Helfert, *Die Gründung der österreichischen Volksschule*, 59–66, 143, 484; Wangermann, *Aufklärung und staatsbürgerliche Erziehung*; Melton, "From Image to Word", 95–124; Melton, *Absolutism*, 7–9, 220–221; Weiss, *Geschichte der österreichischen Volksschule*, 763–797. Theresian School Reform in Bohemia: Kuzmin, *Vývoj školstvi a vzděláni*, 53–73; in Upper Hungary (today Slovakia): Kowalská, *Štátne l'udové školstvo*, 19–30.

66 Allgemeines Verwaltungsarchiv, Wien, Studienhofkommission, F 63, 81 ex 1781, C.85 ex 1781, B. For comparison, see Bruckmüller, *Sozialgeschichte Österreichs*, 288.

67 Neugebauer, *Absolutistischer Staat und Schulwirklichkeit*; Gagliardo, *Germany under the Old Regime*, 177–185; Paulsen, *Geschichte des gelehrten Unterrichts*; La Vopa,

Prussian Schoolteachers, passim.; Schleunes, *Schooling and Society*, 8–48; Engelsing, *Zur Sozialgeschichte deutscher Mittel- und Unterschichten*, 155–179; Wittmann, "Der lesende Landmann", 142–196.

68 Neugebauer, *Absolutistischer Staat und Schulwirklichkeit*, 314–315, 321–335; Schwartz, *Die neumärkischen Schulen*, 10, 52–54.

69 Neugebauer, *Absolutistischer Staat und Schulwirklichkeit*, 317–319, 364–366, 410, 368–369; Fischer, "Der Volksschullehrer", 37–47; Le Cam, "Schulpflicht, Schulbesuch, und Schulnetz", 203–224.

70 Schwartz, *Die neumärkischen Schulen*, 38–40; Pätzold, *Geschichte des Volksschulwesens*, 83–84; Mager, *Geschichte des Bauertums*, 237–238.

71 Leschinsky and Roeder, *Schule im historischen Prozess*, 137.

72 Neugebauer, *Absolutistischer Staat und Schulwirklichkeit*, 505; for comparison, see Brüggemann, *Landschullehrer in Ostfriesland*; Busch-Geertsema, "Elender als auf dem elendsten Dorfe?" 181–189.

73 Laget, *Petites écoles*, 1398; for comparison, see Frijhoff and Julia, *École et société*, 11–37; Chartier, Julia, Compère, *L'éducation en France*, 4–44; Julia and Revel, *Histoire sociale des populations étudiantes*, 303–394; O'Day, *Education and Society*, passim.; Cressy, *Literacy and the Social Order*, 19–41.

74 Chartier, Julia, Compère, *L'éducation en France*, 15–17; Furet and Ozouf, *Lire et écrire*, 69–152; Graff, *Legacies of Literacy*, 195–197.

75 Chartier, Julia, Compère, *L'éducation en France*, 18–25, 41–44; for comparison, see Julia, "L'enseignement primaire", 407–415; Julia, "La réforme post-tridentinne", 311–415.

76 Chartier, Julia, Compère, *L'éducation en France*, 41–44.

Chapter 2

1 Benda, "Felvilágosodás és a paraszti műveltség", 287–308. For methodological problems of research on literacy, see Houston, *Literacy in Early Modern Europe*, 116–129; Houdaille, "Les signatures au mariage", 65–90; Furet and Ozouf, *Lire et écrire*; Schofield, "Measurement of literacy", 311–325; Schofield, "Dimensions of illiteracy", 201–213; Marchesini, "La fatica di scrivere", 83–170; Marchesini, "Sposi e scolari"; Toscani, "L'alfabetismo a Pavia", 353–365; Marchesini, *Il bisogno di scrivere*, passim.; Elena Brambilla, *La misura dell'alfabetizzazione*, 366–374; François, "Die Volksbildung am Mittelrhein", 277–304; Pál, "Írástudás a Székelyföldön", 421–433. For Hungarian cultural history in the early modern period, see Tóth, "Hungarian Culture", 154–225; Bitskey, "Spiritual Life", 229–286.

2 Vas County Archives, XI/604; Sankt Gotthard Abbey Archives, Promissory Bills, Bills of Debt, Deeds of Sale, Village mayors' accounts, passim.; HNA Battyhány Family Archives, P 1322, Village Archives, P 1313, Majoratus; HNA P 275, Festetich Family Archives, Village Archives.

3 HNA P 701, Vidos Family Archives; HNA P 61, Bogyay Family Archives; HNA P 600, Szarvaskendi Sibrik Family Archives. If only three or four crosses or signatures were found from one village, the village was omitted from the statistics.

4 *Első magyarországi népszámlálás*, 238–239.

5 Chartier, "La ville classique", 222–282; Petrucci, *Scrittura e popolo*; Roche, "Les pratiques de l'écrit", 157–179; Quéniart, *Culture et société urbaines*, 31–52; Duglio, "Alfabetismo e società", 485–509.

6 HNA P 533, Ostffy Family Archives, Fasc. 6, No. 57; Péter, "A bibliaolvasás mindenkinek", 1006–1028; Strauss, *Luther's House of Learning*, 193–200; Strauss, "Lutheranism and literacy", 109–123; Strauss and Gawthrop, "Protestantism and literacy", 31–56.

7 Rački, "Acta coniurationem", 207.

8 Schram, *Magyarországi boszorkányperek*, I, 516.

9 Graff, *Legacies of Literacy*, 381–395; Lenhart, "Grundbildung und Modernisierung", 37–48; Parker, "An educational revolution?" 201–222.

10 HNA P 1322, Batthyány Family Archives, Village Archives, 219 (1750), 15 (1809). Similar examples: Vas County Archives, Divisionales, IV/1/v. Fasc. 8, No. 13 (1772).

11 Le Roy Ladurie, *Les paysans*, 345–346; Cabourdin, *Terre et hommes*, 707; Cressy, *Literacy and the Social Order*, 60; Richter, "Zur Schriftkundigkeit", 83.

12 Vas County Archives, XIII/4, Chernel Family Archives, 4, 1767. Peasants did not write only on paper: A cabinetmaker wrote his name in 1762 on the wooden wall of the church at Szentgyőr. HNA Film B 1378, Veszprém County Archives, Acta et fragmenta nobilitaria, Fasc. V/II, 1762.

13 Vas County Archives, XI/604; Sankt Gotthard Abbey Archives, Divisionales, 1762.

14 Some examples: Vas County Archives, Testamenta, IV/1/t, Fasc. 2, No. 38, 1/2 (1756); Vas County Archives, Divisionales, IV/1/v, Fasc. 9, No. 42 (1785); APF SC Moldavia, Vol. 6, Fol. 115, Vol. 3, Fol. 91.

15 ŠOBA Banská Bystrica, Gömör, Criminalia, XII. Fasc. II, No. 24; ŠOBA Košice, Abaúj, Criminalia, XII. Fasc. VI, No. 5; Heves County Archives, Sedis dominalis episcopi Agriensis, XII/3-b, 8, Fasc. No. 12, 1726, 3, Fasc. No. 53, Fasc. No. 69; Heves County Archives, Gyöngyös, V/101/b–129, CL. 27; Borsod County Archives, Miskolc, Sp. XV, 197, 294, 373, 376.

16 ŠOBA Banská Bystrica, Kis-Hont, Processuales, Fons III, Fasc. 4, No. 146, 149.

17 ŠOBA Banská Bystrica, Kis-Hont, Processuales, Fons III, Fasc. 6, No. 258; Fons III, Fasc. 5, No. 228; Fons III, Fasc. 8, No. 364, 386; Fons III, Fasc. 9, No. 461–462.

18 It surely is not by chance that similar "delegated signatures" were found in Poland, Italy and Spain, where much smaller numbers of signatures and crosses are available than, for example, in England or in France. See Urban, "Sztuka pisania", 56–57; Blay, *La escritura*, 10–14; Petrucci, "Scrittura, alfabetismo ed educazione", 181; Wendehorst, "Monachus scribere nesciens", 67, 73; Richter, "Zur Schriftkundigkeit", 83.

19 HNA P 275, Festetich Family Archives, Village Archives, 50, Rezi (1811).

20 HNA P 1322, Batthyány Family Archives, 120, Village Archives, Körmend p. 3; HNA P 1322, Batthyány Family Archives, Instructiones No. 42, p. 8, Familia domini, 1650; HNA P 1314, Batthyány Family Archives, Missiles, 13030.

21 HNA P 1313, Batthyány Family Archives, Majoratus, Lad. 2, No. 24, Szeremleiana 1715.

22 HNA P 1313, Batthyány Family Archives, Majoratus, Lad. 2, No. 31, Faludiana, No. 19, No. 67, Szeremleiana; Vas County Archives, Village Archives, Körmend 1751, 1752; HNA R 307, Village Archives, Körmend 1747; Rába Múzeum, Körmend 13.81/22, 1736; HNA P 1313, Batthyány Family Archives, Majoratus, Lad. 2, No. 21, Szeremleiana, No. 8, Faludiana.

23 HNA P 1313, Batthyány Family Archives, Majoratus, Lad. 2, Majoratus, Lad. 3, No. 73, Körmend, No. 2, Kissiana; HNA P 650, Tallián Family Archives, 5, No. 2, 1706.

24 HNA P 1314, Batthyány Family Archives, Missiles, No. 33878.

25 HNA P 1322, Batthyány Family Archives, Village Archives, Fasc. 182, No. 124, Kukmér 1744, Fasc. 179, No. 80, Hidegkút 1753, Fasc. 181, No. 109, Königsdorf 1754.

26 1830: HNA P 1322, Batthyány Family Archives, Village Archives, 152, Nádasd. 1830, 1845: HNA P 1313, Batthyány Family Archives, Majoratus, Lad. 9/a, No. 85; HNA P 1322, Batthyány Family Archives, Village Archives, 73, Halogy 1830. His signatures from 1832 to 1842: p. 22/a, 29/a, 32, 38/a, 48/a, 50; and his cross in 1838: Ibid., p. 36.

27 Vas County Archives, XI/604; Sankt Gotthard Abbey Archives, Village mayor's accounts, Tótfalu 1834, 1838.

28 HNA P 275, Festetich Family Archives, Village Archives, Fasc. 80, Döbörhegy, Döröske, D. IV, 90/a, p. 69.

29 Vas County Archives, XI/604; Sankt Gotthard Abbey Archives, Village mayor's accounts, Nagyfalu, Kristyán.

30 HNA P 1322, Batthyány Family Archives, Village Archives, Fasc. 75, Haraszti-falu, p. 10, 27/a, 30, 34/a, 39, 43, 46/a, 50, 60, 63, 67/a, 72, 76/a, 81, 1830–1846.

31 HNA P 1322, Batthyány Family Archives, Village Archives, Fasc. 50, p. 9, 17/a, 20, 22.

32 Vas County Archives, XI/604; Sankt Gotthard Abbey Archives, Village mayor's accounts, Nagyfalu, Kristyán.

33 HNA P 1313, Batthyány Family Archives, Majoratus, Lad. 9/a, No. 38. p. 17/a–18, p. 14/a, p. 13/a.

34 HNA P 157, Esterházy Family Archives, 66, Series XIV, No. 10, 1745. Similar cases: Hofkammerarchiv, Wien, Hoffinanz Ungarn, Rote Nummer 235, p. 132, 183, 1671.

35 HNA Film B. 1370, Veszprém County Archives, Acta nobilium, Fasc. K/IV, No. 55, Fol. 110, 1760; Vas County Archives, IV/1/kk, Testimoniales, Fasc. 2, No. 35.

36 The woman in question is Madame Gerencsér Józsefné (born in 1905), grand-mother of the ethnologue Sándor Horváth; many special thanks to both for their help. Similar cases of hidden literacy of widows: Castan, *Honnêteté et relations sociales*, 116–121.

37 von Wartburg-Ambühl, *Alphabetisierung und Lektüre*, 30–31; Norden, "Die Alphabetisierung", 103–164.

38 Vas County Archives, IV/1/f, Orphanalia, Fasc. 4, No. 21, 1786. For comparison, see Ducreux, "Lire à en mourir", 282.

39 Vas County Archives, IV/1/f, Orphanalia, Fasc. 4, No. 45, 1796, Village Archives, Testamenta, 1788. For comparison on peasants who could not write but

bought and read books, see Spufford, *Small books and pleasant histories*, 15–27, 29–35; Spufford, *Great Reclothing*, 85–105; Bollème, "Litérature populaire", 61–92.

40 For extensive and intensive reading: Dann, "Die Lesegesellschaften", 100–101; Chartier, "Du livre au lire", 61–81; Julia, "Lettura e controriforma", 277–316.

41 *A Hét Mennyei Szent Zárok Imádsága*. Special thanks to Gábor Tüskés who drew my attention to this book. See also Tüskés and Knapp, "Fejezetek", 415–437. For similar cases of books and pamphlets speaking to illiterate people, see Chartier, "Culture as Appropriation", 243; Scribner, *Popular culture*, 54; Scribner, "Flugblatt und Analphabetentum", 66–67; Scribner, *For the sake of simple folk*, 1–15; Rössing-Hager, "Wie stark findet", 77–137. The small religious books in eighteenth-century Croatia were intended to be read aloud to the illiterate: Velagić, "Nekoliko vidova", 111–131. "Those good Christians who care for the salvation of their souls can have this book in hand from which even people who cannot read can listen to the good teaching" (Mulih, *Poszel aposztolszki*). "These books when they are read...by the little girl or boy who knows the letters and listened by the simple folk that does not know the letters ... many times made people cry because of their sins" (Gasparotti, *Czvet Szveteh*).

42 Schram, *Magyarországi boszorkányperek*, II, 140.

43 ŠOBA Nitra, Bars, Criminales, XII, Fasc. 9, No. 8, 1772; Heves County Archives, Sedis dominalis episcopi Agriensis, XII/3/b–12, Fasc. Q, No. 14, 16/a.

44 Státny Ústredný Archív, Bratislava, Amadé-Üchtritz 1192, Acta sedis dominalis, Processus. criminales, Lad. 10, sub No. B-p, Horny Bar 1757.

45 ŠOBA Banská Bystrica, Gömör, Criminalia, 644, Fasc. I/P, 1730 (draft).

46 ŠOBA Bratislava, Pozsony, Criminalia, A XII, Sedis criminalis, No. 201, 1796.

47 Táncsics, *Életpályám*, 38–39.

48 HNA P 1314, Batthyány Family Archives, Missiles, No. 31164, No. 5589.

49 Vas County Archives, Archivum Capituli Castriferrei, Testamenta, Fasc. 3, No. 20 (1736); HNA Film 5199, Fol. 937, No. 18 (1756).

50 HNA P 275, Festetich Family Archives, Village Archives, Zalaszántó 1844. For comparison, see Lázár, "A magyarországi kalendáriumirodalom", 5–6; Kovács, *Kis magyar kalendáriumtörténet*, 14–47; Maiello, *Storia del calendario*; Mix, "Lektüre für Gebildete und Ungebildete"; Mix, *Vom Leitmedium zum Lesefutter*, 93–113; Mix, "Der Musenhort in der Provinz", 171–181; Braida, "Les almanachs italiens", 183–206; Braida, "Dall'almanaco all'agenda", 137–167.

51 Schram, *Magyarországi boszorkányperek*, II, 7–302, 563–692; Messerli and Rubini, "Il mestiere del cantastorie", 463–487.

52 HNA P 1322, Batthyány, P 157, Esterházy, P 235, Festetich Family Archives, Vas County Archives, XI. 604; Sankt Gotthard Abbey Archives, passim.; HNA Film 16856, Prothocollum malefactorum Nagykőrös; Csongrád County Archives, IV, A. 53, a. 35, Károlyi Family Archives, Sedis dominalis 1775; Tóth, "Chimes and Ticks", 15–37; Bogucka, "Space and time", 39–52; Whitrow, *Time in history*, 115–138; Peters, "...dahingeflossen", 180–205; Barbu, "Écrire sur le sable", 103–114; Roche, *La France des Lumières*, 68–98.

53 HNA P 235, Festetich Family Archives, Fasc. 136, Acta juris gladii, No. 84, 1755; Houston, *Scottish literacy*, 205.

54 Heves County Archives, Sedis dominalis episcopi Agriensis, XII/3/b–12, Fasc. Q, No. 16/a, 14.

55 ŠOBA Košice, Abaúj, Criminalia, Fasc. VI, No. 48, 1751.

56 Kubinyi, *Bethlenfalvi gróf Thurzó*, I, 261; HNA P 235, Festetich Family Archives, Acta juris gladii, No. 136, No. 154, 1780. On correspondence of illiterate people: Cressy, *"Coming over."* For similar cases, see Štátny Ústredný Archív, Bratislava, Archivum praepositi Jászó, Elenchus III, Fasc. K, No. 13, 1713; ŠOBA Bytča, Turóc, Criminales processus, II, 486, 1769.

57 ŠOBA Bratislava, Pozsony, A XII, Criminales processus, No. 653, 1764, No. 295, 298, 1771.

58 Csongrád County Archives, Criminales processus, b. 21, 1775. Similar cases: Csongrád County Archives, Károlyi Family Archives, Acta sedis dominalis, a. 26, 1756, No. A; ŠOBA Košice, Abaúj-Torna, Criminalia, 91, Fasc. 13, No. 42, 1785.

59 Štátny Ústredný Archív, Bratislava, Pálffy Family Archives, Alm. II. Lad. 9, Fasc. I, No. 12, 1770; ŠOBA Košice, Abaúj-Torna, Criminalia, 90, Fasc. 12, No. 15, 1786. Ibid., Abaúj, Processus criminales 385, Fasc. 4, No. 13, 1793; Heves County Archives, Archivum episcopi Agriensis, XII/3/b–10, Fasc. O, No. 14/c. A, 1766. Borsod County Archives, Miskolc, XV, 325, 1781.

60 Szabó, *A magyarországi úrbérrendezés története*, 407–408, 480–481, 483–484. Similar cases: HNA P 325, Festetich Family Archives, Acta juris gladii, 136, p. 432, 1767; ŠOBA Nitra, Bars, Criminalia, XII, Fasc. 8, No. 46; Csongrád County Archives, Processus criminales, b. 21, 1775.

61 ŠOBA Košice, Abaúj, Criminalia, Fasc. VIII, No. 6, 1763. An almost identical case: ŠOBA Banská Bystrica, Gömör, Processus magistrales, Fasc. X, No. 452, 676, 1770.

62 Csongrád County Archives, Károlyi Family Archives, Acta sedis dominalis, a. 38, No. 5, 1778; Ibid., Csongrád Processus criminales b. 15, 1760; HNA Batthyány P 1313, Majoratus, Lad. 2, No. 31, Faludiana.

63 HNA P 1322, Batthyány Family Archives, Conscriptiones, Körmend 1762, No. 10, 44/a, 44/d, p. 111/a.

64 HNA P 1322, Batthyány Family Archives, Acta sedis dominalis, 197, Fasc. 5, No. 69–4, No. 1, 4.

65 HNA P 1313, Batthyány Family Archives, Majoratus, Lad. 8/a, No. 114, P 1322, 1793, Fasc. 11, No. 96.

66 Ibid., Fasc. 191, p. 472, 1771; HNA Batthyány Family Archives, P 1314, Missiles, No. 24030.

67 Vas County Archives, XI/604; Sankt Gotthard Abbey Archives, "B", Acta sedis dominalis, 1738.

68 ŠOBA Bratislava, Pozsony, Criminalia, Processus criminales, A XII, No. 422, 1779.

69 ŠOBA Košice, Abaúj, Criminalia, Fasc. II, No. 30, 1715.

70 Vas County Archives, VK 36/MV 1, Körmend p. 362, 224, sz.

71 HNA P 623, Széchényi Family Archives, Vol. 379, fol. 95/v, 93/v.

72 HNA P 1322, Batthyány Family Archives, Conscriptiones, Körmend 1762, No. 27, 12.1812, No. 184, 49.

73 ŠOBA Košice, Abaúj, Criminalia, Proc. 217, Inquisitiones, Fasc. I, No. 74, 1737.

74 ŠOBA Banská Bystrica, Gömör, Processus magistrales, 684, Fasc. XIV, No. 587, No. 690, Fasc. XVII, No. 652 (1785).

75 ŠOBA Košice, Abaúj, Criminalia, 395, Fasc. 16, No. 37.

76 ŠOBA Košice, Abaúj, Criminalia, 395, Fasc. 16, No. 37; Pest County Archives, Ráckeve Archives, 1802, No. 136.

77 HNA P 1322, Batthyány Family Archives, Acta sedis dominalis, Fasc. 191, 1768.

78 Takács, *Határjelek, határjárás*, 165–167; Tóth, *Somogyi határvizsgálatok*, 150, 155, 164–165; Függedi, "Oral Culture and Literacy", VI, 1–25.

79 Tóth, *Somogyi határvizsgálatok*, 152.

80 HNA P 1322, Batthyány Family Archives, Conscriptiones, Körmend 1762, No. 10, 24/d, 18/c, No. 27, 1/1, 2/1, No. 12, p. 203/a.

81 HNA P 1322, Batthyány Family Archives, Conscriptiones, Körmend, 1762, Berkifalu.

82 Borsod County Archives, Acta nobilitaria, Mihály alias Rinóth Family, 1638, 1728.

83 APF, SOCG Vol. 218, Fol. 33. See also Tóth, *Relationes missionariorum*, 15.

84 Schram, *Magyarországi boszorkányperek*, II, 171–172. See also Fabre, "Le livre et sa magie", 7–26; Giorgio Raimondo Cardona, *Antropologia della scrittura*, 156–160, 167; Petrucci, *Libri, scritture e pubblico*, 141–143; Cressy, *Literacy and the Social Order*, 50–51; Heves County Archives, Acta sedis dominalis episcopi Agriensis, XII/3-b, 12 doboz, Fasc. Q, No. 16/a, 1768.

85 Schram, *Magyarországi boszorkányperek*, II, 93; See also Heves County Archives, Eger, Sedis dominalis episcopi Agriensis, XII/3-b, 12, Fasc. Q, No. 16/a, 1768.

86 Schram, *Magyarországi boszorkányperek*, II, 227.

87 Štátny Ústredný Archív, Bratislava, Pálffy Family Archives, Sedes dominalis, A VII, Prothocolla, 1701; Alapi, *Bűbájosok és boszorkányok*, 38–48.

88 Schram, *Magyarországi boszorkányperek*, I, 232.

89 Komáromy, *Magyarországi boszorkányperek*, 596.

90 APF Scritture originali riferite nelle Congregazione Generali, vol. 218, Fol. 112.

91 Schram, *Magyarországi boszorkányperek*, I, 516. See also Kristóf, "Istenes könyvek", 67–104.

92 Vas County Archives, IV/5, Inquisitio nobilium, Fasc. 1, No. 57, 1770. See also Boureau, "Adorations et décorations", 25.

93 Schram, *Magyarországi boszorkányperek*, II, 188–191.

Chapter 3

1 Vas County Archives, Szombathely, IV/5, Inquisitio nobilium, Fasc. 1, No. 60, 1728, Fasc. 2, No. 85, 1719, IV/11/c 4, Taxatio nobilium 155–162, IV/5, Inquisitio nobilitatis, Fasc. 4, No. 25, 1/2, 1727; Wirth, "A nemesi kisbirtok", 140–152.

2 HNA P 600, Szarvaskendi Sibrik Family Archives, 8, 26, 10 July 1610. For the sixteenth century: Vas County Archives, XIII/35, Szelestey, Family Archives, Fasc. 1, XIII/37.

3 Vas County Archives, XIII/37, Tolnay–Cziráky Family Archives, Fasc. 1, 19 Sept 1616.

4 HNA P 430, Kisfaludy Family Archives, 9, Letters of Boldizsár Kisfaludy, 19 Aug 1718; Bánkúti, "Egy kuruc nemesifjú útja", 255; Varga, *Szervitorok katonai szolgálata*, 193.

5 HNA P 1322, Batthyány Family Archives, Familia, No. 961, p. 83; Tóth, *Jobbágyok, hajdúk, deákok*, 90–104.

6 HNA P 61, Bogyay Family Archives, 3, 1702, 1710, 1712; Benda, "Egy Zala megyei köznemesi gazdaság", 1–84.

7 Vas County Archives, XIII/35, Szelestey Family Archives, 2, 1655.

8 Ibid., 4, 29 July 1624; HNA P 45, Békássy Family Archives, 8, 24 June 1637.

9 Vas County Archives, IV/1/kk, Fasc. 1, No. 23, No. 18, No. 44, No. 32; HNA P 600, Szarvaskendi Sibrik Family Archives, 8, 26; HNA P 1313, Batthyány Family Archives, 248, Turcica, 1641.

10 Vas County Archives, IV/1/kk, Fasc. 1, No. 29, 1674.

11 Ibid., No. 23, 1653; HNA P 701, Vidos Family Archives, 1.

12 Vas County Archives, XIII/22, Lukinics Family Archives, 1, 1699; Vas County Archives, Vajda Family Archives, XIII/40, 1, 1675, 7, 1681; HNA P 701, Vidos Family Archives, 1, 1662.

13 HNA P 533, Ostffy Family Archives, 4, 22, tétel p. 78/a, 1701.

14 Vas County Archives, IV/1/kk, Fasc. 1, No. 27, 1668.

15 Vas County Archives, IV/1/kk, Fasc. 1, No. 21, 1653; Vas County Archives, Divisionales, Fasc. 2, No. 4, 1648; Vas County Archives, XIII/37, Tolnay–Cziráky Family Archives, 1, 1629.

16 1724: HNA P 157, Esterházy Family Archives, 65, Series XIII, No. 8, 1744; HNA Film B 1392, Zala County Archives, Investigatio nobilium, Fasc. 8, Fol. 45.

17 HNA Film B 1391, Zala County Archives, Investigatio nobilium, Fasc. 6, Fol. 58, No. 8, 1727; HNA P 1322, Batthyány Family Archives, 189, p. 146, 1725; ŠOBA Nitra, Bars, Trestné, Criminalia, proc. XII, Fasc. 1, No. 35, 1704; ŠOBA Banská Bystrica, Districtus minoris Honth, Fons II, Fasc. I, No. 9, 10, 12, 13.

18 HNA P 650, Tallián Family Archives, 5, 1701, 1701.

19 Vas County Archives, Szelestey Family Archives, XIII/35, 2, 1660; HNA P 61, Bogyay Family Archives, 2, 1662. HNA P 701, Vidos Family Archives, 1, 1663.

20 ŠOBA Banská Bystrica, Gömör, Liber inquisitionum nobilitatis, B/7 (22), 1754–57, fol. 13.

21 HNA Film B 1368, Veszprém County Archives, Acta et fragmènta nobilitaria, Fasc. H.I, No. 1, Horváth Fol. 2, 1747.

22 Kolosvári and Óvári, *Corpus Juris Hungarici*, 458.

23 Szegedi, *Tripartitum juris Hungarici Tyrocinium*, 509–12, 709–710.

24 Houston, *Scottish Literacy*, 267–274.

25 Vas County Archives, Archivum capituli Castriferrei, Testamenta, Fasc. 8, No. 12, 1692; HNA P 61, Bogyay Family Archives, 3, 1702, 1710; Ibid., Fasc. 7, No. 8; Vas County Archives, Archivum Capituli Castriferrei, Testamenta, Fasc. 5, No. 16; Vas County Archives, Archivum Capituli Castriferrei, Testamenta, 1583.

26 Szegedi, *Tripartitum juris Hungarici Tyrocinium*, 510. A concrete example: Borsod County Archives, Acta nobilitaria, Hubay 3 Dec 1768.

27 HNA P 650, Tallián Family Archives, 5, 1701.

28 On functional analphabets: Graff, *Legacies of Literacy*, 381–395; Lockridge, *Literacy in Colonial New England*, 7–8, 72–93; Lockridge, "L'alphabétisation en Amérique", 503–18; Graff, *Labyrinths of Literacy*, 158–161.

29 HNA P 600, Szarvaskendi Sibrik Family Archives, 26, 1661; ŠOBA Bytča, Trencsén, Inquisitiones, No. 852, 1743; Ibid., No. 1828, 1747; ŠOBA Banská Bystrica, Gömör, Criminalia, Fasc. I/A, No. 4, 1728; Vas County Archives, IV/1/kk, Fasc. 2, No. 6, 1702.

30 Vas County Archives, IV/1/f, Orphanalia, 22, 28, No. 5, 1797; Vas County Archives, Archivum Capituli Castriferrei, Testamenta, Fasc. 3, No. 47, 1/2, 1783, Fasc. 1, No. 5, 1772; Ibid., Fasc. 3, No. 19, 1702; HNA P 1313, Batthyány Family Archives, 68, Senioratus Alm. 2, Lad. 2, No. 2, 1737.

31 HNA P 1322, Batthyány Family Archives, 196, Sedes dominalis Fasc. 2, No. 28, 1754.

32 Vas County Archives, Archivum Capituli Castriferrei, Testamenta, Fasc. 2, No. 41/a, 1757, Vas County Archives, IV/1/t, Testamenta, Fasc. 1, No. 28, 1728.

33 HNA P 1322, Batthyány Family Archives, 87, Conscriptio dominii, Körmend 1716, p. 284. Similar cases in Poland and in Spain: Urban, "Sztuka pisania", 42–43; Larquié, "L'alphabétisation", 134, 136.

34 Vas County Archives, IV/1/t, Testamenta, 1701. "Manu aliena" subscription of an ill monk: Hungarian Franciscan Archives, Budapest, Gyöngyös monastery, Bosna, 1739; Sv. Duh, Zagreb, Cong. prov. Dalmatiae, passim.

35 Vas County Archives, IV/1/t, Testamenta, Fasc. 2, No. 33, 44, Fasc. 3, No. 14, 10, 23, 24, 34, 46, Fasc. 1, No. 8–1/2, 1734.

36 Vas County Archives, IV/1/t, Testamenta, Fasc. 3, No. 20, 34, 46; HNA P 701, Vidos Family Archives, 1703.

37 Vas County Archives, Divisionales, IV/1/v, Fasc. 8, No. 7, 1771.

38 Ibid., Fasc. 8, No. 13, 1772.

39 Vas County Archives, IV/1/t, Testamenta, Fasc. 2, No. 44/A, 1749.

40 The testaments: Vas County Archives, IV/1/t, Testamenta, IV/1/v, Divisionales, Vas County Archives, Archivum Capituli Castriferrei, Testamenta.

41 Wirth, "A nemesi kisbirtok", 140–148; Benda, "Egy Zala megyei köznemesi gazdaság", 1–7.

42 Hudi, *Nemesvámos története*, 142–144; Hudi, "Alfabetizáció és népi írásbeliség", 16–17; Hudi, "Az írni-olvasni tudás", 38–46.

43 Johansson, "History of literacy", 151–182; Johansson, "Literacy Campaigns", 65–96; Norden, "Die Alphabetisierung", 103–164; von Wartburg–Ambühl, *Alphabetisierung und Lektüre*, 50–99, 30–31.

44 Borsod County Archives, Acta nobilitaria, Mihály 1752. For the well-known beginning formula of early modern documents—*legituris ac legi audituris* ("to those who will read this and to those who will hear this being read")—see some examples: Hofkammerarchiv, Wien, Hoffinanz Ungarn, Rote Nummer 142, 143; APF SOCG, Vol. 333, Fol. 236.

45 ŠOBA Košice, Abaúj, Acta nobilitaria, M. 2, Fol. 19, 1766; ŠOBA Košice, Abaúj, Acta nobilitaria, 207, Fasc. VI, No. 30, No. 21, 1771; ŠOBA Košice, Abaúj, Acta nobilitaria, 702, Fasc. X, No. 36, Kovács 1738; Borsod County Archives, Acta nobilitaria, Czakó 1755.

46 Borsod County Archives, Acta nobilitaria, under the names of these families.

47 ŠOBA Košice, Abaúj, Acta nobilitaria, 418, 882, No. 1, 1745.

48 Szilágyi, *Elmét vidító elegy–belegy dolgok*, 212. On reading glasses in England: Weatherill, *Consumer behaviour*, 195, 201.

49 Vida, *Szerelmes Orsikám*, 235; *Kemény János és Bethlen Miklós*, 491.

50 On György Hertelendy: Vas County Archives, Orphanalia, IV/f, 14, p. 75 (1789). On Zsigmond Botka: Ibid., Fasc. 2, No. 23, p. 379 (1758). On József Laky: Ibid., Fasc. 22, Fol. 230/a, (1797).

51 HNA Film B. 1376; Veszprém County Archives, Fasc. R. I, Acta nobilitaria, No. 16, Fol. 8, Rusa 1747.

52 For solid results drawn from small samples, see also Larquié, "L'alphabétisation", 134; Sallmann, "Alphabétisation et hiérarchie", 79–98.

53 Vas County Archives, Inquisitio nobilium, and Zala County Archives, Investigatio nobilium, passim.

54 HNA Film B 1391, Zala County Archives, Investigatio nobilium, Fasc. 6, Fol. 51, 1718.

55 Vas County Archives, Inquisitio nobilium, IV/1, Fasc. 4, No. 36, 1761.

56 Vas County Archives, Inquisitio nobilium, IV/5, Fasc. 3, No. 39, 1727; HNA Film B 1369, Veszprém County Archives, Acta nobilitaria, Fasc. J/I, No. 3, Fol. 1, 1782.

57 Vas County Archives, Inquisitio nobilium, IV/5, Fasc. 2, No. 93, 1754.

58 HNA Film B 1377, Veszprém County Archives, Acta nobilitaria, Fasc. VI/I, No. 1, Vajda 1733.

59 HNA B 1375, Veszprém County Archives, Acta nobilitaria, Fasc. S/III, Szita 1731.

60 Vas County Archives, Inquisitio nobilium, IV/5, Fasc. 3, No. 16, 1726, Fasc. 1, No. 63, 1728.

61 ŠOBA Košice, Abaúj, Acta nobilitaria, 405. 25. Balogh, Fasc. II, No. 49, 17 Oct 1744.

62 ŠOBA Košice, Abaúj, Acta nobilitaria, 409. 273, 409. 268, 408. 197, 406. 42, 405. 8; ŠOBA Košice, Abaúj, Acta nobilitaria, 405. 25, Balogh 1743.

63 Borsod County Archives, Acta nobilitaria, Fuder 1745.

64 ŠOBA Košice, Abaúj, Acta nobilitaria, 416. 702, Fasc. X, No. 36, 1738, 418. 883, Paitás Fasc. XI, No. 19, 1745.

65 ŠOBA Košice, Abaúj, Acta nobilitaria, Abaúj, 419. 955, Fasc. XI, No. 72, Tóth 1746.

66 ŠOBA Košice, Abaúj, Acta nobilitaria, 418. 880, Borbély alias Pap Fasc. XI, No. 17, 1737.

67 ŠOBA Košice, Abaúj, Acta nobilitaria, 416. 707, 21 Apr 1742, Fasc. X, No. 41, Kornis.

68 ŠOBA Košice, Abaúj, Acta nobilitaria, 418. 881, Fasc. XI, No. 16, Pap 1742.

69 ŠOBA Košice, Abaúj, Acta nobilitaria, 407. 160, Gyarmathy, Fasc. II, No. 29, 466, Fasc. II, No. 45, No. 65, 1743, 418. 881, Fasc. XI, No. 16, 1742, 498, Fasc. III, No. 61, 1752.

70 ŠOBA Košice, Abaúj, Acta nobilitaria, 483, Pócs, Fasc. VI, No. 52, 657, Fasc. III, No. 29, Vitelky 1748.

71 ŠOBA Košice, Abaúj, Acta nobilitaria, 409. 266, Fasc. II, No. 24, 1742, 413. 467, Fasc. II, No. 44, 1743, 407. 116, Fasc. V, No. 10, 1763, Esztáry.

72 ŠOBA Košice, Abaúj, Acta nobilitaria, 414. 610, Tarnóczy, Fasc. V, No. 32, 1766.
73 ŠOBA Košice, Abaúj, Acta nobilitaria, 406. 37, Fasc. V, No. 29, Buko 1766.
74 ŠOBA Košice, Abaúj, Acta nobilitaria, 417. 764, Fasc. X, No. 49, 1749. Kádár: Ibid., 416. 755, Fasc. IX, No. 28, Czeke 1743.
75 ŠOBA Košice, Abaúj Acta nobilitaria, 413. 443, Fasc. III, No. 42, 1753.
76 Borsod County Archives, Acta nobilitaria, Buzgány 1728, Czeglédy 1793, Szilvásy 1774, Lipcse 1752, Lukáts 1752.
77 Borsod County Archives, Acta nobilitaria, Horváth 1740.
78 Borsod County Archives, Acta nobilitaria, 413. 441, Nagy, Fasc. III, No 69, 1752.
79 HNA E 185, Archivum Camerae, Archivum familiae Nádasdy, Tarnóczy–Nádasdy 18 Aug 1566. Komáromy, *Tarnóczy Andrásné levelei*, 549. On her family, see also Borsa, "A gorbonoki", 5–12.
80 HNA E 185, Archivum Camerae, Archivum familiae Nádasdy, Tarnóczy–Nádasdy, passim.
81 Vida, *Szerelmes Orsikám*.
82 Ibid., 36, 38, 264, 123, 134, 98–99; Szathmáry, *Óhajtott szép kincsecském*, 41.
83 Vida, *Szerelmes Orsikám*, 54, 136, 207.
84 Ibid., 221.
85 Kubinyi, *Bethlenfalvi gróf Thurzó*, I, No. IV.
86 Ibid., L. (1593), LI. (1593), CI. (1594), XCIX. (1594).
87 Štátny Ústredný Archív, Bratislava, Zay–Ugróczy Family Archives, 63, 975–976. Special thanks to Péter Kőszeghy who drew my attention this letter.
88 Benda, *Nyári Pál és Várday Kata*, 13; Hargittay, *Régi magyar levelestár*, 317; Eckhardt, *Két vitéz nemesúr*, 9, 11, 27; Kubinyi, *Bethlenfalvi gróf Thurzó*, II 2; Sámuel, *Teleki Mihály levelezése*, I 8.
89 HNA P 1313, Batthyány Family Archives, 68, Senioratus Lad. 2, No. 11, 14/B.
90 Vas County Archives, Archivum Capituli Castriferrei, Testamenta, Fasc. 5, No. 16, Fasc. 5, No. 17.
91 Sámuel, *Teleki Mihály levelezése*, II, 9, 167, 231, 235.
92 Jankovich, *Bethlen Miklós levelei*, I, 200; Kozocsa, *Magyar szerelmes levelek*, 50–51; *Kemény János és Bethlen Miklós*, 625; Sámuel, *Teleki Mihály levelezése*, IV, 159, 153–54; Bethlen, *Erdély története*, 297, 303; Szilády and Szilágyi, *Török–magyarkori államokmánytár*, IV, 383–384.
93 Vas County Archives, XIII/35, Szelestei Family Archives, 3, 1683.
94 Vas County Archives, XIII/40, Vajda Family Archives, 2, 1716, 1724.
95 Signatures: Vas County Archives, XIII/40, Vajda Family Archives, XIII/35, Szelestei Family Archives; HNA P 701, Vidos Family Archives, 2, P 600, Sibrik Family Archives, 8; HNA P 650, Tallián Family Archives, 5, P 533, Ostffy Family Archives, P 61, Bogyay Family Archives, P 430, Kisfaludy Family Archives, 5.
96 Ferenc Kazinczy on his grandmother: Ferenc Kazinczy *Művei*, I, 213.
97 HNA P 430, Kisfaludy Family Archives, 9, 1716, 1720, 1723; Bánkúti, "Egy kuruc nemesifjú útja", 265–266. 270; HNA P 430, Kisfaludy Family Archives, 9, 1722, 1723.
98 Vas County Archives, IV/1/t, Testamenta; Vas County Archives, Archivum Capituli Castriferrei, Testamenta, passim.
99 HNA P 701, Vidos Family Archives, 1, 1657.

100 HNA P 61, Bogyay Family Archives, 2, 1659; Vas County Archives, XIII/35, Szelestei Family Archives, 2, 1632, 1644.

101 HNA P 701, Vidos Family Archives, 2, 1640.

102 Komáromy, *Magyar levelek*, 530, 533, 537, 536.

103 Vas County Archives, XIII/35, Szelestei Family Archives, 4, 1634.

104 HNA P 45, Békássy Family Archives, 8, 1674 and 1635.

105 HNA P 1314, Batthyány Family Archives, Missiles, No. 25443, 25438, 25434.

106 Vas County Archives, IV/1/t, Testamenta, Fasc. 3, No. 42.

107 HNA P 275, Festetich Family Archives, 82, D. IV, 104/a, p. 32, 1834, Personal communication by the anthropologist Sándor Horváth.

108 HNA P 623, Széchényi Family Archives, 190, III, 2, p. 124/a, n.d.

109 Vas County Archives, XIII/35, Szelestei Family Archives, 2, 1673.

110 Vas County Archives, IV/1/v, Divisionales, Fasc. 8, No. 40, 1775.

111 HNA P 275, Festetich Family Archives, 80, D.IV.91.b, 1806.

112 HNA Film 23722, f.165; Rába Múzeum, Körmend 13/81.62; HNA Batthyány Family Archives, P 1313, Majoratus, Lad. 8/a, No. 11/F; Vas County Archives, VK 36/MV 6, Fasc. 4, No. 100, p. 17; HNA P 1322, Batthyány Family Archives, 178, Scholaria, 1.

113 Gvadányi, *Egy falusi nótáriusnak*, XI.

114 Szilágyi, *Elmét vidító elegy–belegy dolgok*, 222.

115 Brown, *Brief account*, 13–14.

116 Szepsi Csombor, *Europica varietas*, 183–184; Pach, *Magyarország története*, 1472–1475 (this chapter was written by László Makkai).

117 Defoe, 236–237.

118 Jankovich, *Bethlen Miklós levelei*, I, 580, 587, 537–538.

119 Olter, "English travellers in Hungary", passim.; Townson, *Travels in Hungary*, 332; Hunter, *Travels through France*, II, 238; Clarke, *Travels in various countries*, 651; Bright, *Travels from Vienna*, 96, 100, 138.

120 APF Roma, SOCG, Visite e Collegi, Vol. 11, Fol. 162–164; APF SOCG, Vol. 76, Fol. 291/r–v, 1634; APF SOCG, Vol.75, Fol.81; Tóth, *Relationes missionariorum*, 16–20.

121 APF Fondo di Vienna, Vol. 6, Fol. 214–214/v.

122 APF SOCG, Vol. 77, Fol. 178, Fol. 208/r–v, Vol. 75, Fol. 217–218, 227. Cima da Conegliano: APF SOCG, Vol. 81, Fol. 254/v.

123 APF SOCG, Vol. 82, Fol. 159, 1639.

124 APF SOCG, Vol. 601, Fol. 581–582, 587–588/v.

125 *Kemény János és Bethlen Miklós*, 55–56, 105. Similarly, the prince of Transylvania and king of Poland (1576–86), Stephen Báthory used the Latin language to communicate with his Polish subjects because he wanted to express himself precisely, as it was befitting to a king. In 1574 he discussed matters at length with the French traveller Pierre Lescalopier in Latin, and on other occasions he admonished the Polish nobles regularly in Latin: *Sum rex vester, nec fictus, nec pictus*. Lescalopier, *Utazása Erdélybe*, 72.

126 Táncsics, *Életpályám*, 61.

127 *Kemény János és Bethlen Miklós*, 61.

128 Pauler, *Wesselényi Ferenc*, II, 128; Cserei, *Erdély históriája*, 225; Táncsics, *Életpályám*, 76–78, 135–136. Even as late as 1793 the Lutheran priest of Lörrach, Rhine region, noted in his diary that the Hungarian soldiers stationed there surprised him not only because they danced all the time and courted all women of all classes, but even more because even noncommissioned officers and private men spoke fluently Latin: *fertig Latein sprechen*. Henner, *Das Tagebuch*, 74.

129 Táncsics, *Életpályám*, 76–78, 135–136.

130 Pest County Archives, Processus criminales, Fasc. 2, No. 53, 1766.

131 Cserei, *Erdély históriája*, 121.

132 Kazinczy, *Művei*, I, 221.

133 Vas County Archives, Archivum Capituli Castriferrei, Testamenta, Fasc. 1, No. 12, 1758; Ibid., Fasc. 2, No. 4, 1755.

134 ŠOBA Bytča, Trencsén, Inquisitiones, sine numero, 1754.

135 Csongrád County Archives, (Szentes), Károlyi Family Archives, Sedes dominalis, a.34, 1771.

136 ŠOBA Banská Bystrica, Gömör, Processus magistrales, 645, Fasc. II, No. 24, 1726.

137 ŠOBA Košice, Torna, Inquisitiones, 405, Fasc. IV, No. 18, 1778.

138 Kazinczy, *Művei*, 255–256.

139 Štátny Ústredný Archív, Bratislava, Pálffy Family Archives, 49, Arm. II, Lad. 9, Fasc. 1, No. 1, Processus criminales, Acta dominii Pozsonyiensis, 4 July 1737.

140 ŠOBA, Košice, Torna, Acta nobilitaria, 213, No. 390; Borsod County Archives, Miskolc, Inquisitiones, XIV, 265, 1755.

141 The best sources for the languages spoken by the population in the eighteenth century are the Catholic and Lutheran church visitations.

142 Vas County Archives, IV/1/v, Divisionalia, Fasc. 5, No. 4, 1740; Istványi, *A magyarnyelvű írásbeliség*, 21, 73; Táncsics, *Életpályám*, 77.

143 Archivum Romanum Societatis Iesu, Roma, Vol. Austria 20, Fol. 42.

144 HNA Film B 1390, Zala County Archives, Investigatio nobilium, Fasc. 5, Kelemen 1748; Cardona, "La linea d'ombra", 39–54.

145 HNA P 1313, Batthyány Family Archives, Majoratus, Lad. 9/a, No. 38, p. 17–18; HNA C 39, Acta fundationalia, Comitatus Castriferrei, Lad. E. Fasc. 12, Egyházashollós.

Chapter 4

1 Similar ancestry investigations took place during the reign of Louis XIV in France: Meyer, *La noblesse bretonne*, 41–60; Chartier and Richet, *Représentation et vouloir politiques*, 114–115; Nassiet, *Noblesse et pauvreté*, 201–211. Ancestry investigations in England: Stone, *Crisis of aristocracy*, 38–43; Holmes, *Gentry in England and Wales*, 6–19. See also Woolf, "Common voice", 39–40; Ong, *Oralità e scrittura*, 139–145; Clanchy, *From memory to written record*, 175–176; Clanchy, "Literacy, law and power", 25–34. In Hungary: Kósa, "Polgárosuló és parasztosodó kisnemesek", 703–710.

2 HNA Film B. 1390, Zala County Archives, Investigatio nobilium, Fasc. 9, Fol. 28, No. 7, 1, 1766.

3 ŠOBA Košice, Abaúj, Processus criminales, Fasc. XIV, No. 1, 1755; Kóta, "Ebül szerzett kutyabőr", 311.

4 HNA Film B 1390, Zala County Archives, Investigatio nobilium, Fasc. 5, Fol. 168, 19 Feb 1728. For the prices: Zimányi, *Der Bauernstand*, appendix. See also HNA Film B 1373, Veszprém County Archives, Acta nobilitaria, Fasc. N, No. 12, Nyúl 1717.

5 HNA Film B 1378, Veszprém County Archives, Acta et fragmenta nobilitaria, IV/1/e/bb, Fasc. V/II, No. 23, Fol. 4, Vörös 1793.

6 HNA B 1377, Veszprém County Archives, Acta nobilitaria, Fasc. V/1, No. 11, 1746.

7 HNA Film B 1371, Veszprém County Archives, Acta nobilitaria, Fasc. M/I, No. 7, Márton 1726.

8 HNA Film B 1392, Zala County Archives, Investigatio nobilium, Fasc. 8, No. 3, Fol. 5, 1760.

9 ŠOBA Košice, Abaúj, Inquisitio nobilium, 407. 84, Czimbalmos 1764.

10 ŠOBA Košice, Abaúj, Acta nobilitaria, 416. 713, Fasc. X, No. 12, 1748; Borsod County Archives, Acta nobilitaria, Barta Varga 1756, Szabó 1776, Pányi 1751.

11 ŠOBA Banská Bystrica, Gömör, Inquisitio nobilium, B/7/22/, sub No. 8/H, 1751.

12 HNA Film B 1257, Győr County Archives, Acta nobilitaria, Beke 1754.

13 HNA Film B 1257, Győr County Archives, Acta nobilitaria, Beke, Fol. 4, 1756; Vas County Archives, IV/5, Inquisitio nobilium, Fasc. 2, No. 89, 1744. See also HNA Film B 1389, Zala County Archives, Investigatio nobilium, Fasc. 4, Fol. 56, 1740; ŠOBA Košice, Abaúj, Acta nobilitaria, 406. 42, Fasc. 11, No. 27, Borbély 1743; HNA Film B 1389, Zala County Archives, Investigatio nobilium, Fasc. 3/M, Fol. 90, Investigatio nobilium, 1736; ŠOBA Košice, Abaúj, Acta nobilitaria, 405. 26, Fasc. IV, No. 23, Balogh "B" 1756; Vas County Archives, IV/5, Inquisitio nobilium, Fasc. 2, No. 70, 1733; Borsod County Archives, Acta nobilitaria, Holló 1792. See also Vas County Archives, IV/5, Inquisitio nobilium, Fasc. 1, No. 51, GG. 1783; HNA Film 1389, Zala County Archives, Investigatio nobilium, Fasc. 2, "SSS", 1733; HNA Film B 1390, Zala County Archives, Investigatio nobilium, Fasc. 5, No. 134, Fol. 480, 1727; Fasc. 5, No. 212, Fol. 542, 1727; HNA Film B 1393, Zala County Archives, Investigatio nobilium, Fasc. 10, No. 5, Fol. 42, 1737.

14 HNA Ft B 1375, Veszprém County Archives, Acta nobilitaria, Fasc. S/IV, No. 34, Szűcs 1772. See also Borsod County Archives, Acta nobilitaria, Berzy 2 Dec 1724.

15 HNA B 1376, Veszprém County Archives, Acta nobilitaria, Fasc. T/I, Tormási 1724.

16 ŠOBA Košice, Abaúj, Inquisitio nobilium, 409. 273, Fasc. II, No. 48, Kovács 1744.

17 Vas County Archives, IV/5, Inquisitio nobilium, Fasc. 2, No. 47–H, 1719.

18 ŠOBA Košice, Abaúj, Inquisitio nobilium, 408. 207, Fasc. VI, No. 21, Hosszú 1771; Vas County Archives, IV/5, Inquisitio nobilium, Fasc. 4, No. 26, 1758; HNA Film B 1375, Veszprém County Archives, Acta nobilitaria, Fasc. S/III, Simon 1733; HNA Film B 1390, Zala County Archives, Investigatio nobilium, Fasc. 5, 1748.

19 HNA Film B 1374, Veszprém County Archives, Acta nobilitaria, Fasc. S/II, Fol. 129, Szabó 1758. See also Vas County Archives, IV/5, Inquisitio nobilium, Fasc. 2, No. 93.

20 HNA Film B 1389, Zala County Archives, Investigatio nobilium, Fasc. 2, Litt. CC, 1728; HNA Film B 1256, Győr County Archives, Acta nobilitaria, Balás 1744.

21 Vas County Archives, IV/5, Inquisitio nobilium, Fasc. 1, No. 22, 1769; HNA Film B 1390, Zala County Archives, Investigatio nobilium, Fasc. 5, Fol. 264, 1733. See also Ibid., Fol. 326, 1728, Uo. Fol. 180, 1727; HNA Film B 1374, Veszprém County Archives, Acta nobilitaria, Fasc. S/II, Fol. 129, 1758, Fasc. R/I, No. 3, Rác 1758; HNA Film B 1391, Zala County Archives, Investigatio nobilium, Fasc. 5, No. 257, Fol. 657, 1757, B 1389, Fasc. 4, No. 225, Fol. 76, 1740; ŠOBA Košice, Abaúj, Inquisitio nobilium, 405. 26, Fasc. IV, No. 23, Balogh 1756.

22 HNA Film B 1375, Veszprém County Archives, Acta nobilitaria, Fasc. S/III, No. 38, 1721; HNA Film 1374, Veszprém County Archives, Acta nobilitaria, Fasc. R/I, No. 13, Répási 1752; Borsod County Archives, Acta nobilitaria, Holló, Kun, Magyari, Herke, Bede, Farkas, Csotka, Nagy; ŠOBA Košice, Abaúj, Inquisitio nobilium, 408. 173, Görgey Fasc. III, No. 35, 1749.

23 ŠOBA Košice, Abaúj, Inquisitio nobilium, 407. 160, Fasc. II, No. 29, Gyarmathy 1743; Borsod County Archives, Acta nobilitaria, Farkas 1776; HNA Film B 1263, Győr County Archives, Acta nobilitaria, Hajduk 1753; ŠOBA Košice, Abaúj, Inquisitio nobilium, 407. 162, Fasc. 11, No. 59, 1744.

24 ŠOBA Košice, Abaúj, Inquisitio nobilium, 413. 466, Fasc. II, No. 64, Pap 1744. Similar cases: 39 HNA Film B 1377, Veszprém County Archives, Acta nobilitaria, Fasc. V/I, No. 11, sub. No. 3, 1746; HNA Film B 1257, Győr County Archives, Acta nobilitaria, Bereczky 1754; HNA Film, Zala County Archives, Investigatio nobilium, Fasc. 9, Fol. 41, 1765, Vas County Archives, IV/5, Inquisitio nobilium, Fasc. 3, No. 45, 1753; HNA Film B 1374, Veszprém County Archives, Acta nobilitaria, Fasc. S, Fol. 46, Szalay 1753; HNA Film B 1369, Veszprém County Archives, Acta nobilitaria, Fasc. K/I, No. 25, Kether 1742; HNA Film B 1376, Veszprém County Archives, Acta nobilitaria, Fasc. I/I, Tormási 1724; HNA Film B 1375, Veszprém County Archives, Acta nobilitaria, Fasc. S/III, No. 38, Sarnóczay 1721, Fasc. S/II, No. 38, Szekér 1763; HNA Film B 1389, Zala County Archives, Investigatio nobilium, Fasc. 3/M, Fol. 90, 1736; ŠOBA Košice, Abaúj, Inquisitio nobilium, 406. 42, Fasc. II, No. 27, 1743; HNA Film B 1391, Zala County Archives, Investigatio nobilium, Fasc. 5, No. 237, Fol. 614, 1715.

25 Fügedi, "Verba volant", 1–25; Takács, *Határjelek, határjárás*, 113–116.

26 ŠOBA Košice, Abaúj, Inquisitio nobilium, 409. 268, Kecskeméti alias Kecskés, 1743, Fasc. X, No. 30, and Ibid., Fasc. II, No. 28 (the document's draft); HNA Film B 1368, Veszprém County Archives, Acta et fragmenta nobilitaria, Fasc. H.I, No. 1, Horváth Fol. 2, 1747.

27 Vas County Archives, Inquisitio nobilium, Fasc. 1, No. 7, Antal 1733; Borsod County Archives, Acta nobilitaria, Poczik 1767; HNA Film B 1377, Veszprém County Archives, Acta nobilitaria, Fasc. V/I, Fol. 96, Varga 1773. Pálffi: Vas County Archives, IV/5, Inquisitio nobilium, Fasc. 3, No. 45, 1753, Borsod County Archives, Acta nobilitaria, Pető 1724.

28 HNA Film B 1378, Veszprém County Archives, Acta nobilitaria, Vörös Fol. 7, 1775.

29 HNA Film B 1370, Veszprém County Archives, Acta nobilitaria, Fasc. K/IV, No. 55, Fol. 76, Kozma 1759.

30 HNA Film B 1379, Veszprém County Archives, Processus nobilium, Bodor 1753.

31 HNA Film B 1390, Zala County Archives, Investigatio nobilium, Fasc. 5, Fol. 326, 1728; Takács, *Határjelek, határjárás*, 177–192; Tóth, *Somogyi határvizsgálatok*, 152, 154; ŠOBA Košice, Abaúj, Acta nobilitaria, 416. 699, Fasc. X, No. 33, Kis Mester 1741.

32 HNA Film B 1389, Zala County Archives, Investigatio nobilium, Fasc. 2/CC, 1728; ŠOBA Košice, Abaúj, Acta investigationis nobilium, 417. 768. See also Ibid., 416. 744, Fasc. IX, No. 20, Batha 1748; HNA Film B 1376, Veszprém County Archives, Acta nobilitaria, Fasc. T/I, Tormási 1724; HNA Film B 1390, Zala County Archives, Investigatio nobilium, Fasc. 5, No. 140, 1750.

33 Vas County Archives, IV/5, Inquisitio nobilium, Fasc. 2, No. 93, 1754.

34 Vas County Archives, IV/5, Inquisitio nobilium, Fasc. 2, No. 97.

35 Vas County Archives, IV/5, Inquisitio nobilium, Fasc. 2, No. 3, 1757.

36 Vas County Archives, IV/12/I, Fasc. 3, No. 11, 1760.

37 Vas County Archives, IV/5, Inquisitio nobilium, Fasc. 2, No. 50, 1728, Fasc. 2, No. 82, 1768.

38 HNA Film B 1368, Veszprém County Archives, Acta nobilitaria, Fasc. H/I, No. 1, Horváth Fol. 100, 1748. Almost identical cases: HNA Film B 1378, Veszprém County Archives, Acta nobilitaria, Fasc. Z./I, No. 12, Zsigmond Fol. 1, 1749; HNA Film B 1392, Zala County Archives, Investigatio nobilium, Fasc. 9, No. 7, Fol. 28, No. 1; HNA Film B 1377, Veszprém County Archives, Acta nobilitaria, Fasc. V/I, Fol. 111, Varga 1753; HNA Film B 1379, Veszprém County Archives, Acta nobilitaria, Fasc. A. Ács "B", 1801; Vas County Archives, Processus nobilium, IV/1/d, Fasc. 3, No. 14, 1733; HNA Film B 1369, Veszprém County Archives, Acta nobilitaria, Fasc. K/I, No. 1, 1743, Kámi; HNA Film B 1372, Veszprém County Archives, Acta nobilitaria, Fasc. N/II, No. 5, Fol. 10, 1700, Borsod County Archives, Acta nobilitaria, Havas 1747, Beke 1728.

39 HNA Film B 1392, Zala County Archives, Investigatio nobilium, Fasc. 8, No. 1, Fol. 10, 1743.

40 HNA Film B 1393, Zala County Archives, Investigatio nobilium, Fasc. 10, No. 6, Fasc. 2, Litera X.

41 HNA Film B 1930, Zala County Archives, Investigatio nobilium, Fasc. 2/GG, 1733.

42 Vas County Archives, Processus nobilium, IV/1/d, Fasc. 4, No. 3/E.

43 HNA Film B 1392, Zala County Archives, Investigatio nobilium, Fasc. 7, No. 2, Fol. 34.

44 Vas County Archives, IV/12/I, Fasc. 7, No. 10/A, 1779.

45 HNA Film B 1374, Veszprém County Archives, Acta nobilitaria, Fasc. R/I, No. 16, 1747, Fasc. K/IV, No. 55, Fol. 87; HNA Film B 1392, Zala County Archives, Investigatio nobilium, Fasc. 7, No. 2, Fol. 34; Borsod County Archives, Acta nobilitaria, Fónyi 1742; Ibid., Nagy Mády 1779, Bihary 1737, Káló 1737, Rácz 1752, Koródi 1781, Janka 1779; APF SOCG, Vol. 624, Fol. 207–208, 1720, Vol. 601, Fol. 587/v, 591. 589, 1715, Vol. 630, Fol. 75–76, 1720.

46 Vas County Archives, IV/12/I, Fasc. 1, No. 11, 1746.

47 HNA Film B 1391, Zala County Archives, Investigatio nobilium, Fasc. 6, Fol. 51; Borsod County Archives, Acta nobilitaria, Kozma 1778, Szőcs 1762.

48 HNA Film B 1390, Zala County Archives, Investigatio nobilium, Vol. 4, Tik 1736.

49 HNA P 1313, Batthyány Family Archives, Majoratus, Lad. 6, No. 16, Metalia.

50 Vas County Archives, IV/5, Inquisitio nobilium, Fasc. 3, No. 7, No. 36, No. 41.
51 HNA Film B 1392, Zala County Archives, Investigatio nobilium, Fasc. 7, No. 2, Fol. 43. 46; HNA Film B 1365, Veszprém County Archives, Acta nobilitaria, Fasc. B/IV, No. 43, B 1369, Fasc. K/I, No. 6, 1742.
52 ŠOBA Košice, Torna, Acta nobilitaria, 208. 214/192 Oláh, 1767; Borsod County Archives, Acta nobilitaria, Fekete 1755.
53 ŠOBA Košice, Abaúj, Acta nobilitaria, 417. 816, Fasc. IX, No. 56, Fazakas 1742, 416. 737, Fasc. IX, No. 13, 1745, Bodolai, 417. 866, Rácz 1743.
54 ŠOBA Košice, Abaúj, Acta nobilitaria, 417. 802, Morvay Fasc. X, No. 74, 1741, Fasc. X, No. 53, Kosdy 1750.
55 ŠOBA Košice, Abaúj, Inquistiones Fasc. I, No. 84, 1737.
56 Borsod County Archives, Acta nobilitaria, Mihály alias Rinóth 1638 (Mályinka).
57 Borsod County Archives, Acta nobilitaria, Nagy, Kazai, Szabó, Rigó, Rácz, Kun, Kósa, Pázmándi.
58 ŠOBA Košice, Torna, Acta nobilitaria, 211. 315, No. 3, Czélia 1794.
59 ŠOBA Banská Bystrica, Gömör, Processus magistrales, 678, Fasc. XI, No. 481–482, 1776. On Jánosik see *Encyklopédia Slovenská II*, 479.
60 Vas County Archives, IV/5, Inquisitio nobilium, Fasc. 3, No. 5, 1754; Borsod County Archives, Acta nobilitaria, Bordás 1740.
61 Vas County Archives, IV/5, Inquisitio nobilium, Fasc. 3, No. 39, 1727.
62 ŠOBA Košice, Abaúj, Acta nobilitaria, 413. 448, Fasc. V, No. 27, 1766, Abaúj, Inquisitiones, Criminalia, Fasc. II, No. 22; Pest County Archives, IV/31/f, Processus criminales, Fasc. 2, No. 45; See also Ibid., 405, No. 22, Árvay–Lengyel 1742.
63 HNA Film B 1259, Győr County Archives, Acta nobilitaria, Cséri 1763.
64 Borsod County Archives, Acta nobilitaria, Rácz 1748, Kis 1793. See also Pinczés 1741; HNA P 1322, Batthyány Archives, Majoratus, Lad. 6, No. 40, Metalia; ŠOBA Bratislava, Pozsony County Archives, Éleskő, Sedes dominalis, Lad. 6, Fasc. 3, No. 1, No. 437.
65 HNA Film B 1374, Veszprém County Archives, Acta nobilitaria, Fasc. S/I, No. 5, Fol. 64–68, Szakál 1792; ŠOBA Košice, Abaúj, Acta nobilitaria, 415. 677, Fasc. VII, No. 35, Zádeczky 1784. See also Borsod County Archives, Acta nobilitaria, Nagy 1784, Hagyárosi 1785, Császár 1783, Pázmándi 1752, Fegyverneki 1771; Heves County Archives, Sedes dominalis episcopi Agriensis, 17, XII/3-b–17, 1781.
66 ŠOBA Košice Abaúj, Acta nobilitaria, 415. 677, Fasc. VII, No. 35.
67 HNA Film B 1390, Zala County Archives, Investigatio nobilium, Vol. 4, Tik.
68 ŠOBA Košice, Abaúj, Acta nobilitaria, 415. 686, Fasc. X, No. 19, Idrányi 1742.
69 Vas County Archives, Inquisitio nobilium, IV/5, Fasc. 1, No. 65/a, 1775; Borsod County Archives, Acta nobilitaria. Kiss 1779.
70 HNA Film B 1371, Veszprém County Archives, Acta nobilitaria, Fasc. M. I, No. 43, 1766; Vas County Archives, Inquisitio nobilium, IV/5, Fasc. 4, No. 41, 1754.
71 Werbőczy, *Tripartitum Juris Hungarici*, 58–60.
72 Vas County Archives, Inquisitio nobilium, IV/5, Fasc. 1, No. 51/GG, 1783; Varga, *Szervitorok katonai szolgálata*; Iványi, *Képek Körmend múltjából*; Zimányi, "Adatok a dunántúli hajdúk történetéhez", 294–296. See also Borsod County Archives, Acta nobilitaria, Pányi 8 March 1747.

73 HNA Film B 1389, Zala County Archives, Investigatio nobilium, Fasc. 4, No. 220, 1735. See also Vas County Archives, IV/5, Inquisitio nobilium, Fasc. 2, No. 70, 1733.

74 HNA Film B 1370, Veszprém County Archives, Acta nobilitaria, Fasc. K/II, No. 32, Kis Fol. 10, 1733.

75 HNA Film B 1390, Zala County Archives, Investigatio nobilium, Vol. 4, Fol. 52, No. 16/L.

76 Vas County Archives, Processus nobilium, IV/1/d Fasc. 1, No. 4/E, 1765.

77 Some examples: HNA Film B 1259, Győr County Archives, Acta nobilitaria, Csicsay 1764; HNA Film B 1369, Veszprém County Archives, Acta nobilitaria, Fasc. K/I, No. 6, 1742, Fasc. N/I, No. 4, Fol. 46, 1726, Fasc. N, No. 5, Fol. 95, 1756, Fasc. J/I, No. 1, Joó 1729, Fasc. K/II, No. 32, Fol. 10–11, 1733.

78 Borsod County Archives, Acta nobilitaria—Balogh, Kun families.

79 HNA Film B 1369, Veszprém County Archives, Acta nobilitaria, Fasc. K/I, No. 6, Kalocza 1742, B. 1365, Fasc. B/IV, No. 43, 1742.

80 HNA Film B 1390, Zala County Archives, Investigatio nobilium, Fasc. 5, Fasc. 5, Fasc. 5, No. 207, Fasc. 5, Fol. 300.

81 Vas County Archives, IV/5, Inquisitio nobilium, Fasc. 4, No. 46, 1758. Further examples: Borsod County Archives, Acta nobilitaria—Pap, Beke, Bencsik families.

82 Vas County Archives, IV/5, Inquisitio nobilium, Fasc. 1, No. 52, 1733.

83 ŠOBA, Košice, Abaúj, Acta nobilitaria, 408. 173, Fasc. III, No. 35, Görgey 1749.

84 ŠOBA, Košice, Abaúj, Acta nobilitaria, 408. 207, Fasc. VI, No. 21, Hosszú 1771.

85 Vas County Archives, IV/5, Inquisitio nobilium, Fasc. 2, No. 89, 1744; HNA Film B 1372, Veszprém County Archives, Acta nobilitaria, Fasc. N/I, No. 3, Nagy 1771, Fol. 190.

86 HNA Film B 1332, Sopron County Archives, Acta nobilitaria, Csajtai, 1779; Borsod County Archives, Acta nobilitaria, Csizmadia 1763.

87 ŠOBA Košice, Torna, Inquisitiones nobilium, Fragmenta 405, No. 19; Borsod County Archives, Acta nobilitaria, Miskolczy 1755.

88 ŠOBA Košice, Abaúj, Acta nobilitaria, 405. 24, Balogh, 1753.

89 ŠOBA Košice, Abaúj, Acta nobilitaria, Inquisitio nobilium, 409. 247, Kőszeghy 1745.

90 HNA Film B 1389, Zala County Archives, Investigatio nobilium, Fasc. 3, No. 13, 1735.

91 HNA Film B 1389, Zala County Archives, Investigatio nobilium, Fasc. 3, No. 13, 1735. For comparison: HNA Film B 1366, Veszprém County Archives, Acta nobilitaria, Fasc. F/I, Fábján 1717. Further examples: HNA Film B 1365, Veszprém County Archives, Acta nobilitaria, Fasc. C/I, No. 4, Fol. 1, 1733; HNA Film B 1261, Győr County Archives, Acta nobilitaria, Filep 1754.

92 HNA Film B 1332, Sopron County Archives, Acta nobilitaria, Csajtai.

93 Vas County Archives, Inquisitio nobilium, IV/5, Fasc. 2, No. 102. A very similar case happened at this time in Miskolc, too. A certain András Balogh, coming from Veszprém County, tried to prove his title of nobility in Borsod County. However in the village, where he was supposedly born, nobody had ever heard of him. True, a nobleman named Balogh attested to be his parent and thus proved his noble genealogy; however, this man "would accept anybody as his close parent, if

he only received some gifts from him," as other witnesses declared to the judges. The presumed father of this Balogh, seeking his nobility, was a Várad tailor, just as in the other already quoted case; however, this man was only the stepfather of the supposed nobleman, whose real father was hanged as a criminal. Borsod County Archives, Acta nobilitaria, Balogh 1749.

94 In the well-known case of Martin Guerre in Southern France in the sixteenth century, suspicion arose in the village because the real Martin Guerre could not read, but the person who returned from the war as his alterego and took over his propriety even wrote fluently. Davis, Carrière, Vigne, *Le retour de Martin Guerre*, 118.

95 Nagy, *Magyar drámaírók*, 703–705.

Chapter 5

1 *Vas vármegye 1870*; *A Magyar Korona országaiban az 1870...*, 227–232, 239; *A Magyar Korona országaiban az 1881...*, 226–227, 228–235; *A Magyar Korona országaiban az 1891...*, 151–158; *A Magyar Korona országainak 1900...*, 96–99, 101–113, 132–153; *A Magyar Korona országainak 1910...*, 50–71; Vörös, *A művelődés*, 1399–1402.

2 Benda, "Iskolázás és az írástudás", 123–133; Le Roy Ladurie, "De la crise ultime", 520–526; Cressy, *Literacy and the Social Order*, 175–188.

3 Benda, "Iskolázás és az írástudás", 132. See also Furet and Sachs, "La croissance de l'alphabétisation", 714–737; Cressy, *Literacy and the Social Order*, 118–140.

4 *Vas vármegye 1870*; see the given villages.

5 Cressy, *Literacy and the Social Order*, 72–81, 98–103.

6 Cressy, *Literacy and the Social Order*, 175–201; Schofield, "Measurement of literacy", 437–545; Sanderson, "Education and the factory", 266–79; Sanderson, "Literacy and social mobility", 75–104; Stephens, "Illiteracy and schooling", 27–48; West, "Literacy and the industrial revolution", 369–383; Smout, "New evidence on popular religion", 114–127; Houston, *Scottish Literacy*; Vincent, *Literacy and Popular Culture*, 22–32, 53–92; and recently: Vincent, *Coming of Mass Literacy* (forthcoming at Polity Press; special thanks to the author for the manuscript). For further European countries, see Van de Woude, "Der alfabetisering", 256–267; Kamen, *The Iron Century*, 302; Parker, *The Dutch Revolt*, 21; Graff, *Legacies of Literacy*, 191–192; Kagan, *Students and society*; Larquié, "L'alphabétisation", 132–136; Le Flem, "Instruction, lecture et écriture", 29–43; Ruwet and Wellemans, *L'analphabétisme en Belgique*, 15, 21–29.

7 Furet and Ozouf, *Lire et écrire*; Houdaille, "Les signatures au mariage", 65–72; Chartier, Julia, Compère, *L'éducation en France*, 87–105; Graff, *Legacies of Literacy*, 265–266. For Germany: François, "Alphabetisierung in Frankreich und Deutschland"; Hinrichs, "Zum Alphabetisierungsstand", 21–42; Hinrichs, "Leben, Schulbesuch und Kirchenzucht", 15–33; Norden, "Die Alphabetisierung", 122–124, 140–144; Hinrichs, "Wie viele Menschen", 85–103; Engelsing, *Zur Sozialgeschichte*; Schenda, "Alphabetisierung und Literarisierungsprozesse", 154–163; Richter, "Zur Schriftkundigkeit", 79–102; Bödeker, "Lesestoffe, Lesebedürfnisse und Leseverhalten", 51–58; Bödeker, "Invisible Commerce of

Hearts", 583–612; Winnig, "Unterschriften aus der Altmark", 90–119; Winnig, "Alphabetisierung in der Frühen Neuzeit", 82–97; Siegert, "Zur Alphabetisierung", 283–308; Hofmeister, Prass, Winnige, "Elementary Education, Schools", 329–384.

8 Cipolla, *Literacy and Development*, 14–19, 85; Neugebauer, *Absolutistischer Staat und Schulwirklichkeit*; Graff, *Legacies of Literacy*, 285–291, 294–297; Katus, "A népesedés és a társadalmi szerkezet."

9 Sallmann, "Alphabétisation et hiérarchie", 79–98; Pelizzari, "Alfabeto e fisco", 99–152; Toscani, "L'alfabetismo nelle campagne", 549–610; Duglio, "Alfabetismo e società", 485–509; Marchesini, *Il bisogno di scrivere*, 3–32; Lucchi, "La Santacroce", 593–630; Anelli, Maffini, Viglio, *Leggere in provincia*, passim.; de Fort, *Scuola e analfabetismo*, 39–102; Pelizzari, *La penna*, 51–112; Marchesini, Qualis, 437.

10 Wyczański, "Alphabétisation et structure sociale", 705–713; Urban, "Sztuka pisania", 39–80; Urban, "Umiejetność pisania w Malopolsce", 231–256; Potkowski, "Écriture et société", 47–100.

11 Brooks, *When Russia Learned to Read*, 3–30; Marker, *Publishing, Printing, and the Origins*, 184–211; Cipolla, *Literacy and Development*, 116–118. On Estonia's literacy: Aarma, *Kirjaoskus Eestis*, 234–236; Raun, *The development*, 115–126; Popoff, *La Bulgarie économique*, passim.; Mishkova, "Literacy and nation–building", 63–93; Daskalova, *Literacy and Reading*, 7–22; Daskalova, *B'lgarskijat ucitel*, 223–237.

12 APF SOCG, Vol. 219, Fol. 179–182, Vol. 539, Fol. 129.

13 Sundhaussen, *Historische Statistik Serbiens*, 525–549; Adler, "Habsburg School Reform", 22–24.

Conclusion

1 Cressy, *Literacy and the Social Order*, 44; Kamen, *The Iron Century*, 302–303.

2 Kováts, *Mindenes gyűjtemény*, 313–363; Kosáry, *Művelődés*, 553.

3 Mályusz, *Sándor Lipót főherceg*, 827–828, 847–848; Engelsing, *Zur Sozialgeschichte*, 199; Schenda, "Alphabetisierung und Literarisierungsprozesse", 160; Chartier, Julia, Compère, *L'éducation en France*, 37–38; Chisick, *Limits of Reform in the Enlightenment*, 137–147, 166–167.

4 Bél, "Vas vármegye leírása", 123.

5 Misztótfalusi Kis, "Erdélyi féniks", 85.

6 APF Fondo di Vienna, Vol. 6, Fol. 111.

7 APF SOCG, Vol. 581, Fol. 76–77.

8 Notizie del mondo, Napoli, 11 May 1790 and 14 May 1790. Quoted in Rao, "Esercito e società", 660.

REFERENCES

I. Archival Sources

1. Hungarian National Archives, Budapest (HNA)

Archivum Camerae: Archivum familiae Nádasdy
Archivum Consilii Locumtenentialis: Acta fundationalia, Acta nobilitaria, Departamentum nobilitare, Departamentum scholarum nationalium
Batthyány Family Archives: Majoratus, Senioratus, Missiles, Instructiones, Conscriptiones, Village Archives, Acta sedis dominalis
Békássy Family Archives
Bogyay Family Archives
Esterházy Princes Family Archives: Acta sedis dominalis
Festetich Family Archives: Acta juris gladii, Village Archives
Hertelendy Family Archives
Kisfaludy Family Archives
Ostffy Family Archives
Szarvaskendi Sibrik Family Archives
Széchényi Family Archives: Acta dominii Sárvárfelvidék
Tallián Family Archives
Vidos Family Archives
Zichy Family Archives: Acta sedis dominalis, Missiles

2. Hungarian National Archives, Budapest, Microfilm Collection

Győr County Archives: Acta nobilitaria (on microfilm)
Nagykőrös: Prothocollum malefactorum (on microfilm)
Sopron County Archives: Acta nobilitaria (on microfilm)
Szombathely Diocesan Archives, Szombathely: Visitationes canonicae 1697–1782 (on microfilm)
Veszprém County Archives: Acta et fragmenta nobilitaria (on microfilm)
Zala County Archives: Investigatio nobilium (on microfilm)

3. Vas County Archives, Szombathely

Archivum Capituli Castriferrei: Litterae instrumentae, Testamentales, Metales
County Assembly Protocols, Insurrectionales, Orphanalia, Testamenta, Boundary
    investigations, Taxatio nobilium, Taxatio ignobilium, Processuales
Egervári Family Archives
Hertelendy Family Archives
Jakabfai Bernáth Family Archives
Lukinich Family Archives
Sankt Gotthard (Szentgotthárd) Cistercian Abbey Archives
Szegedy Family Archives
Szelestey Family Archives
Szentgyörgyi Horváth Family Archives
Tömördi Chernel Family Archives
Vajda Family Archives
Vépi Erdődy Family Archives
Village Archives: Alsóőr, Telekes, Ják, Kisunyom, Körmend, Molnaszecsőd, Szent-
    gotthárd
Vidos Family Archives
Weöres Family Archives

4. Hungarian Franciscan Archives, Budapest

Gyöngyös Monastery Archives: Bosna Argentina, Acta Varia

5. Heves County Archives, Eger

Acta sedis dominalis episcopi Agriensis
Gyöngyös Town Archives
Heves County: Prothocollum judiciarium

6. Borsod-Abaúj-Zemplén County Archives, Miskolc

Borsod County Archives: Acta nobilitaria
Miskolc Town Archives

7. Csongrád County Archives, Szentes

Csongrád County Archives: Criminalia
Károlyi Family Archives: Acta sedis dominalis

8. Pest County Archives, Budapest

Pest County Tribunal: Criminalia
Ráckeve Town Archives

9. Rába Múzeum, Körmend

Historical Collection

10. Szombathely Diocesan Library

Manuscripts: Schematismus Dioecesis

11. Lutheran Church Archives, Körmend

Acta Varia

12. Berényi Family Archives, Simaság (Private Collection)

Acta familiae

13. Hofkammerarchiv, Wien

Hoffinanz Ungarn

14. Neues Verwaltungsarchiv, Wien

Studienhofkommission

15. Archivum Romanum Societatis Iesu, Roma

Provincia Austria

16. Archivio di Sacra Congregazione de Propaganda Fide, Roma (APF)

Acta Sacrae Congregationis de Propaganda Fide
SC Bosna, SC Bulgaria, SC Dalmazia, SC Moldavia, SC Serbia, SC Ungheria e
   Transilvania
Fondo di Vienna
Scritture Originali riferite nelle Congregazioni Generali

17. Štátny Ústredný Archív, Bratislava

Amadé-Üchtritz Family Archives
Archivum praepositi Cisterciensis (Jászó)
Pálffy Family Archives

18. Štátny Oblastný Archív (=ŠOBA) (County District Archives), Bratislava

Acta sedis dominalis dominii Éleskő
Pozsony County Archives: Criminalia
Archivum Provinciae Marianae ordinis Sancti Francisci

19. Štátny Oblastný Archív (County District Archives), Košice

Abaúj County Archives: Acta Nobilitaria, Criminalia, Investigationes
Torna County Archives: Acta Nobilitaria, Criminalia, Investigationes

20. *Štátny Oblastný Archív (County District Archives), Prešov*

Sáros County Archives: Criminalia

21. *Štátny Oblastný Archív (County District Archives), Nitra*

Bars County Archives: Criminalia
Kis-Hont County Archives: Acta nobilitaria
Komárom County Archives: Criminalia

22. *Štátny Oblastný Archív (County District Archives), Bytča*

Trencsén County Archives: Inquisitiones
Turóc County Archives: Criminalia

23. *Štátny Oblastný Archív (County District Archives), Banská Bystrica*

Gömör County Archives: Criminalia, Inquisitio nobilitatis

24. *Samostan Sveti Duh, Zagreb*

Archivum provinciae Dalmatiae

II. Printed Sources

A Hét Mennyei Szent Zárok Imádsága (Prayers of the seven heavenly Saint Locks). n.p.: n.d.

A Magyar Korona országaiban az 1870. év elején végrehajtott népszámlálás eredményei (Census at the beginning of the year 1870 in the countries of the Hungarian Crown). Pest: 1871.

A Magyar Korona országaiban az 1881. év elején végrehajtott népszámlálás (Census at the beginning of the year 1881 in the countries of the Hungarian Crown). Budapest: 1882.

A Magyar Korona országaiban az 1891. év elején végrehajtott népszámlálás eredményei (Census at the beginning of the year 1891 in the countries of the Hungarian Crown). Budapest: 1893.

A Magyar Korona országainak 1900. évi népszámlálása (Census in the year 1900 in the countries of the Hungarian Crown). Budapest: 1902.

A Magyar Korona országainak 1910. évi népszámlálása (Census in the year 1910 in the countries of the Hungarian Crown). Budapest: 1912.

Aarma, Liivi. *Kirjaoskus Eestis 18. sajandi lopust 1880. aastateni*. Tallin: 1990.

Adler, Philip J. "Habsburg School Reform among the Orthodox Minorities." *Slavic Review* 33 (1974).

Alapi, Gyula. *Bűbájosok és boszorkányok Komárom vármegyében* (Sorcerers and witches in Komárom County). Komárom: 1914.

Andritsch, Johann. *Studenten und Lehrer aus Ungarn und Siebenbürgen an der Universität Graz*. Graz: 1965.

Anelli, Vittorio, Luigi Maffini, and Patrizia Viglio. *Leggere in provincia*. Bologna: 1986.

Az első magyarországi népszámlálás (1784–1787) (The first Hungarian census). Budapest: 1960.

Bánkúti, Imre. "Egy kuruc nemesifjú útja a laki udvarháztól a francia emigrációig" (The way of a young Kurutz noble from the manor house of Lak to French emigration). *Arrabona* 13 (1971).

Barbu, Daniel. "Écrire sur le sable. Temps, histoire et eschatologie dans la société roumaine à la fin de l'Ancien Régime." In *Temps et changement dans l'espace roumain*, edited by A. Zub, 103–14. Iaşi: 1991.

Bél, Mátyás. "Vas vármegye leírása" (Description of Vas County). *Vasi Szemle* 30: 1 (1976).

Benda, Gyula. "Egy Zala megyei köznemesi gazdaság és család a XVIII. század közepén" (Economy and family of a nobleman in Zala County in the middle of the eighteenth century). *Agrártörténeti Szemle* (Budapest) XXVI (1984): 1–84.

Benda, Kálmán. "A felvilágosodás és a paraszti műveltség a XVIII. századi Magyarországon" (Enlightenment and peasant culture in Hungary in the eighteenth century). In *Emberbarát vagy hazafi?* (Philanthrope or Patriot?), 292–296. Budapest: 1978.

—, "A magyar köznemesség művelődési törekvései a XVIII. században" (Cultural aspirations of Hungarian gentlefolk in the eighteenth century). In *Nógrád megyei Múzeumok Évkönyve VII*, 87–92. Salgótarján: 1981.

—. "Az iskolázás és az írástudás a dunántúli parasztság körében az 1770–es években" (Schooling and literacy among peasants in Transdanubia in the 1770s). In *Somogy megye múltjából 8*, 123–132. Kaposvár: 1977.

—, ed. *Nyári Pál és Várday Kata levelezése 1600–1607* (Correspondence of Pál Nyári and Kata Várday). Kisvárda: 1975.

Bethlen, János. *Erdély története 1629–1673* (History of Transylvania). Budapest: 1993.

Bitskey, István. "Spiritual Life in Early Modern Hungary." In *A Cultural History of Hungary*, edited by László Kósa, 229–286. Budapest: 1999.

Blay, Francisco Gimeno. "La escritura en la diocesis de Segorbe." *Alfabetismo e cultura scritta*. 1984.

Bödeker, Hans Erich. "The Invisible Commerce of Hearts and Minds. Authors, the literary market and the Public in Eighteenth-century Germany." In *Le livre et l'historien. Mélanges Henri-Jean Martin*, edited by Frédéric Barbier et al., 583–612. Genève: 1997.

—, "Lesestoffe, Lesebedürfnisse und Leseverhalten im 'Kreis von Münster'." In *Meine Seele ist auf der Spitze meiner Feder*, edited by Petra Schulz, 51–58. Münster: 1998.

Bogucka, Maria. "Space and time as factors shaping Polish mentality from the 16th until the eighteenth century." *Acta Poloniae Historica* 66 (1992): 39–52.

Bollème, Geneviève. "Littérature populaire et littérature de colportage au 18e siècle." In *Livre et société dans la France du XVIIIe siècle*, edited by François Furet, 61–92. Paris: 1965.

Borsa, Iván. "A gorbonoki, majd belosovci Kerhen család történetéhez" (To the history of the Kerhen family). *Somogy megye múltjából* (Kaposvár) 22 (1991): 5–12.

Boureau, Alain. "Adorations et décorations franciscaines. Enjeux et usages des livrets hagiographiques." In *Les usages de l'imprimé*, edited by Roger Chartier. Paris: 1987.

Braida, Lodovica. "Dall'almanaco all'agenda. Lo spazio per le osservazioni del lettore nelle 'guide del tempo' italiane." *Annali della Facoltà di Lettere e Filosofia dell'Università degli Studi di Milano.* LI: 1998.

—, "Les almanachs italiens. Évolutions et stéréotypes d'un genre." In *Colportage et lecture populaire. Imprimés de large circulation en Europe. XVIe–XIXe siècles,* edited by Roger Chartier and Hans Jürgen Lüsebrink, 183–206. Paris: 1998.

Brambilla, Elena. "La misura dell'alfabetizzazione nella Lombardia del primo Ottocento." *Archivo storico lombardo* vol. 1: CX (1984): 366–374.

Bright, Richard. *Travels from Vienna through Lower Hungary.* Edinburgh: 1818.

Brooks, Jeffrey. *When Russia Learned to Read: Literacy and Popular Literature 1861–1917.* Princeton: 1985.

Brown, Edward. *A brief account of some travels in Hungaria,* edited by Karl Nehring. München: 1975.

Bruckmüller, Ernst. *Sozialgeschichte Österreichs.* Münster–Wien: 1985.

Brüggemann, Sibylle. *Landschullehrer in Ostfriesland und Harlingerland während der ersten preussischen Zeit (1744–1806).* Köln: 1988.

Busch-Geertsema, Bettina. "Elender als auf dem elendsten Dorfe? Elementarbildung und Alphabetisierung in Bremen am Beginn des 19. Jahrhunderts." In *Alphabetisierung und Literalisierung in Deutschland in der frühen Neuzeit,* edited by Hans Erich Bödeker and Ernst Hinrichs, 181–189. Tübingen: 1999.

Cabourdin, Guy. *Terre et hommes en Lorraine 1550–1635.* Nancy: 1974.

Cardona, Giorgio Raimondo. *Antropologia della scrittura.* Torino: 1981.

Cardona, Giorgio. "La linea d'ombra dell' alfabetismo. Ai confini tra oralità e scrittura." In *Sulle vie della scrittura. Alfabetizzazione, cultura scritta, e instituzioni in età moderna,* edited by Maria Rosaria Pelizzari, 39–54. Napoli: 1989.

Castan, Yves. *Honnêteté et relations sociales en Languedoc (1715–1780).* Paris: 1974.

Chartier, Roger. "Culture as Appropriation: Popular Cultural Uses in Early Modern France." In *Understanding Popular Culture,* edited by Steven L. Kaplan. New York: 1984.

—, "Du livre au lire." In *Pratiques de la lecture,* edited by Roger Chartier, 61–81. Marseille: 1985.

—, "La ville classique." In *Histoire de la France urbaine,* edited by Georges Duby, 222–282. Tome III. Paris: 1981.

Chartier, Roger, Dominique Julia, and Marie-Madelaine Compère. *L'éducation en France du XVIe au XVIIIe siècle.* Paris: 1976.

Chartier, Roger and Denis Richet. *Représentation et vouloir politiques autour des États Généraux de 1614.* Paris: 1982.

Chisick, Harvey. *The Limits of Reform in the Enlightenment. Attutides toward the Education of the Lower Classes in Eighteenth Century France.* Princeton: 1981.

Cipolla, Carlo. *Literacy and Development in the West.* Hardmonsworth: 1969.

Clanchy, Michael. *From Memory to Written Record. England 1066–1307.* London: 1979.

—, "Literacy, Law, and the Power of the State." In *Culture et idéologie dans la genèse de l'État moderne.* École Française de Rome: 1985.

Clarke, Edward. *Travels in Various Countries of Europe.* London: 1816.

Cressy, David. *Coming Over. Migration and Communication between England and New England in the Seventeenth Century.* Cambridge: 1987.

—, *Literacy and the Social Order. Reading and Writing in Tudor and Stuart England.* Cambridge: 1980.

Cserei, Mihály. *Erdély históriája* (History of Transylvania), edited by Bánkúti Imre. Budapest: 1983.

Csokonai Vitéz, Mihály. *Minden munkája* (Complete works). Vol. I. Budapest: 1973.

Defoe, Daniel. "The Compleat English Gentleman." Quoted in *God's Playground* by Norman Davies, 236–237. Oxford: 1981.

Dann, Otto. "Die Lesegesellschaften des 18. Jahrhunderts und der gesellschaftliche Aufbruch des deutschen Bürgertums." In *Die Bildung des Bürgers*, edited by Ulrich Herrmann. Basel: 1982.

Daskalova, Krassimira. *B'lgarskijat ucitel prez vzrazdaneto* (The teachers in Bulgarian national revival). Sofia: 1997.

—, *Literacy and Reading in Nineteenth Century Bulgaria.* Washington: 1997.

Davis, Natalie Zemon, Jean-Claude Carrière, and Daniel Vigne. *Le retour de Martin Guerre.* Paris: 1982.

de Fort, Ester. *Scuola e analfabetismo nell'Italia del '900.* Bologna: 1995.

Ducreux, Marie-Élisabeth. "Lire à en mourir. Livres et lecteurs en Bohème au XVIIIᵉ siècle." In *Les usages de l'imprimé*, edited by Roger Chartier. Paris: 1987.

Duglio, R. "Alfabetismo e società a Torino nel secolo XVIII." *Quaderni storici* 17 (1971): 485–509.

Eckhardt, Sándor. *Két vitéz nemesúr* (Two brave noblemen). Budapest: 1944.

Encyklopédia Slovenská II. Bratislava: 1978.

Engelbrecht, Helmut. *Geschichte des österreichischen Bildungswesens.* Vols. II–III. Wien: 1984.

Engelsing, Rolf. *Zur Sozialgeschichte deutscher Mittel- und Unterschichten.* Göttingen: 1973.

Evans, Robert J.W. *The making of the Habsburg Monarchy, 1550–1700.* Oxford:1979.

Fabre, Daniel. "Le livre et sa magie." In *Pratiques de le lecture*, edited by Roger Chartier, 182–206. Marseille: 1985.

Fináczy, Ernő. *A magyarországi közoktatás története Mária Terézia korában* (History of Hungarian public education in the time of Maria Theresia). Budapest: 1899.

Fischer, Wolfram. "Der Volksschullehrer. Zur Sozialgeschichte eines Berufsstandes." *Soziale Welt* 12 (1961): 37–47.

François, Étienne. "Alphabetisierung in Frankreich und Deutschland während des 19. Jahrhunderts." *Zeitschrift für Pedagogik* 30 (1983).

—, "Die Volksbildung am Mittelrhein im ausgehenden 18. Jahrhundert. Eine Untersuchung über den vermeintlichen 'Bildungsrückstand' der katholischen Bevölkerung Deutschlands im Ancien Régime." *Jahrbuch für westdeutsche Landesgeschichte* 3 (1977): 277–304.

Frijhoff, Willem and Dominique Julia. *École et société dans la France d'Ancien Régime.* Paris: 1975.

Fügedi, Erik. "'Verba volant…': Oral Culture and Literacy among the Medieval Hungarian Nobility." In *Kings, Bishops, Nobles and Burghers in Medieval Hungary.* Vol. IV. London.

Furet, François and Jacques Ozouf. *Lire et écrire: l'alphabétisation des Français de Calvin à Jules Ferry.* I–II. Paris: 1977.

Furet, F. and W. Sachs. "La croissance de l'alphabétisation en France, XVIIIe–XIXe siècle." *Annales ESC* (1974): 714–737.

Gagliardo, John. *Germany under the Old Regime*. London: 1991.

Gasparotti, Hilarion. *Czvet Szveteh*. Graz: 1752.

Graff, Harvey J. *The Labyrinths of Literacy*. Philadelphia: 1987.

—, *The Legacies of Literacy*. Bloomington: 1987.

Guttormsson, Loftur. "The development of popular religious literacy in the seventeenth and eighteenth centuries." *Scandinavian Journal of History* 15 (1990).

Gvadányi, József. *Egy falusi nótáriusnak budai utazása* (Travel to the capital by a village notary). Pozsony: 1790.

Hargittay, Emil, ed. *Régi magyar levelestár (XVI–XVII. sz.)* (Old Hungarian letters from the sixteenth and seventeenth centuries). Budapest: 1981.

Házi, Jenő. *Die kanonische Visitation des Stefan Kazó* (Burgenländische Forschungen, Heft 37). Eisenstadt: 1958.

Hébrard, Jean. "Comment Valentin Jamerey-Duval apprit-il à lire? L'autodidaxie exemplaire." In *Pratiques de la lecture*, edited by Roger Chartier, 24–60. Marseille: 1985.

Heiss, Gernot. "Konfession, Politik und Erziehung. Die Landschaftsschulen in den nieder- und innerösterreichischen Ländern vor dem Dreissigjährigen Krieg." In *Bildung, Politik und Gesellschaft. Wiener Beiträge zur Geschichte der Neuzeit*, Bd. 5., edited by Grete Klingenstein and Heinrich Lutz, 13–63. Wien: 1978.

Helfert, Joseph. *Die Gründung der österreichischen Volksschule durch Maria Theresia*. Prague: 1860.

Henner, Adolf Schmitt. *Das Tagebuch meines Urgrossvaters (1790–1799)*. Freiburg: 1908.

Hinrichs, Ernst. "Leben, Schulbesuch und Kirchenzucht im 17. Jahrhundert. Eine Fallstudie zum Prozess der Alphabetisierung in Norddeutschland." In *Mentalitäten und Lebensverhältnisse. Beispiele aus der Sozialgeschichte der Zeuzeit*, 15–33. Göttingen: 1982.

—, "Wie viele Menschen konnten um 1800 lesen und schreiben?" In *Alte Tagebücher und Anschreibebücher. Quellen zum Alltag der ländlichen Bevölkerung in Nordwesteuropa*, edited by Helmut Ottenjann and Günter Wiegelmann, 85–103. Münster: 1982.

—, "Zum Alphabetisierungsstand im Norddeutschland um 1800." In *Sozialer und kultureller Wandel in der ländlichen Welt des 18. Jahrhunderts*, edited by Ernst Hinrichs and Günter Wiegelmann, 21–42. Wolfenbüttel: 1982.

Hofmeister, Andrea, Reiner Prass, and Norbert Winnige. "Elementary Education, Schools and the Demands of Everyday Life: Northwest Germany in 1800." *Central European History* 31 (1999): 329–384.

Holmes, Felicity. *The Gentry in England and Wales 1500–1700*. Stanford: 1994.

Houdaille, Jacques. "Les signatures au mariage de 1740 à 1829." *Population* 32 (1977).

Houston, Rab A. *Literacy in Early Modern Europe. Culture and Education 1500–1800*. London: 1992.

—, *Scottish Literacy and the Scottish Identity*. Cambridge: 1985.

Hudi, József. "Alfabetizáció és népi írásbeliség a 18–19. században" (Literacy and popular use of written record in the eighteenth and nineteenth centuries). *Rubicon* (Budapest) 5 (1990).

—, "Az írni-olvasni tudás helyzete Veszprém megyében a 18. század végén" (The reading and writing capacity in Veszprém County at the end of the eighteenth century). *Levéltári Szemle* (Budapest) 4 (1995): 38–46.

—, *Nemesvámos története* (A history of Nemesvámos). Veszprém: 1994.

Hunter, William. *Travels through France, Turkey, and Hungary to Vienna*. London: 1803.

Huszty, Stephanus. *Jurisprudentia practica*. Tyrnaviae: 1766.

Istványi, Géza. *A magyarnyelvű írásbeliség kialakulása* (Making use of Hungarian written records). Budapest: 1934.

Iványi, Béla. *Képek Körmend múltjából* (Pictures from the past of Körmend), Körmend: 1943.

Jankovich, József, ed. *Bethlen Miklós levelei* (Letters of Miklós Bethlen). Budapest: 1987.

Johansson, Egil. "The history of literacy in Sweden." In *Literacy and Social Development in the West*, edited by Harvey J. Graff, 151–182. Cambridge: 1981.

—, "Literacy Campaigns in Sweden." In *National Literacy Campaigns*, edited by Robert F. Arnove and Harvey J. Graff, 65–96. London–New York: 1987.

Juhász, Kálmán. *A licenciátusi intézmény Magyarországon* (The institution of licentiatus in Hungary). Budapest: 1921.

Julia, Dominique. "L'enseignement primaire dans le diocèse de Reims à la fin de l'Ancien Régime." *Actes du 95e Congrès des Sociétés Savantes* (Reims 1970). Paris: 1974.

—, "La réforme post-tridentinne en France d'après les procès verbaux de visites pastorales." In *La società religiosa nell'età moderna*, 311–415. Napoli: 1973.

—, "Lettura e controriforma." In *Storia della lettura*, edited by Guiglelmo Cavallo and Roger Chartier, 277–316. Roma: 1995.

Julia, Dominique and Jacques Revel. *Histoire sociale des populations étudiantes* II. Paris: 1989.

Kagan, Richard. *Students and Society in Early Modern Spain*. Baltimore: 1974.

Kamen, Henry. *The Iron Century. Social Change in Europe 1550–1660*. London: 1971.

Katus, László. "A népesedés és a társadalmi szerkezet változása" (Changes in demography and social structure). In *Magyarország története 1848–1890* (History of Hungary 1848–1890), edited by Endre Kovács. Budapest: 1979.

Kazinczy, Ferenc. *Művei* (Works). Budapest: 1979.

Kemény János és Bethlen Miklós művei (Works of János Kemény and Miklós Bethlen). Budapest: 1980.

"Kis János Emlékezései." In *Berzsenyi Dániel művei–Kis János Emlékezései* (Works of Dániel Berzsenyi and memories of János Kis). Budapest: 1985.

Klingenstein, Grete. "Akademikerüberschuss als soziales Problem im aufgeklärten Absolutismus." In *Bildung, Politik und Gesellschaft. Wiener Beiträge zur Geschichte der Neuzeit*, Bd. 5., edited by Grete Klingenstein and Heinrich Lutz, 165–203. Wien: 1978.

Kolosvári, Sándor and Kelemen Óvári, eds. *Corpus Juris Hungarici. 1608–1657, 1657–1740*. Budapest: 1900.

Komáromy, Andor (András). *Magyarországi boszorkányperek oklevéltára* (Documents of Hungarian witch trials). Budapest: 1910.

Komáromy, Andor. *Magyar levelek a XVI. századból* (Hungarian letters from the sixteenth century). Történelmi Tár Budapest: 1907.

Komáromy, András. *Tarnóczy Andrásné levelei Nádasdy Tamáshoz* (Letters of Madame Tarnóczy Andrásné to Tamás Nádasdy). Történelmi Tár Budapest: 1907.

Kósa, László. "Polgárosuló és parasztosodó kisnemesek" (Lower nobles on the way to the bourgeoisie and to the peasantry). *Világosság* (Budapest) 9 (1991): 703–710.

Kosáry, Domokos. *Művelődés a XVIII. századi Magyarországon* (Culture in Hungary in the eighteenth century). Budapest: 1980.

Kóta, Péter. "'Ebül szerzett kutyabőr,' avagy címerlevél-hamisítások a XVIII. században" (Falsified letters patent of nobility in the eighteenth century). In *Vas megyei levéltári füzetek* 6. Szombathely: 1993.

Kovács I., Gábor. *Kis magyar kalendáriumtörténet 1880-ig*. (Small Hungarian calendar history until 1880). Budapest: 1989.

Kovács, Péter, E. *Estei Hippolit püspök egri számadás könyvei 1500–1508* (The Eger account book of Bishop Ippolito d'Este, 1500–1508). Eger: 1992.

Kovács, Tibor. *Das südliche Burgenland in den Volkszählungen der Jahre 1857. und 1869*. Eisenstadt: 1972.

Kováts, Ferenc. *Mindenes gyűjtemény* (Miscellaneous collection). II. 1789.

Kowalská, Eva. *Štátne l'udové školstvo na Slovensku na prelome 18. a 19. stor.* Bratislava: 1987.

Kozocsa, Sándor, ed. *Magyar szerelmes levelek* (Hungarian love letters). Budapest: 1976.

Kristóf, Ildikó. "Istenes könyvek—ördöngős könyvek" (Godly books—diabolical books). *Népi kultúra—népi társadalom* (Budapest) XVIII (1995): 67–104.

Kubinyi, Miklós. *Bethlenfalvi gróf Thurzó György levelei nejéhez, Czobor-Szent-Mihályi Czobor Erzsébethez* (Letters of Count György Thurzó to his wife, Erzsébet Czobor). Budapest: 1876.

Kuzmin, Michail N. *Vývoj školstvi a vzděláni v Československu*. Praha: 1981.

La Vopa, Anthony J. *Prussian Schoolteachers: Profession and Office 1763–1848*. Chapel Hill: 1980.

Laget, Mireille. *Petites écoles en Languedoc au XVIIIᵉ siècle*. Annales ESC: 1971.

Larquié, Claude. "L'alphabétisation à Madrid en 1650." *Revue d'histoire moderne et contemporaine* 28 (1981).

Lázár, Márta Gellériné. "A magyarországi kalendáriumirodalom a kapitalizmus korában" (Hungarian calendars in the capitalist period). *Századok* (Budapest) 108 (1974).

Le Cam, Jean Luc. "Schulpflicht, Schulbesuch, und Schulnetz im Herzogtum Braunschweig-Wolfenbüttel im 17. Jahrhundert." In *Alphabetisierung und Literalisierung in Deutschland in der frühen Neuzeit*, edited by Hans Erich Bödeker and Ernst Hinrichs, 203–224. Tübingen: 1999.

Le Flem, Jean-Paul. "Instruction, lecture et écriture en Vieille-Castille et Extremadure aux XVIe–XVIIe siècles." In *De l'alphabétisation aux circuits du livre en Espagne (XVIe–XIXe siècles)*. Paris: 1987.

Lenhart, Volker. "Grundbildung und Modernisierung in Entwicklungsländern." In *Allgemeinbildung als Modernisierungsfaktor*, edited by Norbert Reiter and Holm Sundhaussen, 37–48. Berlin: 1994.

Le Roy Ladurie, Emmanuel. "De la crise ultime à la vraie croissance." In *Histoire de la France rurale*, edited by Georges Duby and Armand Wallon, 520–526. Vol. 2. Paris: 1975.

—, *Les paysans de Languedoc*. Paris: 1966.

Lescalopier, Pierre. *Utazása Erdélybe* (The travel of Pierre Lescalopier to Transylvania), edited by Kálmán Benda and Lajos Tardy. Budapest: 1982.

Leschinsky, Achim and Peter Martin Roeder. *Schule im historischen Prozess*. Stuttgart: 1976.

Lexicon locorum Regni Hungariae. Budapest: 1920.

Lockridge, Kenneth. A. "L'alphabétisation en Amérique." *Annales ESC* 32 (1977): 503–518.

—, *Literacy in Colonial New England: An Enquiry into the Social Context of Literacy in the Early Modern West*. New York: 1974.

Lucchi, Piero. "La Santacroce, il Salterio e il Babuino. Libri per imparare a leggere nel primo secolo della stampa." *Quaderni storici* 38 (1978): 593–630.

Mager, Friedrich. *Geschichte des Bauertums und Bodenkultur im Lande Mecklenburg*. Berlin: 1955.

Maiello, Francesco. *Storia del calendario. La misurazione del tempo. 1450–1800*. Torino: 1994.

Mályusz, Elemér, ed. *Sándor Lipót főherceg nádor iratai 1790–1795* (Documents of Palatin Archduke Alexander Leopold). Budapest: 1926.

Marchesini, Daniele. "Copier à l'école en Italie." In *Copies et modèle: usages, transmissions, appropriation de l'écrit*, edited by Christine Barré-De Miniac, 29–33. Paris: 1996.

—, *Il bisogno di scrivere. Usi della scrittura nell'Italia moderna*. Roma: 1992.

—, "La fatica di scrivere. Alfabetismo e sottoscrizioni matrimoniali in Emilia tra Sette e Ottocento." In *Il catechesimo e la grammatica*, edited by Gian Paolo Brizzi, 83–170. Bologna: 1985.

—, "Qualis pater...? La trasmissione dell' alfabetismo nell'Italia otto-novecentesca." *Annali di storia moderna e contemporanea* 3 (1997): 435–447.

—, "Sposi e scolari. Sottoscrizioni matrimoniali e alfabetismo tra Sette e Ottocento." *Quaderni storici* 53, (1983).

Marker, Gary. *Publishing, Printing and the Origins of Intellectual Life in Russia, 1700–1800*. Princeton: 1989

Melton, James Van Horn. *Absolutism and the Eighteenth-Century Origins of Compulsory Schooling in Prussia and Austria*. Cambridge: 1988.

—, "From Image to Word: Cultural Reform and the Rise of Literate Culture in Eighteenth-Century Austria." *Journal of Modern History* 58 (1986): 95–124.

Messerli, Alfred and Luisa Rubini. "Il mestiere del cantastorie." In *Hören, Sagen, Lesen, Lernen. Festschrift für Rudolf Schenda zum 65. Geburtstag*. Wien and New York: 1995. 463–87.

Mészáros, István. *A tankönyvkiadás története Magyarországon* (History of school book editions in Hungary). Budapest: 1989.

—, *Az iskolaügy története Magyarországon 996–1777 között* (School history of Hungary from 996 to 1777). Budapest:1981.

—, *Középszintű iskoláink kronológiája és topográfiája 996–1948* (Chronology and topography of Hungarian grammar schools). Budapest: 1988.

—, "Népoktatás Nyugat-Magyarországon a XVII. században" (Elementary schooling in western Hungary in the seventeenth century). *Soproni Szemle* (Sopron) 30 (1976).

—, ed. *Ratio Educationis*. Budapest: 1987.

Meyer, Jean. "Alphabétisation, lecture et écriture. Essai sur l'instruction populaire en Bretagne du XVIe au XIXe siècle." In *Histoire de l'enseignement de 1610 à nos jours. Actes du 95e congrès national des sociétés savantes*. Paris: 1974.

—, *La noblesse bretonne*. Paris: 1972.

Mikes, Kelemen. *Összes Művei* (Complete works). Vol. I. Budapest: 1966.

Mishkova, Diana. "Literacy and nation-building in Bulgaria", *East European Quarterly* 28: 1 (1994), 63–93.

Misztótfalus Kis, Miklós. *Erdélyi főniks* (Phoenix of Transylvania), edited by Zsigmond Jakó. Bucharest: 1974.

Mix, York-Gothart: "Der Musenhort in der Provinz. Literarische Almanache in den Kronländern der österreichischen Monarchie im ausgehenden 18. und beginnenden 19. Jahrhundert." *Archiv für Geschichte des Buchwesens* 27 (1986): 171–181.

—, "Lektüre für Gebildete und Ungebildete." In *Almanach und Taschenbuchkultur des 18. und 19. Jahrhunderts*, edited by York-Gothart Mix, 7–20. *Wolfenbütteler Forschungen Tübingen* Vol. 69. (1996).

—, "Vom Leitmedium zum Lesefutter." *Jahrbuch des Freien Deutschen Hochstifts* 93–113. Tübingen: 1997.

Morineau, Michel. "Budgets populaires en France au XVIIIe siècle." *Revue d'histoire économique et sociale* (1972): 204–212.

Mulih, Juraj. *Poszel aposztolszki*. Zagreb: 1742.

Nagy, Péter, ed. *Magyar drámaírók. 16–18. század* (Hungarian drama writers in the sixteenth to eighteenth centuries). Budapest: 1981.

Nassiet, Michel. *Noblesse et pauvreté. La petite noblesse en Bretagne, XVe–XVIIIe siècle*. Rennes: 1993.

Neugebauer, Wolfgang. *Absolutistischer Staat und Schulwirklichkeit in Brandenburg-Preussen*. Berlin: 1985.

Norden, Wilhelm. "Die Alphabetisierung in der oldenburgischen Küstenmarsch im 17. und 18. Jahrhundert." In *Regionalgeschichte. Probleme und Beispiele*, edited by Ernst Hinrichs and Wilhelm Norden. Hildesheim: 1980.

O'Day, Rosemary. *Education and Society 1500–1800*. London: 1982.

Olter, László. "English travellers in Hungary 1792–1815." Manuscript, Central European University History Department. Budapest: 1996.

Ong, Walter J. *Oralità e scrittura*. Bologna: 1986.

Pach, Zsigmond Pál, ed. *Magyarország története. 1526–1686* (History of Hungary). Budapest: 1985.

Pál, Judit. "Írástudás a Székelyföldön a XVIII. században" (Literacy in Székely lands in the eighteenth century). In *Emlékkönyv Jakó Zsigmond születésének nyolcvanadik évfordulójára* (Festschrift for Zsigmond Jakó). Kolozsvár (Cluj) 1996. 421–433.

Parker, Geoffrey. "An Educational Revolution? The Growth of Literacy and Schooling in Early Modern Europe." *Tijdschrift voor Geschiedenis* 93 (1980): 201–222.

—, *The Dutch Revolt*. London: 1985.

Pätzold, W. *Geschichte des Volksschulwesens im Königreich Sachsen*. Leipzig: 1908.

Pauler, Gyula. *Wesselényi Ferenc nádor és társainak összeesküvése* (The conspiracy of the Palatin Ferenc Wesselényi and his confederates). Budapest: 1876.

Paulsen, Friedrich. *Geschichte des gelehrten Unterrichts auf den deutschen Schulen und Universitäten*. Vol. I. Leipzig: 1919.

Payr, Sándor. *A dunántúli evangélikus egyházkerület története* (History of the Transdanubian Lutheran Church district). Vol. I. Sopron: 1924.

—, *Egyháztörténeti emlékek* (Documents of Church history). Vol. I. Sopron: 1910.

Pelizzari, Maria Rosaria. "Alfabeto e fisco. Tra cultura scritta e oralità nel Regno di Napoli a metà Settecento." In *Sulle vie della scrittura*, edited by Maria Rosaria Pelizzari, 99–152. Salerno: 1989.

—, *La penna e la zappa. Alfabetizzazione, culture e generi di vita nel Mezzogiorno moderno.* Salerno: 2000.

Péter, Katalin. "A bibliaolvasás mindenkinek szóló programja Magyarországon a 16. század második felében" (The program of reading the Bible by everybody in Hungary in the second half of the sixteenth century). *Századok* (Budapest) 119 (1985): 1006–1028.

—, *Papok és nemesek* (Priests and nobles). Budapest 1995.

Peters, Jan. "'…dahingeflossen, ins Meer der Zeiten.' Über frühmodernes Zeitverständnis der Bauern." In *Frühe Neuzeit—Frühe Moderne?*, edited by Rudolf Vierhaus, 180–205. Göttingen: 1992.

Petrucci, Armando, ed. *Libri, scritture e pubblico nel rinascimento.* Roma: 1979.

Petrucci, Armando. "Scrittura, alfabetismo ed educazione grafica nella Roma del primo cinquecento." *Scrittura e civiltà* 2 (1978).

—, *Scrittura e popolo nella Roma barocca.* Rome: 1981.

Pferschy, Gerhard, ed. *Atlas zur Geschichte des steirischen Bauerntums.* 59/I–IV. Graz: 1975.

Pietsch, Walter. *Die theresianische Schulreform in der Steiermark.* Graz: 1977.

Popoff, Kiril G. *La Bulgarie économique. 1879–1911.* Sophia: 1920.

Potkowski, Edward. "Écriture et société en Pologne du Bas Moyen Age (XIVe–XVe siècles)." *Acta Poloniae Historica* 39 (1979): 47–100.

Quéniart, Jean. *Culture et société urbaines dans la France de l'Ouest au XVIIIe siècle.* Paris: 1978.

—, "Les apprentissages scolaires élémentaires." *Revue d'histoire moderne et contemporaine* 24 (1977): 3–27.

Rački, F. *Acta coniurationem bani Petri Zrinio et comitis Francisci Frangepan illustrantia.* Zagreb: 1873.

Rao, Anna Maria. "Esercito e società a Napoli nelle riforme del secondo Settecento." *Studi storici* 28 (1987): 3.

Raun, Toivo U. "The development of Estonian literacy in the 18th and 19th centuries." *Journal of Baltic Studies* X (1979) 2: 115–126.

Richter, Jochen. "Zur Schriftkundigkeit mecklenburgischer Bauern im 17. Jahrhundert." *Jahrbuch für Wirtschaftsgeschichte* (Berlin) 3 (1981).

Roche, Daniel. *La France des Lumières.* Paris: 1994.

—, "Les pratiques de l'écrit dans les villes françaises du XVIIIe siècle." In *Pratiques de la lecture*, edited by Roger Chartier, 157–179. Marseille: 1985.

Rössing-Hager, Monika. "Wie stark findet der nicht-lesekundige Rezipient Berücksichtigung in den Flugschriften?" In *Flugschriften als Massenmedien der Reformationszeit*, edited by Hans-Joachim Köhler, 77–137. Stuttgart: 1981.

Ruwet, Joseph and Yves Wellemans, eds. *L'analphabétisme en Belgique.* Louvain: 1978.

Sallmann, Jean Michel. "Alphabétisation et hiérarchie sociale à Naples à la fin du XVIe et au début du XVIIe siècle." In *Sulle vie della scrittura. Alfabetizzazione, cultura scritta e instituzioni in età moderna*, edited by Maria Rosaria Pelizzari, 79–98. Salerno: 1989.

Sámuel, Gergely, ed. *Teleki Mihály levelezése* (Correspondence of Mihály Teleki). Budapest: 1906–1908.

Sanderson, Michael. "Education and the Factory in Industrial Lancashire 1780–1840." *Economic History Review* 20 (1966): 266–279.

—, "Literacy and Social Mobility in the Industrial Revolution in England." *Past and Present* 56 (1972): 75–104.

Schenda, Rudolf. "Alphabetisierung und Literarisierungsprozesse in Westeuropa im 18. und 19. Jahrhundert." In *Das pädagogische Jahrhundert*, edited by Ulrich Hermann, 154–163. Basel: 1981.

—, *Volk ohne Buch. Studien zur Sozialgeschichte der populären Lesestoffe*. Frankfurt am Main: 1970.

Schleunes, Karl. *Schooling and Society: The Politics of Education in Prussia and Bavaria.* New York: 1989.

Schofield, R. S. "Dimensions of Illiteracy 1750–1850." In *Literacy and Social Development in the West*, edited by Harvey J. Graff, 201–213. Cambridge 1981.

—, "The Measurement of Literacy in Pre-Industrial England." In *Literacy in Traditional Societies*, edited by J. Goody, 311–325. Cambridge: 1968.

Schram, Ferenc, ed. *Magyarországi boszorkányperek* (Witchcraft trials in Hungary). Vols. I–III. Budapest: 1970.

Scribner, Robert W. "Flugblatt und Analphabetentum.Wie kam der gemeine Mann zu reformatorischen Ideen?" In *Flugschriften als Massenmedien der Reformationszeit*, edited by Hans-Joachim Köhler. Stuttgart: 1981.

—, *For the Sake of Simple Folk. Popular Propaganda for the German Reformation*. Cambridge: 1981.

—, *Popular Culture and Popular Movements in Reformation Germany*. London: 1987.

Schutte, Anne Jacobson. "Teaching Adults to Read in Sixteenth-Century Venice." *The Sixteenth-Century Journal* 17: 1 (1986).

Schwartz, Paul. *Die neumärkischen Schulen am Ausgang des 18. und am Anfang des 19. Jh.* Landsberg: 1905.

Smout, T. C. "New Evidence on Popular Religion and Literacy in Eighteenth-Century Scotland." *Past and Present* 97 (1982): 114–127.

Spufford, Margaret. "First Steps in Literacy: The Reading and Writing Experiences of the Humblest Seventeenth-Century Spiritual Autobiographers." *Social History* 4 (1979): 407–436.

—, *The Great Reclothing of Rural England. Petty Chapmen and Their Wares in the Seventeenth Century*. London: 1984.

—, *Small Books and Pleasant Histories: Popular Fiction and Its Readership in Seventeenth-Century England*. Athens, Ga.: 1982.

Stephens, W. B. "Illiteracy and Schooling in the Provincial Towns 1640–1870." In *Urban Education in the Nineteenth Century*, edited by David Reeder, 27–48. London: 1977.

Stone, Lawrence. *The Crisis of Aristocracy. 1558–1641*. Oxford: 1986.

Strauss, Gerald. *Luther's House of Learning: Indoctrination of the Young in the German Reformation*. Baltimore: 1978.

—, "Lutheranism and Literacy: A Reassessment." In *Society in Early Modern Europe*, edited by Kaspar von Greyerz, 109–23. London: 1984.

Strauss, Gerald and Richard Gawthrop. "Protestantism and Literacy in Early Modern Germany." *Past and Present* 104 (1984): 31–56.

Stromp, László, ed. *Magyar Protestáns Egyháztörténeti Adattár* (Data on Hungarian Protestant Church History). Budapest: 1907.

Sundhaussen, Holm. *Historische Statistik Serbiens 1834–1914*. München: 1989.

Szabó, Dezső, ed. *A magyarországi úrbérrendezés története Mária Terézia korában* (History of Hungarian serfdom regulations in the age of Maria Theresia). Budapest: 1933.

Szathmáry, Éva, ed. *Óhajtott szép kincsecském!* (My desidered little treasury) Budapest: 1988.

Szegedy, Joannes. *Bipartita cynosura universi juris Ungarici*. Vols. I–II. Jaurini: 1749.

—, *Rubricae sive synopses titulorum, capitum, et articulorum universi juris Ungarici*. Tyrnaviae: 1734.

—, *Tripartitum juris Hungarici tyrocinium*. Tyrnaviae: 1751.

Szentiványi, Martinus. *Turris Babel seu confusio doctrinae fidei inter modernos acatholicos*. Tyrnaviae: 1731.

Szepsi Csombor, Márton. *Europica varietas*. Budapest: 1979.

Siegert, Reinhard. "Zur Alphabetisierung in den deutschen Regionen am Ende des 18. Jahrhunderts." In *Alphabetisierung und Literalisierung in Deutschland in der frühen Neuzeit*, edited by Hans Erich Bödeker and Ernst Hinrichs, 283–308. Tübingen: 1999.

Szilády, Áron and Sándor Szilágyi, eds. *Török–magyarkori államokmánytár* (State documents of Turkish Hungary), Vol. IV. Pest: 1870.

Szilágyi, Ferenc, ed. *Elmét vidító elegy-belegy dolgok* (Varied and funny stories). Budapest: 1983.

Takács, Lajos. *Határjelek, határjárás a feudális kor végén Magyarországon* (Boundary marks, boundary inspection at the end of the Old Regime in Hungary). Budapest: 1987.

Táncsics, Mihály. *Életpályám* (My life). Budapest: 1978.

Thirring, Gusztáv. *Magyarország népessége II. József korában* (The population of Hungary in the time of Joseph II). Budapest: 1938.

Toscani, Xenio. "L'alfabetismo a Pavia agli inizi dell'Ottocento." *Annali di storia pavese* No. 6–7 (1981): 353–365.

—, *Scuole e alfabetismo nello Stato di Milano da Carlo Borromeo alla rivoluzione*. Brescia: 1993.

Tóth, István György. "Chimes and Ticks: The Concept of Time in the Minds of Peasants and the Lower Gentry in Hungary in the Seventeenth and Eighteenth Centuries." In *Central European University, History Department Yearbook 1994–1995*, 15–37. Budapest: 1996.

—, "Deákok (licenciátusok) a moldvai csángó magyar művelődésben a XVII. században" (Licentiati in the culture of Hungarians in Moldavia in the seventeenth century). In *Az értelmiség Magyarországon a 16–17. században* (Intellectuals in

Hungary in the sixteenth and seventeenth centuries), edited by István Zombori, 139–148. Szeged: 1988.

—, "Hungarian Culture in the Early Modern Age." In *A Cultural History of Hungary*, edited by László Kósa, 154–225. Budapest: 1999.

—, "Iskola és reformáció Körmenden a 16–18. században" (Schools and reformation in Körmend in the sixteenth through eighteenth centuries). In *Ráday Gyűjtemény Évkönyve VI*, 10–21. Budapest: 1989.

—, *Jobbágyok, hajdúk, deákok. A körmendi uradalom társadalma a 17. században* (Serfs, haiducks, scribes. The society of the Körmend estate in the seventeenth century). Budapest: 1992.

—, ed. *Relationes missionariorum de Hungaria et Transilvania (1627–1707)*. Rome and Budapest: 1994.

Tóth, Péter. "Somogyi határvizsgálatok tanulságai." (Boundary inspections in Somogy County). *Somogy megye múltjából*. Kaposvár: 1987.

—, *Vas vármegye közgyűlési jegyző könyveinek regesztái* (Protocols of county assemblies in Vas County). Vol. II. Szombathely: 1992.

Townson, Robert. *Travels in Hungary with a Short Account of Vienna in the Year 1793*. London: 1797.

Tüskés, Gábor and Éva Knapp. "Fejezetek a XVIII. századi vallásos ponyvairodalom történetéből" (From the history of small religious books in the eighteenth century). *Irodalomtörténeti Közlemények* (Budapest) (1985): 415–437.

Urban, Wacław. "Sztuka pisania w województwie krakowskim w XVII i XVIII wieku." *Przegląd historyczny* 75 (1984).

—, "Umiejetność pisania w Malopolsce w drugiej polowie XVI wieku." *Przegląd historyczny* 68 (1977), 231–256.

Van de Woude, A. M. "Der alfabetisering." In *Algemeine Geschiedenis der Nederlanden*, 256–267. Haarlem: 1980.

Varga, Imre. "A győri székesegyházi főesperesség egyházlátogatási jegyző könyvei 1698-ból" (Protocols of church visitations in Győr church district). *Arrabona* 13 (1971): 177–221.

Varga, János J. *Szervitorok katonai szolgálata a XVI–XVII. századi dunántúli nagybirtokokon* (The military service of serving noblemen in sixteenth and seventeenty-century Transdanubian estates). Budapest: 1981.

Vas vármegye 1870. évi népszámlálása (Census of Vas County in 1870). Szombathely: 1871.

Velagić, Zoran. "Nekoliko vidova prosvjetnog rada na hrvatskom sjeveru osamnaestog stoljeća." *Zbornik Odsjeka za povijesne znanosti* (Zagreb) 17 (2000): 111–131.

Vida, Tivadar, ed. *Szerelmes Orsikám* (My beloved Orsolya). Budapest: 1988.

Vigo, Giovanni. "Quando il popolo cominciò a leggere. Per una storia dell'alfabetismo in Italia." *Storia e società* 6 (1983).

Vincent, David. *Literacy and Popular Culture: England 1750–1914*. Cambridge: 1989.

—, *The Coming of Mass Literacy*. Cambridge: 2000 (forthcoming).

von Wartburg-Ambühl, Maria-Louise. *Alphabetisierung und Lektüre. Untersuchung am Beispiel einer ländichen Region im 17. und 18. Jahrhundert*. Bern: 1984.

Vörös, Károly. "A művelődés" (Cultural history). In *Magyarország története 1848–1890* (History of Hungary 1848–1890), edited by Endre Kovács, Budapest: 1979: 1399–1402.

Vovelle, Michel. "Y-at-il eu une révolution culturelle au XVIIIe siècle? A propos de l'éducation populaire en Provence." *Revue d'histoire moderne et contemporaine* 22 (1975): 89–141.

Wangermann, Ernst. *Aufklärung und staatsbürgerliche Erziehung. Gottfried van Swieten als Reformator des österreichischen Unterrichtswesens.* München: 1978.

Weatherill, Lorna. "Consumer Behaviour and Social Status in England. 1660–1750." *Continuity and Change* (1986).

Weiss, Anton. *Geschichte der österreichischen Volksschule unter Franz I. und Ferdinand I.* Graz: 1904.

Wendehorst, Alfred. "Monachus scribere nesciens." *Mitteilungen des Instituts für österreichische Geschichtsforschung* 71 (1963).

Werbőczy, István. *Tripartitum Juris Hungarici.* Budapest: 1897.

West, E. G. "Literacy and the industrial revolution." *Economic History Review* 31 (1978): 369–383.

Whitrow, G. J. *Time in History.* Oxford: 1988.

Winnig, Norbert. "Alphabetisierung in der Frühen Neuzeit, oder: Wie visualisiere ich raumbezogene historische Daten?" In *Historisch-thematische Kartographie*, edited by Dietrich Ebeling, 82–97. Bielefeld: 1999.

—, "Unterschriften aus der Altmark. Zur Alphabetisierung in Stendal und Umgebung um 1800." In *Leben und arbeiten auf märkischem Sand*, edited by Ralf Röve and Bernd Kölling, 90–119. Bielefeld: 1999.

Wirth, Zsuzsanna. "A nemesi kisbirtok differenciálódása Vas megyében a XVIII. század közepétől a polgári forradalomig" (The differentiation of lower nobility's possessions in Vas county from the middle of the eighteenth century until 1848). In *Vas megye múltjából*, III. Szombathely: 1986.

Wittmann, Reinhard. "Der lesende Landmann." In *Der Bauer Mittel- und Osteuropas*, edited by Dan Berindei, 142–196. Köln: 1973.

Woolf, D. R. "The 'Common Voice.' History, Folklore and Oral Tradition in Early Modern England." *Past and Present* 120 (1988).

Wyczański, Andrzej. "Alphabétisation et structure sociale en Pologne au XVIe siècle." *Annales ESC* 29 (1974): 705–713;

Zimányi, Vera. "Adatok a dunántúli hajdúk történetéhez" (Data on the history of the Haiducks in Transdanubia). *Századok* 94 (1960).

—, *Der Bauernstand der Herrschaft Güssing im 16. und 17. Jahrhundert.* Eisenstadt: 1962.

INDEX

Albania 137
Alexander Leopold, archduke, palatine 209
Alsace 130, 204–205
amulet 79
arithmetics 24, 26
Astori da Ferrara, Giovanni Battista, Italian missionary 138
Augustinians 12
Austria 9, 38–39, 45, 204–205

Balassa, Zsuzsanna, aristocrat 127
Bánffy, Borbála, aristocrat 126
Bánffy, Dénes, aristocrat 139
Batthyány, Ádám, aristocrat 62, 73, 98, 127
Bél, Mátyás, polymath 209, 210
Belgrade 75, 88, 91
Benda, Kálmán, historian 32, 199
Benedictines 12
Beregszász (Berehovo, Ukraine) 170
Besztercebánya (Banská Bystrica, Slovakia) 60, 168
Bethlen, Miklós, chancellor and writer 114, 128, 136
Bible 76–77, 110, 111, 128, 209
Bohemia 9, 38, 39, 45, 205

book: owned by illiterates 69–70; prize of, 76
Bosnia 87, 207–208
Bosnian Franciscans 88, 91–92, 137
Brandenburg 41
Breznóbánya (Brezno, Slovakia) 60
Bright, Richard, English traveler in Hungary 136–137
Britanny (Bretagne) 43–44
Brooks, Jeffrey, historian 206–207
Brown, Edward, English traveler in Hungary 136–137, 139, 143
Buda 12, 101, 139, 173, 179
Bukovina 205
Bulgaria 207–208

calendar 72–77, 90
Calvinists 26–27, 43, 46, 66–67, 71, 76–77, 118, 163
Carinthia 39
Carlowitz, Peace Treaty of 172
Carniola 39
Charles VI, emperor 55
Cistercians 16, 58
Clarke, Edward, English traveler in Hungary 136–137

Cologne 57
correspondence: between illiterates 78–79
Cracow 206, 207
Cressy, David, historian 202–203
Croatia 123, 211
cross, difficult to draw 59–60; of literates
   as signatures 61–63, 105–106
Csáky, István, aristocrat 124
Csokonai Vitéz, Mihály, poet 35
Czobor, Erzsébet, aristocrat 125–126

Dalmatia 205
Damokos, Kázmér, missionary 137
Defoe, Daniel 136
devil: book of 89–93; speaking Latin 91;
   taking away false witnesses 176
Dominicans 12
Dupin, Charles, Baron 43

Eger 60, 77, 79, 178, 180
England 135–136, 202–203, 209
Enlightenment: school reforms of, 20–
   22, 35, 37, 39, 41–43, 45–46
Eötvös, József, minister of education 193
Eperjes (Prešov, Slovakia) 28
Esterházy, Borbála, aristocrat, 103, 127
Esterházy, Pál, palatine 127
Esztergom 126
eyeglasses 113–114

Febronius, Justinus (Johann Nikolaus
   von Hontheim) 129
Fejérvár (Székesfejérvár) 179
Felbiger, Johann Ignaz abbot, school
   reformer 6, 37, 38, 39
Ferdinand II, emperor 138, 150
Ferdinand III, emperor 162, 171, 182
Fermo 208
finger-print: as signature 59
Finland 110
forgery of documents: by lower noble-
   men 150; by peasants 81–83,
France 39, 43–45, 58, 129, 204–205
Francis II, emperor 36, 209
Franciscans 79, 88, 91–92, 137–138, 210
Frangepán, Anna, aristocrat 125
Frederick William II, Prussian king 41

Galgóc (Hlohovec, Slovakia) 30
Galicia 39, 205
Genova, Bonaventura da, missionary
   137–138
Gotthal, Nikolaus, vicar of Zagreb 210
Graz 30, 36
Greece 208
Gvadányi, József, general and poet 134
Győr (Raab) 30, 32, 34, 35, 112, 134

Heisler, Donatus, general 139
Hercegszőllősi, János, illiterate priest 7
Hódmezővásárhely 28, 80
Holland 203, 210
Houston, Rab, historian 102
Hunter, William, English traveler in
   Hungary 136–137

Ibrishimovich, Marino, bishop of Bel-
   grade 88
Illésházy, Kata, aristocrat 127
Istanbul 79, 124
Italy 205, 210, 211

Jászó (Jasov, Slovakia) 113
Jesuits 20, 30, 208
John I. (Szapolyai), Hungarian king 88
Joseph II, emperor 21, 36, 38, 45, 46,
   77, 96, 115, 139

Kanizsa (Nagykanizsa) 87, 164, 165, 179
Kanizsai, Orsolya, aristocrat 114, 123–125
Kaposvár 89
Kassa (Košice, Slovakia) 79, 143
Kazinczy, Ferenc, writer 129, 139, 142
Kemény, János, prince of Transylvania
   138–139
Kerhen, Borbála, aristocrat 123
Keszthely 74, 78, 152, 186
Kis, János, writer 31
Kisfaludy, Boldizsár, Hungarian officer
   in France 97–98, 129–130
Komárom (Komárno, Slovakia) 28
Königshegg, Antónia, aristocrat 105
Köprülü, Ahmed, Grand Visier 165
Kőszeg (Güns) 9, 12, 15, 20
Kun, Ilona, aristocrat 128

Latin language: pronunciation of 139,
142; spoken by children 137; by merchants 139–141; by peasants 137, 141,
143; by soldiers 139; taught in village
schools 24, 32, 144; used without understanding it, 133–135, 191
Latvia 110
legends: on King Matthias 88; on Turkish wars 179–181
Leone da Modica, Francesco, missionary
138
Leopold I , emperor 113, 149, 158, 173,
180, 181, 184
licenciatus 6, 7, 144
Lippa (Lipova, Roumania) 210
Lőcse (Levoča, Slovakia) 136
London 135
Louis I , Hungarian king 181
Louis II, Hungarian king 88, 180–181
Louis XIV, French king, 43, 205
Louis XV, French king 43
Lutherans 7–8, 10, 25, 27, 30–31, 32, 70,
71, 76, 108, 110, 118, 163

Magyaróvár 83
Mainz 9, 12
Majláth, István, aristocrat 124
Maria Theresia, queen, 12, 22, 36, 39, 45
Massarecchi, Pietro, Albanian mission-
ary 137
Mathias I. Corvinus, Hungarian king,
87–88, 170
Maximilian II, emperor 155, 164, 165, 166
memory: boundaries of, 86–87, 165–166;
credibility of 167–169
Mikes, Kelemen, writer 29
Miloš, Serbian prince 208
Miskolc 76, 112, 119, 154, 160, 178,
183, 186
Misztótfalusi Kis, Miklós, printer 210
Mohács, battle 180, 181
Moldavia 59, 206–207
monogram: as signature 58–59, 100
Montecuccoli, Raimondo, general 179
Moore, Thomas 209
Moravia 9–10, 38, 39, 139, 205

Munkács (Mukačevo, Ukraine) 139
Murány (Muraň, Slovakia) 139

Nádasdy, Tamás, palatine, 114, 123–
125, 131–132
Nagykőrös 74
Nagyszombat (Trnava, Slovakia) 137
Nagyvárad (Oradea, Roumania) 187,
188, 189
Naples 211
Natale, Luca, bishop of Belgrade 138
nationalities: literacy of, 54–55, 196–197

oral tradition: among noblemen 162–163,
177–179, 181; among peasants 86–89
Ovid 31
Oxford 136

Pál, Gáspár, school refomer 20
Pápa 79, 117, 163, 164
Paris 44
Pataki, István, Transylvanian professor
139
Paulines 191
Pázmány, Péter, cardinal, 76
Pécs 144
Poland 170, 206–207
pope, popular image of 77, 78
Pozsony (Bratislava, Slovakia) 8, 26, 79, 142
prayer, synonym of reading 72
prayer-book 69–72, 90
primer 28–29
Protestants: founding schools 46; literacy
of, 18, 43, 54–55, 60; persecution of
55–56; see also: Lutherans, Calvinists
Prussia 39–42
Putnok 71

Rákóczi, Francis II, prince of Transylvania, 97, 129, 148, 158, 182, 190
Rákóczi, Georges II, prince of Transylvania 170
reading: aloud 70–71; aloud to illiterates
76–78; common 70; extensive 70;
only of printed texts 57, 72, 80; without understanding 144

reading capacity: prestige of 115, 117,
    118–120; without writing capacity 7–
    8, 10–11, 22–24, 57, 69–71, 201
Regensburg 78
Rome 72, 210
Roumania 207
Russia 19, 207–208

Salzburg 9
Sárospatak 139, 142
Sárvár 11, 123
Scotland 102
seal: as signature 61–63, 96–97, 100,
    157, 184
Selmecbánya (Banská Štiavnica, Slova-
    kia) 211
semi-illiterates 56–59, 80, 97–99
Serbia 208
servant-maids: reading books, 73, 211
Sigismund, emperor 120
signature: false, by illiterates 61, 99;
    false, by literate persons 61–63, 65;
    with guided hand 104–106; written
    with blood 90–91
Silesia 9, 12
Smodics, Mihály, illiterate priest 7
Sopron (Ödenburg) 30, 31
Styria 9, 36
Sweden 110
Szatmár (Satu Mare, Roumania) 138
Szeged 90
Szegedy, János, Jesuit jurist 102, 104
Szentgotthárd (Sankt Gotthard) 16, 18,
    51, 58, 82, 179
Szepsi (Moldava nad Boldou, Slovakia)
    121, 142, 159, 184
Szepsi Csombor, Márton, Hungarian
    traveller in England 135–136, 142
Szikszó 79, 120
Szily, János, bishop 5, 11, 12, 13, 15, 21, 45
Szombathely (Steinamanger) 12, 16, 20,
    70

Tállya 84, 120, 153
Táncsics, Mihály, writer 27, 28, 72, 138–
    139

teachers: illiterates 10–12; migration of
    9–11; not teaching at all 5–6; prestige
    of 10–11, 15–19; remuneration of 15–
    17, 40–41
Telegdy, Pál, aristocrat 126
Teleki, Mihály, chancellor 127–128
Thököly, Imre, prince of Transylvania
    178
Thurzó, György, palatine 30, 78, 125–
    126
time: concept of 72–75, 168–169
Tokaj 83, 139
Tomka Szászky, János, writer 31
Townson, Robert, English traveller in
    Hungary 136–137
Transylvania 29, 30, 135, 137–138, 138–
    139, 170, 196, 198, 199, 210
Trento 38
tuition fee 15–17
tutor: in private house 27–30
Tyrol 39

United States of America 68

Várday, Kata, aristocrat 126
Veér, Judit, aristocrat 127–128
Veszprém 169
Vienna 9, 10, 27, 30, 31, 32, 37, 130,
    136, 149, 177, 180
Visegrád 137

Wallachia 207
Wimpassing 26
witch: illiteracy of 57, 75, 89–93
women: altering their age, 173; not
    understanding Latin 140; reading ca-
    pacity of, 125, 156, 201; writing ca-
    pacity of, 123–124, 127
written document: and illiterates 69–70,
    78–80, 82–85, 153, 155–162; healing
    power of, 92

Zagreb 210
Zay, Ferenc, aristocrat 126
Zernyest, Battle of, 139
Zrínyi, Péter, aristocrat 57